DISCOVER THE ISLANDS OF THE PACIFIC

Reader's
Digest

PUBLISHED BY THE READER'S DIGEST ASSOCIATION LIMITED

LONDON   NEW YORK   SYDNEY   MONTREAL

DISCOVER THE ISLANDS OF THE PACIFIC

Translated and edited by Toucan Books Limited, London
for Reader's Digest, London

Translated and adapted from the French by Antony Mason

For Reader's Digest
Series Editor: Christine Noble
Editorial Assistant: Lucy Murray
Production Controller: Martin Hendrick
Reader's Digest General Books
Editorial Director: Cortina Butler
Art Director: Nick Clark

First English language edition Copyright © 2002
The Reader's Digest Association Limited
11 Westferry Circus, Canary Wharf, London E14 4HE
www.readersdigest.co.uk

Reprinted with amendments 2004

We are committed to both the quality of our products and
the service we provide to our customers. We value your
comments, so please feel free to contact us on 08705 113366,
or via our web site www.readersdigest.co.uk
If you have any comments about the content of our books,
you can contact us at gbeditorial@readersdigest.co.uk

ISBN 0 276 42518 9

Discover the World: THE ISLANDS OF THE PACIFIC
was created and produced by
AMDS (ATELIER Martine et Daniel SASSIER), Paris for
Selection Reader's Digest S.A., Paris, and first published
in 2000 as *Regards sur le Monde:* LE PACIFIQUE ET SES ÎLES

©2000 Selection Reader's Digest, S.A.
212 boulevard Saint-Germain, 75007, Paris

CONTENTS

INTRODUCING
THE ISLANDS
OF THE
PACIFIC

Like stars in the night sky, the islands of the Pacific lie scattered across a vast expanse of sea. Although numbered in thousands, each island has its distinctive qualities: bewitching and infinitely varied combinations of surf-fringed reefs, serene lagoons, dazzling sands and volcanic hills ragged with tropical vegetation. Along with this physical diversity, there is also a remarkable unity to the region, the product of extraordinary human courage and endeavour.

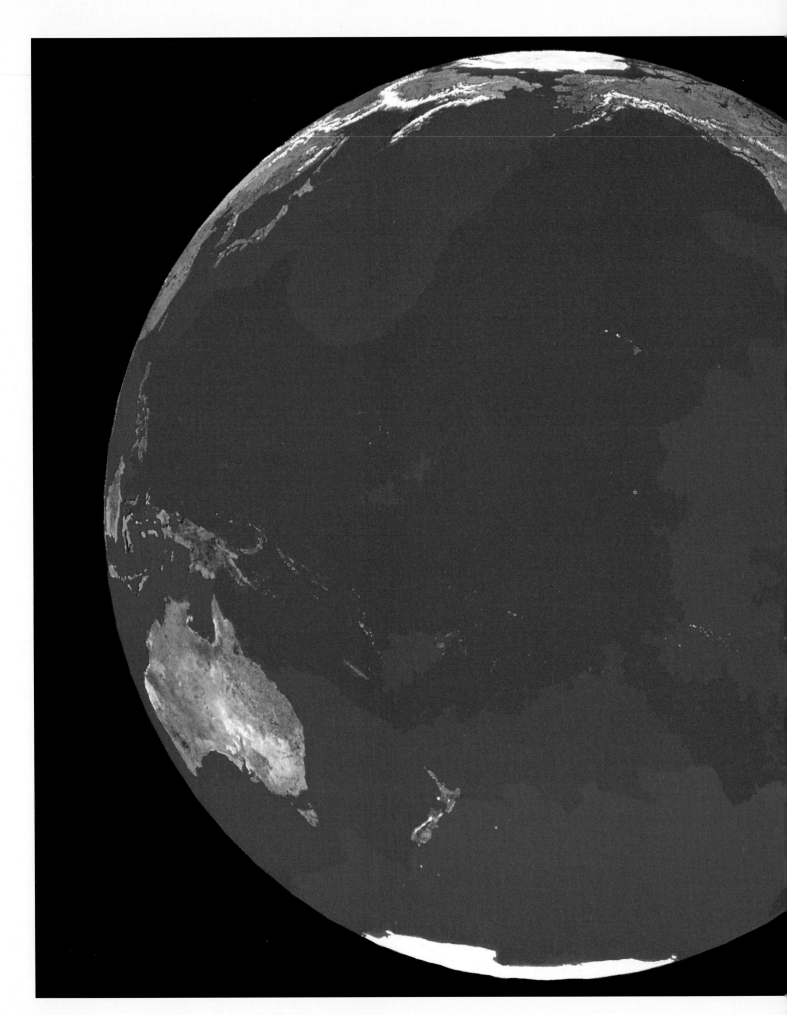

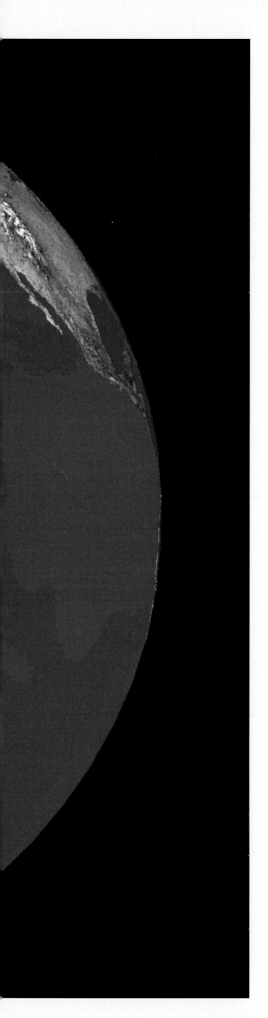

Specks in the ocean

The Pacific is the world's largest ocean, covering almost one-third of the surface of the globe. Easter Island in the eastern Pacific and Palau in the west are separated by a time difference of nine hours. Sprinkled across this vast area are 25 000 or so islands – but only 3000 are of any significant size. Almost all owe their origin to volcanic activity: they are, or were, the tips of volcanoes that have been thrust up from the ocean floor. Many are coral islands, formed on the flanks and peaks of volcanoes that have disappeared beneath the waves. The biggest islands lie in the western Pacific, like chunks of the Asian continent that have slipped their mooring. But even with these, the total land area of all the Pacific islands is equivalent only to the size of France.

Consistent patterns of winds and currents sweep seasonally across the region. These could be read by early migrants, who in ancient times travelled increasingly vast distances in their outrigger sailing boats, gradually peopling the region. This has given the islands a surprising degree of uniformity, despite their enormous geographical range. In the 19th century the islands were grouped geographically and ethnically into three regions: Melanesia, the 'black islands' (so named after the darker complexions of its people); Micronesia, the 'small islands' that stretch across the north of the region, mainly to the north of the equator; and Polynesia, the 'many islands' scattered across the east. We now know that neither the geography of the region nor the history of settlement conforms to this categorisation, but nonetheless the terms persist.

Water world Atlases traditionally focus selectively on land and countries. By contrast, the neutral lens of a camera in space gives a quite different perspective on the world, and, from this angle, demonstrates the immense size of the Pacific Ocean. It also underlines the minute scale of most of the Pacific islands, only a handful of which are big enough to feature in this picture.

The traditional image of the Pacific islands is one of balmy tropical tranquillity: white sandy beaches with coconut palms; turquoise lagoons fringed by coral reefs mirroring the wispy clouds that float across an unfathomably blue sky. In reality, the forces of nature at work are far from tranquil. Volcanic action surges to the surface along the 'Ring of Fire' that encircles the Pacific. Cyclones frequently lash the sea and flatten the islands' vegetation and settlements. Drought and floods visit the region in equal measure. Now the rise of sea levels associated with global warming appears to threaten the lowest-lying islands, some of which barely stand above the sea at all.

Neither are these islands socially or politically tranquil. Since their first contact with Europeans in the 18th century, the islanders have been subjected to imported diseases, war, colonial coercion, the demands of plantation economies, immigration and missionaries. The trauma of the Second World War still haunts them: the resumption of nuclear testing by France on the island of Mururoa in French Polynesia in 1995 seemed like the ultimate foreign-imposed indignity. But most of the islands have at least shaken off their colonial rulers, and so are free – in principle, at least – to choose their own destinies.

Today, the islands of the Pacific include 12 independent nations, and 12 islands or groups of islands that have retained links with, and dependency on, other powers (France, USA, New Zealand, Britain, Chile and Japan). Independence has brought questions about economic development, which are acute in a region that is short of resources. The import of consumer goods – from canned food to video cassettes – has undermined traditional culture, while also raising expectations and aggravating the frustrations of island life. The physical beauty of the Pacific islands remains a key asset, and not just for its tourism potential: in this fast-changing world, the natural features that have shaped the islands and set them apart remain an enduring and reassuring constant.

Desert island dreams *Many of the countless tiny islands of Fiji are protected by a fringe of coral, which waves have pulverised over time into the banks of white sand, where coconut palms take root. For any creatures that can reach them, such islands represent havens amid the vast expanses of deep, sapphire-blue sea. A number of early European and American visitors portrayed the Pacific islands as paradise on Earth, and the image of the region as an ideal, pristine natural environment has remained part of Western folklore ever since.*

Between sea and sky *From afar, most Pacific islands are the merest punctuation on the horizon. On Aitutaki atoll in the Cook Islands (right), palm trees raise the profile of the sand bordering the lagoon, which is made turquoise by its bed of coral sand. The Pacific sky is often brushed by clouds that are lit by sunlight bouncing off the surface of the sea. Navigators of old could read the distinctive colours of the lagoons in the clouds, which helped them to locate islands.*

Perfect beach *A coral-sand beach on the Fijian island of Ovalau provides an idyllic Pacific island image. The shallow lagoon water may warm up to bath-like temperatures of 30°C (86°F). Tourist brochures exploit such images, but are less keen to draw attention to the downsides, such as the swarms of mosquitoes that emerge at dusk, and the venomous stonefish, cone shells and jellyfish that may live in a lagoon.*

Coral empires A wall of dead and heavily eroded coral on the Rangiroa atoll, in the Tuamotu archipelago of French Polynesia, demonstrates what a formidable barrier coral reefs create between land and sea. Left high and dry by falling sea levels, all that remains here are jagged and lacerating encrustations that were built up over hundreds of years by generations of coral polyps. Although tiny, soft and delicate, coral polyps are capable of building some of nature's largest structures, including the foundation blocks of whole islands. The Tuamotus form the world's largest group of coral atolls, spanning an area 310 miles (600 km) wide and 930 miles (1500 km) long. When submerged and living, the coral reefs create a protective wall around islands in which a rich range of sealife can prosper, providing a vital element in a complex food chain.

Ring of surf Moorea, sister island to Tahiti and the second largest island of French Polynesia, rises to a volcanic cone 3960 ft (1207 m) above sea level. It represents a coral-atoll in the making. Coral reefs have built up on submerged flanks of this mountain, creating a lagoon that all but surrounds the island, as well as the islets of Motu Faroehe and Motu Tiahura in the foreground. Over a period of about 10 million years, the volcanic cone will become submerged, but the coral – constantly building upwards – will create a ring-like atoll. This cycle creates an exceptional diversity in animal and plant life in both habitats: the warm waters of the lagoon and the fertile volcanic slopes of the mountain.

11

Keeping watch *The white spots of a moray eel provide camouflage in its reef home off Vanuatu. Morays spend most of the day in their lairs with only their heads protruding, watching for passing prey. They continuously open and close their mouths to pass water over their gills. If attacked, they can use their tails to grip on to the sides of their lairs, making it virtually impossible to dislodge them. They will usually risk swimming out only under the cover of darkness. Such strategies, and their ferocious jaws, designed to take chunks of flesh out of larger fish, mean that morays have few predators and enjoy a privileged place at the upper end of the lagoon food chain.*

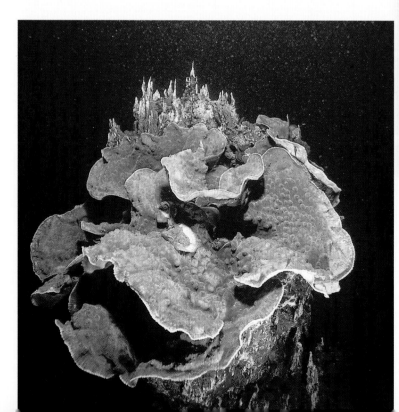

Springing surprises *The world beneath the surface of the ocean presents an almost infinite number of niches for life. Here, off the coast of New Caledonia, a cluster of lettuce coral has grown on top of a limestone column that has formed around a submarine freshwater spring. On top of the coral, limestone concretions form delicate spires, inching the column towards the surface. Such submarine springs are not unusual. They are fairly easy to spot: visible on the surface as a disc of fresh water. Divers can also see them, because the different densities of fresh water and salt water make a spring visible.*

Mesmerising diversity   A coral reef contains a rich diversity of life, with outcrops of staghorn and finger coral growing on the eroded remains of older stands of coral, and surmounted with a crown of flamboyant feather stars. Reefs represent a highly dynamic environment, changing over time according to the currents and their distance from the reef crest on the seaward side. At the interface with the ocean, the surf and surge of water prevent the more delicate forms of coral from taking hold. But by the same token, the swirling water carries with it rich supplies of plankton – food for coral polyps. In calmer waters, the sea is clearer and activity less frantic. The colour of a reef is a measure of its health. Living coral may be red, green, blue or yellow, and the polyps themselves may be even more vivid shades. The algae that encrust and bind together abandoned clumps of coral add their touches of purple, brown, green and red. Dead coral is white.

Unrestrained growth   Aerial views of the Seventy Islands, a nature reserve in the Rock Islands of Palau (Micronesia), reveal the complex patterns created by coral islands. Here, free of human exploitation, the vegetation grows to the rocky shorelines, which plunge straight into the sea. Despite the shallow depth of the lagoon, detectable by the ascending shades of blue, there are few beaches. This is a feature of many of the Pacific islands, and the lack of access to humans has been a determining feature of their habitat. Today, most of the traffic between these islands is for tourists who come to marvel at the natural tropical gardens and crystal clear waters – home to some 1500 species of fish alone.

Local variety   Some landscapes of the Pacific islands are the reverse of the stereotypical coral-sand, brochure image. Much of the coast of Hawaii (below) reflects the volcanic origins of the islands, where lava flows running down to the sea have left fields of tortured black rock onto which coral has only sometimes fastened. The vegetation reflects the varying ability of the soil to retain moisture. Here, tough scrub and succulents, which store reserves of moisture in their bulbous leaves, predominate. The only obvious clue that this is a tropical landscape is the sparse scattering of coconut palms.

Unwelcoming shores The coast of Easter Island has virtually no protection from coral reefs, and as a result its remnants of ancient lava flows receive the full erosive force of the ocean. The resulting formidable barrier of sharp rocks and surf means that there are very few safe landing places on Easter Island, and beaches are similarly rare. Easter Island is a Pacific island like no other, not only for its mysterious stone sculptures, but also for its isolation in the far south-east. Its subtropical climate is cooled by constant winds and the cold Humboldt Current. There were forests on the island before the arrival of the first Polynesian settlers in about AD 600, but these were cut down long ago, leaving a windswept landscape of sheep-cropped grasslands and scrub, often shrouded in mist and drizzle.

Volcanic beginnings   *In their youth, many islands of the Pacific probably resembled Lopevi, which lies close to the centre of the Vanuatu group. Rising to 4636 ft (1413 m) in an almost-perfect cone, the volcano is still active: an eruption in the 1970s forced all its inhabitants to abandon the island. The ash-coated flanks of the cone still have a raw look, and have yet to be fully colonised by vegetation. And, for the present, the drop-off from the shore is too steep for extensive colonisation by coral, which cannot grow at depths greater than 150 ft (45 m). In the distant future, however, the volcanic peak will become submerged, and probably be succeeded by a coral atoll.*

Danger zone   *The Lombenden volcano (below) on the island of Ambae (which was called Aoba until 1980), in Vanuatu, is also still active, and possesses two of the world's rare examples of warm, sulphurous crater lakes. An eruption took place beneath Lake Vui in 1991, causing the water to boil, and destroying the surrounding vegetation. Following several other signs of increased volcanic activity in the 1990s, a full-scale eruption is now considered inevitable and evacuation plans for the island's population have been put in place.*

Front line The Hawaiian islands have formed over a shifting hotspot that pierces the Earth's crust in the middle of the Pacific Plate. The current position of the hotspot is marked by Mauna Loa, and by the younger volcano of Kilauea, both in the south of Hawaii and the centrepieces of the Hawaii Volcanoes National Park. The name Kilauea means 'much spreading', and its treacle-like lava frequently oozes down its south slope to meet the sea, as here.

Unique growth   Little can grow in the volcanic desert around the Haleakala crater on the Hawaiian island of Maui, but a unique plant has found a niche. The leaves of the aptly named silversword (Argyroxiphium sandwicense) reflect the damaging rays of sunlight and conserve moisture. Between 15 and 50 years old, the plant produces a massive sword-like spike bearing hundreds of daisy-like flowers, then dies. Silverswords are believed to be related to a Californian daisy, so the seeds of their ancestors must have arrived on the island by sea, or been carried by birds. The silversword is under threat of extinction from goats and ants, and from hikers who used to take pleasure in seeing it roll down the slopes. It is now a protected species.

Silent sentinels   There is a timeless quality to the marshlands of Wallis, in the Wallis and Futuna Islands, the smallest and least-known of France's Overseas Territories in the Pacific. The island has a comparatively high level of rainfall, at 118 in (3000 mm) a year. In the forested wetlands the trees grow from widely splayed bases, the roots of which anchor them in the marsh. This is the kind of scene that would have greeted the first settlers, who came to these islands some 3500 years ago. The pigs introduced by those first settlers were the precursors of today's feral animals, which number 11 000 – more than the human population.

Primal forest *The highland tropical forests of Papua New Guinea (right) produce an extraordinary abundance of growth. The trees reach up to the light on columnar trunks with few branches, and form a high canopy of leaves that keeps the forest floor in semi-darkness. The cycle of fertility is maintained by falling trees and leaves, which decompose into a rich humus. Ferns and mosses prosper in the warm, damp atmosphere, colonising logs, tree-stumps and the trunks of living trees. Papua's dense tropical forests offer natural refuges to a number of unique bird species, such as the spectacular birds of paradise and the related bowerbirds.*

Running water By and large, rivers are a feature only of the larger, more mountainous islands, where increasing altitude causes rising tropical air to cool and condense as rain. Pohnpei, in the Federated States of Micronesia, has several reasons to be thankful for its abundant rainfall. The numerous rivers fed by the rain supply the islanders with fresh water. Heavy rainfall also feeds the island's cloak of vegetation, which is lush even by the standards of the south Pacific. The thick forest persuaded US military planners to bypass the island during the Second World War, so sparing it the violence that still troubles the memory of many other islanders. By contrast, low-lying coral atolls usually have to depend for their rain on passing storms and showers, and many suffer from chronic shortages of fresh water.

Plant heaven The continuous rumble of waterfalls breaks the silence of the botanical reserve that surrounds the Chutes de la Madeleine on Grande Terre, the largest island of New Caledonia and one of the largest islands in the south Pacific. The reserve lies in the region around Yaté, close to the southern tip of the island, which is known as the 'Botanical Paradise' for its rich concentration of flora. New Caledonia has some 2500 native species of plants and animals, which share much in common with those in its nearest neighbour to the west, Australia. The Yaté region includes the 22 000 acre (9000 ha) Parc Provincial de la Rivière Bleue, which has one of the few surviving populations of the endangered kagu (Rhynochetos jubatus), which has become New Caledonia's national bird.

A brief history

When the first Europeans sailed into the Pacific in the 16th century, virtually all of the ocean's thousands of habitable islands were already occupied. The history of this occupation remains one of the world's most extraordinary tales of migration and settlement – so extraordinary in its manner and timing that it mystified the Western world until the 20th century.

Origins

It now seems fairly certain that the first settlers of the region migrated from Southeast Asia between 33 000 and 40 000 years ago, about the time that similar peoples moved across a land bridge to Australia. This was during the Ice Age, when sea levels were lower and more of the land was exposed, making such migrations possible. In New Guinea, people settled on the coasts, and later turned their hands to agriculture in the forested hills.

Many thousands of years later, in about 2000 BC, a new wave of migrants, lighter-skinned Austronesian-speakers from Southeast Asia, began to move into the region, also settling on the coasts of New Guinea and in the neighbouring Bismarck archipelago. With improvements to their outrigger sailing canoes, they began the island-hopping that led them ever farther into the ocean. They found other large islands fairly close to New Guinea, and then the scattering of the thousands of smaller islands beyond. They turned northwards into Micronesia, southwards to the Solomons, Vanuatu and New Caledonia, then eastwards to Fiji, Samoa and Tonga (considered to be the Polynesian homelands, known as Havaiki). While tribal and family groups settled and colonised the islands, new generations, perhaps prompted by over-population, perpetuated the tradition of expansion in the image of their forebears – whose exploits had now been woven into their clan myth. They eventually reached the Marquesas Islands, possibly by the 2nd century BC.

Spiritual guardians Tikis, *ancestral figures carved in stone or wood, played a central role in religious rites.*

Route finder Early Pacific navigators found their way by 'reading' the currents, the swell, stars, clouds and the flight of birds. They recorded navigational information in 'maps' made from wood, twine and shells.

Reconstructing the past The achievements of the first pioneers are still treated with great respect and wonder. This reconstruction of a traditional sailing vessel was exhibited at a festival in Port Moresby, Papua New Guinea.

Settlement map

Hawaii · Marshall Islands · Equator · Pacific Ocean · New Guinea · Solomans · Marquesas · Coral Sea · Vanuatu · Samoa · Fiji · Tahiti · Tonga · New Caledonia · Pitcairn · Easter Island · AUSTRALIA · NEW ZEALAND

120° · 140° · 160° · 160° · 140° · 120°

Settlement
- First settlers, over 5000 years ago
- Lapita culture

Trans-oceanic migrations
- c. 3000-200 BC
- after 200 BC

Ocean-going craft   An 1861 engraving shows a double-hulled canoe from Tongaptapu, in the Tonga archipelago. Such boats could travel 150 miles (240 km) in a day.

This phase of migration lasted 2000 years; the next phase began in about AD 300. Fleets of large Polynesian canoes departed from the Marquesas and began exploring and settling the farthest extremities of their region. They reached the Hawaiian islands perhaps in about AD 300, Easter Island in AD 400, the Society Islands (in French Polynesia) in about AD 800 – at about the same time that the forebears of the Maoris began settling in New Zealand.

Canoes and outriggers

The journeys achieved by these Polynesian sailors were without precedent. The distances involved, much of which was out of sight of land, put their skills of navigation to the test. Relying on knowledge accumulated by generations of sailors, they steered by the sun, the stars, the flight of birds, the shape and colour of the clouds, and a feel for the swell. They travelled on catamaran-like 'canoes' consisting of two long and heavy hulls, joined together by a deck furnished with a shelter. Capable of carrying 100 adults and all their provisions, the larger canoes were well equipped to transport sustainable populations of settlers to any islands that favoured them. With them, they took the basics of farming that had been developed in New Guinea: taro roots and yams, cuttings of banana and breadfruit trees, of coconut and pandanus palms, as well as pigs, chickens and dogs. Their culture was essentially Stone Age: they never developed metals but made all they needed from plant matter, bone, stone, and shells.

*Staple diet
Taro plants arrived with the first settlers.*

Some Polynesian travellers evidently reached South America, returning with the sweet potato, the only New World product to reach Oceania before the 16th century. This, and other indications, gave rise to the belief that perhaps Oceania had been peopled by South Americans, not by Asians – a theory tested by the Norwegian explorer and ethnologist Thor Heyerdahl in his famous *Kon Tiki* raft expedition of 1947, which sailed from South America to Polynesia. But, despite his successful crossing, the theory has since been convincingly discredited by other data, including that derived from studying languages, inherited diseases and DNA.

In 1976, a reconstruction of an ocean-going canoe, the *Hokule'a*, sailed the 3000 miles (4800 km) from Hawaii to Tahiti and successfully proved the feasibility not only of the journey, but also of traditional Polynesian navigation achieved entirely by reading natural phenomena.

Lapita culture

Lapita is the name of a site near Koné in northern New Caledonia, where in 1951 the American archaeologist Edward W. Gifford discovered fired pottery decorated with distinctive bands of stamped or incised geometric markings. Similar examples of this 'Lapita' pottery were subsequently found in other parts of Melanesia (New Guinea, Fiji), and in western Polynesia (Tonga, Samoa). The oldest date to about 1600 BC, but they appear to represent a culture that lasted over 1000 years. All signs of pottery then vanished on many islands. The conclusion is that these 'Lapita people' had spread eastwards from New Guinea, but were then absorbed by a new wave of migrants.

Adapting to the environment

Landscapes vary hugely across the Pacific, from the dense forests of New Guinea to the coral beaches of the Tuamotu archipelago in French Polynesia. The migrant groups that settled fashioned their survival strategies according to their habitat, pursuing agriculture, animal husbandry and fishing, thus creating their own individual island cultures.

All the island communities were to some degree isolated, and some by vast expanses of open water. All the more surprising,

Enduring ways   A boy takes a lesson in traditional navigation on the island of Satawal, Federated States of Micronesia.

23

Walking the pig *Pigs are the principal domestic animal in the Pacific islands. They are sometimes treated virtually as pets, as here on Tubuai Island, French Polynesia.*

therefore, is the amount of features that these scattered communities have in common, such as their language links, kinship ties, their taboos and religious practices, and their veneration of nature. In addition, they all shared a taste for warfare, and most, it seems, practised cannibalism.

First contact

During the 15th century, on the other side of the world, the Ottoman Turks cut off European access to the eastern Mediterranean ports, the terminals of the Asian spice trade and silk routes. Western merchants decided to seek for themselves sea routes that led to the sources of these valuable goods. Just about all they knew was that they came from the East, which was described as Cathay (or China) and the Indies. Most of their knowledge was derived from medieval copies of Ptolemaic maps made during Roman times.

In this initial stage, the main contenders in the field were Spain and Portugal. In the search for the spices of the East, the Spanish stumbled on the Americas, while the Portuguese headed eastwards around Africa, found India, and first entered the Pacific from the west in 1511. In 1520 the Portuguese captain Ferdinand Magellan, on a Spanish-sponsored expedition that eventually completed the first circumnavigation of the world, rounded the southern tip of South America and named the ocean he entered *Mar Pacifico* (Peaceful Sea). He underestimated the scale of the Pacific, believing he would reach the Philippines in a matter of days, but sailing westwards he encountered virtually no land at all – just

Cannibalism

Much of the fearsome reputation attributed to Pacific islanders by early European voyagers derived from the widespread practice of cannibalism. Each society had its own contexts, taboos and rituals relating to the practice. It was not conducted out of some kind of sadistic bloodlust: cannibal victims were often defeated warriors, whose power and prestige (*mana*) was said to transfer to those who ate their flesh – but eating another person could also be a way of displaying disrespect. There was also a simple dietary logic: human flesh was a useful source of protein: in Melanesian pidgin it was known as 'long pig'. Fingers and feet were particularly prized.

Shelling out *Cowries were used as money in New Guinea. The bag is made of orchid fibre.*

Mutual interest *A 17th-century engraving pictures contact between a Spanish ship and people of the Marianas, in Micronesia.*

Concentric circles *The circular focus of this village in the Trobriand Islands, off Papua New Guinea, becomes evident from the air. The islanders live by growing taro, sweet potatoes, pumpkins and yams, and by fishing.*

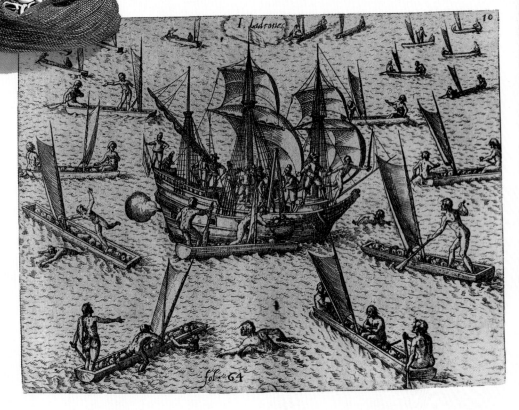

Drinking ceremony This print illustrates a kava-drinking ceremony on the ill-fated French expedition under La Pérouse in 1785-8.

War dance Traditional dancing remains one of the most enduring cultural traditions of Melanesia.

one isolated and uninhabited island in the Tuamotu chain, probably Pukapuka. Eventually, after a crossing of 8000 miles (13 000 km) he reached the Marianas, where he received a hostile reception and had to fight for fresh supplies. Magellan was killed in the Philippines, but his expedition eventually limped home.

The Portuguese and Spanish now sailed not simply for spices, but for gold and territorial possessions – and the possibility of turning the native peoples into Christians. With the Pope's assistance, under the Treaty of Tordesillas of 1494, they divided the world into two hemispheres in which each could claim possession of all newly discovered lands. The line of division ran through the middle of the Atlantic and Brazil on one side of the world, and through the unexplored Pacific on the other. Spain ended up with the Americas, Portugal with Africa and Asia.

The vast, empty expanses of the Pacific, and its islands inhabited by Neolithic people, held little interest when there appeared to be greater spoils elsewhere. But one conundrum still exercised the European navigators: inscribed on the Ptolemaic maps was a massive continent named the Unknown Southern Land, the *Terra australis incognita*, purportedly introduced to give balance to the landmasses of the Northern Hemisphere. Many expeditions set off in search of this elusive goal. With this in mind, and also lured by an Inca legend of gold-rich Pacific islands, the Spaniard Álvaro de Mendaña de Neira sailed westwards from Mexico in 1567. He passed between the Marquesas and the Tuamotu islands apparently

without seeing them, and in 1568 became the first European to reach the Solomons.

In 1595 Mendaña organised a second expedition, which took him to the Marquesas, but he was unable to find the Solomons again and died on the expedition. His pilot, the Portuguese Pedro Fernández de Quirós, brought the fleet to safety in the Philippines, then in 1603 set out again in search of the Unknown Southern Land. He thought he had found it when he reached present-day Vanuatu which he named La Austrialia [sic] del Espiritu Santo. De Quirós abandoned an attempt to colonise the island, brought his starving crew back to South America, and died in Peru. With his death the ambition of Spain and Portugal to explore the remoter parts of the south Pacific also expired.

Memories A circle of stone commemorates the arrival of the first canoes, bringing ancestral settlers.

Visual record A drawing of 1822 attempts to show styles of dress and tattooing among islanders.

Dutch, French and English

The Dutch took over where the Spanish and Portuguese left off. They saw the Pacific as a business venture, and installed trading posts in Indonesia, which they reached via the route around southern Africa. More through mishap than design, their ships were occasionally swept by currents and winds onto the west coast of Australia, but they dismissed it as a wasteland. In 1615-16 Jacob Le Maire and Willem Schouten, in search of the Unknown Southern Land, discovered Tonga and New Ireland in the Bismarck archipelago. Abel Tasman visited Tonga, the Fijian islands and New Britain, the largest island of the Bismarck archipelago, in 1642–3. In 1722 Jacob Roggeveen, crossing the ocean from east to west, was the first to visit Easter Island, the Society Islands (in French Polynesia), and some of the Samoan islands. Essentially, though, the Dutch concentrated on their valuable trade in the East Indies (Indonesia).

One of the obstacles to exploration of the Pacific was that no one could determine longitude with any degree of accuracy. Maps from these early years were extremely inaccurate, making it hard for subsequent navigators to find islands in the great expanse of blue – sometimes with dire consequences when food and water ran low. The solution lay with the invention of the ship's chronometer in the late 18th century, which enabled local time and time at Greenwich to be accurately compared.

By then, exploration of the Pacific formed part of the age-old rivalry between the French and the English. The English captain Samuel Wallis was the first European to reach Tahiti in 1768, a few months before Frenchman Louis-Antoine de Bougainville. After a journey that

The French Cook
Bougainville gained a deep admiration for the peoples and cultures of Oceania during his round-the-world voyage of 1767-9.

also took him to Samoa, Vanuatu and the Solomon Islands to complete the first French circumnavigation of the globe. Before long Bougainville's exploits had been eclipsed by the greatest explorer of the Pacific, James Cook.

Captain Cook

Between his first visit to Tahiti in 1769 and his death ten years later in Hawaii, Captain James Cook, in the course of three British naval expeditions, covered the greater part of the Pacific. Between 1768 and 1771, on board the *Endeavour*, he reconnoitred the Society Islands (now in French Polynesia), New Zealand, and the west coast of Australia. In his 1772-5 expedition, with the *Resolution* and the *Adventure*, he visited the Marquesas, the New Hebrides (Vanuatu), and New Caledonia. He also circumnavigated the globe in southern latitudes and determined that no habitable southern continent existed south of Australia. By the time he died, almost all of the Pacific had been mapped. The expedition led by French aristocrat Jean-François de La Pérouse marked the last in the era of great voyages of discovery. He

Jumping ship

The beauty and 'hospitality' of the women of the Pacific islands was something that European sailors found hard to resist. After months at sea, they were easily won over by the accommodating young women who appeared all-but naked on their decks and welcomed them into their homes. Sailors often deserted their ships to remain permanently on the islands, but they faced severe penalties. Their captains, who could not afford to lose crew, put pressure on local chiefs to hand over absconders, and punished those caught with floggings or death – all of which seemed barbaric to the islanders. However, some of those who jumped ship did succeed in settling and carving out new lives for themselves.

reached the Hawaiian islands, Easter Island, Tonga and Samoa in 1786, but disappeared near Vanikoro in the Solomons in 1788.

In the wake of Cook's discoveries, the first English colony was established on the east coast of Australia in 1788, swiftly followed by waves of settlers. They opened up a direct trade with the islands, buying pigs from Tahiti, for example. European merchants toured the islands in search of goods to feed into a triangular trade with China. They exchanged muskets, alcohol and glass beads for pearls, turtle shells, *bêche-de-mer* (sea cucumber, a food delicacy), and scented sandalwood. These they took to China to exchange for silk, tea and porcelain. Meanwhile, hundreds of

Different rules
While some officers of La Pérouse's French expedition to Easter Island in 1786 make preliminary studies of the statues, others tolerate the islanders' making free and easy with their possessions.

whaling ships now came into the Pacific, in pursuit of the source of oil for lamps.

Relations between traders and islanders were generally fraught with mistrust; as well as firearms and alcohol, the traders brought European diseases against which the

sent a mission to Tonga in 1822 and Fiji in 1835. In the 1830s, French Catholics began work in New Caledonia. Soon, Christianity had spread across most of the region.

The Polynesians, in particular, were generally welcoming: these foreigners were interested neither in their women nor their possessions, and they brought various useful craft skills along with their religion. There was often a social price to pay: the

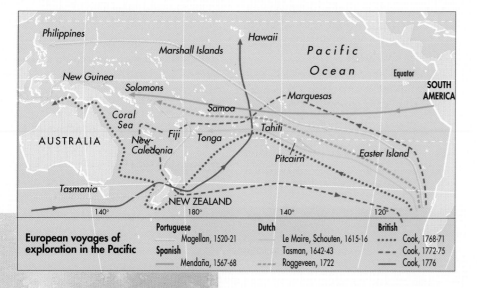

European voyages of exploration in the Pacific

	Portuguese	Dutch	British
	Magellan, 1520-21	Le Maire, Schouten, 1615-16	..... Cook, 1768-71
	Spanish	Tasman, 1642-43	– – – Cook, 1772-75
	Mendaña, 1567-68	Roggeveen, 1722	—— Cook, 1776

islanders had no resistance. They also took advantage of the different moral code practised by the islanders. The genetic heritage of this is more evident in Polynesia than in Melanesia, where the tribes defended their homelands more ferociously and were less accommodating.

For God and king

Until about 1800, most Europeans were just passing visitors, with the rare exception of castaways and those who jumped ship. A new era dawned with the arrival of the missionaries. The London Missionary Society was the first to reach the region, arriving on Tahiti in 1797. The Methodists

Show of strength *An impressive array of Tahitian war canoes, painted by William Hodges on Cook's second expedition.*

On display *These New Caledonians were photographed at a colonial exhibition in Paris in 1907. The woman is wearing a 'missionary dress'.*

missionaries discouraged traditions such as cannibalism, polygamy, kava-drinking and the semi-nudity of traditional dress. There was also a political price – the missionaries, once they had converted tribal chiefs, established power bases and took an increasing say in government. This was the case, for example, in Tahiti, Hawaii and Tonga, where chiefs adopted missionary codes of

Missionary fervour Catholicism and other forms of Christianity sought converts among Pacific islanders from the beginning of the 19th century.

law, and had close missionary advisers. The missionaries, meanwhile, maintained links with their own countries, laying the foundations for full-scale colonisation.

Changing society

Meanwhile, the basis of foreign trade had switched from sandalwood and muskets to copra, the dried kernels of coconut which supplied the oil used to manufacture soap and candles. The scale of this trade encouraged the foundation of port settlements, such as Papeete in Tahiti, Levuka in Fiji and Apia in Samoa. This in turn gave rise to a growing community of Europeans seeking not just trade, but also minerals and land for coffee, coconut palm, cotton, sugar and vanilla plantations.

The development of plantations, particularly for sugar cane, brought fundamental changes. From their introduction, it was clear that the local populations could not supply all the labour needed. Plantation owners looked abroad to make up the shortfall. Thousands of Indians were recruited to work in the sugar cane plantations of Fiji after the 1870s; workers from China, Japan and the Philippines went to Hawaii. In New Caledonia at the end of the 19th century, labour was needed for the nickel mines and this was provided by convicts and by Indonesians, Malays and Vietnamese.

'Blackbirding'

The economic development of the region also involved a flow of labour away from the islands. From the 1840s on, islanders from the New Hebrides (Vanuatu), the Solomons, and New Caledonia were recruited to work on sugar cane plantations in Australia and Fiji. Unscrupulous plantation owners often used intimidation and violence to acquire labourers, and many islanders were kidnapped and sold into slavery. This practice, known as 'blackbirding', was condemned in the West, mainly because of the troubles it provoked as agents tried to force local islanders to sign up. The need for security to prevent it was one of the pretexts for escalating colonial rule. Nonetheless, the practice did not cease until the end of the 19th century.

Exploiting the land

By the beginning of the 20th century, agriculture in Europe and America was consuming increasing quantities of phosphates. Guano, bird dung that had accumulated in deep deposits on some islands, was a rich source of phosphate. Local communities, notably on Makatea in French Polynesia and Nauru, reaped

Asian input Descendants of the thousands of Indians brought to Fiji to work on sugar cane plantations.

Sweet success Volcanic soil and tropical heat provide the ideal combination for sugar cane, as here on Kauai, in the Hawaiian islands.

Prospects of wealth Minerals attracted a rush of adventurers, in search of quick riches.

slim but easy benefits by allowing big business to take over extraction, but this had a corrosive effect on traditional life. Parallel damaging effects were seen on the larger Melanesian islands, where valuable metals were mined. Unscrupulous operators profited from the islanders' notions of land ownership to purchase land and negotiate exploitation leases, often at a pittance, generating problems over land rights.

Colonial rule

The rapid development of the plantations, mines, trading ports and immigrant communities created widespread tensions that undermined the stability once offered by chiefs and missionaries. European colonial governments stepped in, happy to secure a foothold in a region that had become increasingly important, both economically and strategically. Tahiti became a French protectorate in 1843, New Caledonia was annexed by France in 1853, Fiji became a British colony in 1874, and

Germany in the Pacific

In 1856, Johann Caesar Godeffroy, a wealthy shipowner and merchant from Hamburg, set up a trading station in Apia, Samoa. Before long his ships had forged a network of trade routes, making Samoa a key trading hub in the Pacific. The business was taken over by the Deutsche Handel und Plantagengesellschaft (German Trading and Plantation Company) in 1879 and the following year the newly united Germany under Otto von Bismarck gave its political backing. Germany's drive to empire accelerated: between 1884 and 1888, it annexed the north-east of New Guinea and the Bismarck archipelago, and extended into Micronesia by annexing the Marshall Islands in 1885. In 1899 it purchased the Caroline Islands, Palau and the Marianas (excluding Guam) from Spain. By 1900 Germany had a regional presence almost as extensive as Britain's.

Trusting foreigners This tribe in Vanuatu has developed a 'cargo cult' around the Duke of Edinburgh since his visit to the islands in 1974.

Germany took possession of territories in Melanesia, Polynesia and Micronesia.

In the 1870s, Australia and New Zealand began agitating for annexation of New Guinea and the Cook Islands respectively, and in the end Britain made both protectorates – south-east New Guinea in 1884, and the Cooks in 1888. Australia took over south-east New Guinea in 1906 and attached the name Papua to the territory. Britain and France agreed to share influence in the New Hebrides (Vanuatu) in 1887, and declared it a condominium in 1906. Britain granted Germany control of Nauru in 1887, but retained its presence in the Gilbert (Tuvalu) and Ellice Islands (Kiribati), and took possession of the southern Solomons in 1893. Tonga remained virtually an independent kingdom, albeit with British protection from 1900.

The USA took Guam from Spain in the Spanish-American War of 1898. It also annexed Hawaii in 1898, and negotiated with Germany and Britain for control of eastern Samoa in 1899, when the rest of Samoa became a German protectorate.

After the First World War, Germany lost its colonial possessions under the Treaty of Versailles, and the cake was redivided under mandates issued by the League of Nations. Papua New Guinea, the Bismarck Islands and the Solomon Islands were placed under an Australian mandate. The USA held sway in Hawaii and a part of Samoa, while Japan took control of Micronesia, with the exception of US-held Guam.

There was, however, some shift in the sensitivities of the colonial powers towards the welfare of the islanders during the interwar years, but the south Pacific had now been irreversibly drawn into the web of world affairs. The Panama Canal had opened in 1914, greatly improving shipping links with the east coast of the USA and with Europe. Air links began to develop in the 1930s. But when war broke out in Europe in 1939, Japan took the opportunity to impose its own Asia-centric vision on the region – and unleashing the cataclysm of the Second World War on these tranquil islands.

Raising the flag The French tricolour has flown over Tuamotu, in French Polynesia, for over a century. France is the last of the European nations to retain substantial possessions in the South Pacific.

29

Illustrated news
A letter dated 1846 depicts the French painter Charles Giraud in Tahiti, reading his mail in the shade of a coconut palm.

Objects of fascination The French writer and traveller Pierre Loti (1850-1923) made this sketch of Easter Island statues.

The region's myths

Virtually from the moment that Europeans first set eyes on the south Pacific, the islands caught their imagination. Their travel reports inspired reverie back home – a dream of far-off places, untainted by the complexities of life in Europe. Here, so the myth suggested, was a vast, warm ocean dotted with lush islands, that provided miniature gardens of Eden for simple people living without the blemish of sin or the corruption of civilisation. In the years of the Enlightenment during the 18th century, such reports provided an idealised backdrop for the concept of the 'noble savage', as envisaged by the French philosopher Jean-Jacques Rousseau (1712-78).

Several of the mariners who travelled in the Pacific were not just expert navigators, but subtle observers and talented writers. Valuable records were left by the Italian Antonio Pigafetta, who survived Magellan's circumnavigation of 1519-22; by the Spaniards Andres de Urdaneta and Alonso de Arellano (who crossed the Pacific in 1564-5); by Mendaña and his Portuguese pilot Quirós; and by the Dutchman Abel Tasman. *A New Voyage Round the World* (1697) by the piratical but systematic William Dampier triggered widespread interest in the Pacific in Britain and led to his appointment to lead a further expedition in 1703. The French explorer Bougainville had a similar impact on the reading public with his *Voyage autour du monde* (*A Voyage round the World*, 1772).

From reality to fiction

In 1704, during his second expedition to the Pacific, Dampier put a quarrelsome Scottish crew member ashore, at his own request, on an uninhabited island in the Juan Fernández group, off Chile. This was Alexander Selkirk (1676-1721), whose account of his five-year stay on the island until his rescue formed the basis of one of the best-known tales of the Pacific: *Robinson Crusoe* (1719) by Daniel Defoe. Over a century later, the American writer Herman Melville served on whaling ships in the Pacific islands, experience which he put to use in his masterpiece *Moby Dick* (1851).

Perhaps the most famous resident-writer of the Pacific is the Scottish author Robert Louis Stevenson. Already celebrated for his adventure stories *Treasure Island* and *Kidnapped*, he came to the Pacific in 1888 and recorded his experiences sailing round the Marquesas and the Tuamotus in his book *In the South Seas* (1896). He settled in Samoa in 1890, where he worked until his death in 1894, aged 44.

American author Jack London echoed this experience with his voyages in his ketch the *Snark* in 1907-9. He recorded these in *The Cruise of the Snark and South Sea Tales* (1911), and went on to write ten books set in the Pacific.

In 1880, French writer and traveller Pierre Loti published his romanticised *The*

Whaling and literature

Whaling took off in the Pacific in the 18th century when American ships started hunting sperm whales there. This very tough life brought a new kind of ruffian-adventurer to the Pacific islands, many of whom exploited the islanders ruthlessly. Herman Melville's book *Moby Dick* can be read as a parable of the times.

Famous resident The Scottish author Robert Louis Stevenson spent the last four years of his life (1890-4) in Samoa.

Marriage of Loti, about the love of a young French naval officer for a Polynesian girl. The French painter Paul Gauguin was persuaded by Loti's writings to leave France and head for Polynesia, where he lived in Tahiti (1891-3 and 1895-1901), and then in the Marquesas Islands until his death, lonely, impoverished and syphilitic, in 1903.

British author W. Somerset Maugham later wrote a novel based on Gauguin's life, *The Moon and Sixpence* (1919), having visited Polynesia as part of his research. He subsequently wrote a number of short stories set in the Pacific, including the highly charged *Rain* (1921) set in Pago Pago in the Samoan islands.

Anthropologists lent some respectability to the South Seas myth. The Polish-born American, Bronislaw Malinowski, considered the founder of social anthropology, spent two years among the people of the Trobriand Islands in Melanesia between 1915 and 1918, and produced a series of

Painter of the isles *The work of the French painter Paul Gauguin helped to promote an image of Tahiti's sensuous beauty.*

Truth and fiction *Daniel Defoe's book* Robinson Crusoe, *published in 1719, was based on a real-life tale of desert island survival.*

works on the region, including his famous *Sexual Life of Savages* (1929). This followed on the heels of *Coming of Age in Samoa* (1928), by American anthropologist Margaret Mead, which was celebrated for its observation of alternative sexual mores, though her methods and conclusions were later the subject of controversy.

Writing transformed by war

The Second World War inspired a new assessment of the Pacific. American novelist James A. Michener served as a war historian in the US navy, a posting that took him to more than 50 islands. His *Tales of the South Pacific* (1947) explores the impact of war on the islands and the servicemen. It also provided the basis of *South Pacific*, the hit Broadway musical by Rodgers and Hammerstein. Michener's compatriot Norman Mailer served in the US army in the Pacific from 1944 to 1946, and his novel *The Naked and the Dead* (1948) was greeted as one of the best to emerge from the war. Similarly, the American writer James Jones drew on his military experience for his novels *From Here to Eternity* (1951) and *The Thin Red Line* (1962).

One author who has questioned the Pacific myth is American travel writer Paul Theroux, whose ironically titled *The Happy Isles of Oceania* (1992) recounts his travels around the islands of Melanesia and Polynesia. But, like the first European visitors, he admires the islands' natural beauty, and occasionally discovers a kind of contentment akin to paradise.

Greeting sailors with offers of free love

'As soon as we approached land, the islanders surrounded the ships. There were so many canoes around our vessels that we had difficulty mooring amid all the crowd and noise. They were all shouting "*tayo*", which means "friend", and they were lavish in their signs of friendship; they all demanded nails and earrings. The canoes were filled with women who, in terms of facial charm, would be a match for the majority of European women, while their bodies were of a beauty unsurpassed. Most of these nymphs were naked, for the men and older women who accompanied them had removed the loin cloth that they normally wore. They began by addressing us from their canoes with provocative gestures and taunts, in which, despite their naivety, we could detect at least some inhibition; either nature had generally imbued their sex with a genuine timidity, or, even in these lands where the freedoms of the Golden Age still ruled, women like to appear not to want what they most desire. The men, more direct and less inhibited, soon made clear what they had in mind: they urged us to choose a woman, to follow her ashore, and their unequivocal gestures showed us how we were expected to become better acquainted. I put it to you: how, in the midst of such a show, do you keep 400 young French sailors, who have had no sight of a woman for six months, focused on their work?' Louis-Antoine de Bougainville, Tahiti, 1768.

Covered up
A contemporary print of island women.

The Second World War in the Pacific

→ Japanese advance or attack → U.S. advance or attack
■ Japanese base ■ U.S. base

The Pacific War

Between 1941 and 1945 the Pacific islands were the theatre of the war between the USA and Japan. The populations of the islands became victims in a conflict over which they had little control.

From 1919 on Japan had power over most of Micronesia (the Marshall Islands, the Caroline Islands and the Marianas), which it ruled as if they were part of Japan

Shock tactics Japan's pre-emptive air raid on the US naval base at Pearl Harbor marked the entry of America into the war. This picture is taken from the 1970 film Tora! Tora! Tora!

The Kokoda Trail

Port Moresby, the capital of Papua New Guinea, lies on the south coast of the island. The Kokoda Trail links it to the north coast, across mountainous terrain cloaked in thick forest. In July 1942, the Japanese landed on the north coast of New Guinea and pushed down the trail in an attempt to take Port Moresby. For four months Australian troops opposed them: although numerically inferior, they had the support of the Papuans, who operated supply routes and helped to repatriate the wounded. On October 30, the Australians raised their flag over Kokoda, halfway along the trail, and the Japanese were forced out of Papua in January 1943. It was a key early success in the Pacific campaign, but cost the lives of 5700 Australians, 2800 Americans and 10 000 Japanese.

Pushing on A Japanese base is destroyed by fire on the island of Bougainville.

itself. The Japanese developed trade and other commercial activities, and also set up military bases. While Japan reinforced the legitimacy of its presence in the region, Germany began to agitate for the return of the possessions it had lost under the Treaty of Versailles in 1918.

When war broke out in Europe in 1939, the south Pacific territories under British and French rule declared solidarity with

Carrier hit The Battle of Guadalcanal, which began in August 1942, was America's first offensive.

their colonial powers, and volunteers signed up to serve in their defence. The threat of war grew closer in September 1940, when Tokyo signed a non-aggression pact with Berlin. Japan's aggression in Asia, meanwhile, provoked US-led embargoes on raw material exports.

On December 7, 1941, the Japanese launched a surprise air attack on the American fleet at Pearl Harbor on the Hawaiian island of Oahu, destroying or severely damaging 18 battleships (including eight aircraft carriers) and 300 aircraft, and killing 2400 Americans. The aim was to destroy US naval power in the western Pacific, and leave British, Dutch, French and American possessions unprotected.

End of the road A Japanese soldier surrenders on the island of Namur, in the Kwajalein atoll of the Marshall Islands, in 1944. Other Japanese-held islands capitulated after the Hiroshima and Nagasaki bombs.

The cost of war A US poster asks citizens to subscribe to a loan to assist in the war against Japan.

Barbed wire on the beaches

Pearl Harbor precipitated all-out conflict. The USA responded swiftly: the Hawaiian islands were reinforced; barbed wire barricades erected on the beaches; a curfew imposed; and the large Japanese population interned. For the next four years, Hawaii was transformed into a vast military camp, the headquarters of the US military effort for the entire Pacific theatre of war.

Meanwhile, the Japanese continued to score successes in their advance across the Pacific, taking the Gilbert Islands and Guam, and landing in north-eastern New Guinea and New Britain. But the tide

began to turn for the Japanese at the Battle of the Coral Sea, in May 1942, and the Battle of Midway, in June 1942. The Americans consolidated their gains by building bases. Under the direction of General Douglas MacArthur, hundreds of thousands of GIs were sent to the Melanesian islands that Japan had not yet occupied – the New Hebrides (Vanuatu), New Caledonia and Fiji – islands that were generally spared the extreme violence of the front line.

The defeat of Japan

The heavy action was taking place to the north, notably in the Solomon Islands. After the Japanese had been forced out of Guadalcanal, New Guinea and Bougainville, an 'island-hopping' counter-offensive opened up in Micronesia under Admiral Chester Nimitz. For the islanders, conditions deteriorated as the Japanese supply lines crumbled. They were subjected to requisition-

Pouring ashore The USA poured vast resources of men and materials into winning the war in the Pacific.

ing and forced labour. Conditions often worsened with the arrival of the Americans, who used heavy bombardments to oust the Japanese. The US campaign drove on, taking the Gilbert Islands, then the Marshall Islands, then Guam, the Marianas and Palau. Japanese resistance was fierce, often suicidal. Heavy American casualties in taking the Japanese islands of Iwo Jima and Okinawa was one of the factors leading to the decision to drop atom bombs on Hiroshima and Nagasaki. Japan finally capitulated on August 15, 1945.

The path to independence

The region was one of the last to retain a significant colonial presence. Nonetheless, the writing was on the wall from the close of the Second World War. The United Nations granted a resumption of rule by the victorious colonial powers, but on the understanding that independence and

Scars of battle In Pago Pago, in the Samoan islands, rusting reminders of the war remain.

Guadalcanal: battle of attrition

The Japanese invaded the island of Guadalcanal on July 6, 1942, and began building an airfield. On August 7, the USA launched a massive attack and captured the airfield. The Japanese reinforced with 36 000 troops, while six separate battles raged around the coasts. The US marines at the airfield held out, and were eventually reinforced by 38 000 troops. Battle now raged across the forested island, until, on February 8,1943, the Japanese were forced to evacuate.

self-rule was the ultimate goal. With this in view, postwar colonial rule involved a greater level of participation by the islanders, and by the 1950s many of the islands were enjoying a considerable degree of autonomy.

Intent The Maohi (people of East Polynesia) began to agitate against French rule in the 1950s.

Many had achieved full independence by 1980, but a number opted to remain under the control of the former ruling power, such as French Polynesia and Guam. Of the 24 Pacific archipelagoes, nine became fully independent: Samoa (in 1962), Nauru (1968), Fiji (1970), Tonga (1970), Papua New Guinea (1975), Solomon Islands (1978), Tuvalu (1978), Kiribati (1979) and Vanuatu (1980). Three are independent republics with a Compact of Free Association with the USA: Federated States of Micronesia, the Marshall Islands and Palau. Two islands are provinces or states forming an integral part of their mother country: Hawaii (USA) and Easter Island (Chile). Eight are territories administered directly by, or in conjunction with, the mother country: New Caledonia,

French Polynesia, Wallis and Fortuna (France); American Samoa, Guam, Northern Marianas (USA); Pitcairn (UK); Tokelau (New Zealand). And two are self-governing states in free association with New Zealand: Cook Islands and Niue.

Styles of government vary across the region, but largely reflect the influence of the former colonial power, mixed with local tradition. Of the independent states formerly associated with Britain, Tonga has its own monarchy; Samoa has a president elected from among four royal families; the British sovereign remains the head of state of the Solomons and Tuvulu; Kiribati and Nauru are republics. All are members of the British Commonwealth.

By and large, the transition to the current state of affairs was achieved peacefully,

through negotiation. In part, this was due to the Pacific islands' traditional pattern of government, which puts consensus above confrontation. On the other hand, the region's complex geography, its long history of migration, foreign intrusion and

Armed conflict Separatists on the island of Bougainville, Papua New Guinea, precipitated the intervention of government troops in 1988.

Campaign trail An election candidate in tribal dress attempts to win over the crowd at Tari, central Papua New Guinea.

Head of state The Queen visited Tuvalu in 1982, four years after it had achieved independence from Britain.

Economic dependence

Most of the Pacific islands depend on aid from former colonial masters, neighbouring countries and international organisations. Few have the resources to make a significant contribution to their domestic income or development needs, the exceptions being New Caledonia (through its nickel), Papua New Guinea (oil, gas, gold and copper), Guam and Hawaii (tourism).

On the march   The FLNKS (Kanak national and socialist liberation front) maintain resistance to French rule in New Caledonia.

Strategic crossroads

The Americans have military bases in Micronesia and Hawaii; the French have outposts in New Caledonia and French Polynesia. Between 1945 and 1996, the French, British and Americans carried out nuclear tests in the region. The islanders are aware of the strategic importance of their region and constantly fear that any international conflict will spill over into it.

local rivalries have made identity an issue in many islands and left a legacy of tension.

The islands of the Pacific have had comparatively few single-issue nationalist movements. One exception is in Papua – the western half of New Guinea, annexed by Indonesia in 1969 – where a separatist movement has been fighting to be free of Indonesian rule. Autonomy was granted to Papua (formerly Irian Jaya but renamed when autonomy was given) in 2002, but for some this is not enough.

Fiji has had upheavals largely because the native Fijians have found themselves an economic minority, thanks to the legacy of the 19th century immigration of Asian workers. To defend their position against the power of the Indian vote, the army took over in October 1987. In 2000, the prime minister, an Indian, was ousted in a coup and native Fijians took over the government, although democratic elections soon followed in 2001. Even in Hawaii, a fully integrated state of the USA since 1959, a movement called 'Ka Pae'aina Hawai'i' presses for a Polynesian nation.

Troubles in paradise

French rule in the South Pacific continues to cause friction, notably in New Caledonia, which suffered a decade of confrontation and conflict before the Matignon Accords of 1988 ushered in a period of relative calm. The Nouméa Accord of 1998 anticipates a progressive and irreversible transfer of authority. A referendum, set for 2013, or a second in 2018, will allow the population to choose between independence or autonomy within the French system.

Since 1996 French Polynesia has had broad powers of autonomy, with decentralised local institutions. But those pressing for total independence remain a significant force, and the local government wants to see its powers increased.

Wallis and Futuna is a French *pays d'outremer* (overseas country) co-administered by France with a council of elders and an elected local assembly.

All Pacific islands are troubled to some degree by a conflict of interests: struggling to retain traditional values but also tempted to join the modern world. They have to come to terms with unemployment, overcrowding and a mismatch between ambitions and the opportunities available. As the first European explorers found, these islands are not paradise, but sometimes something resembling it may be found among them.

Home pride   A T-shirt slogan voices an islander's pride in his ethnic identity.

THE PLACE
AND ITS
PEOPLE

By dint of the ocean's vast scale and the scarcity of land amid so much water, the islands of the Pacific were among the last places on Earth to be settled. They were in a state of pristine nature when the first migrants arrived, bringing with them their own plants and animals – a trend that continued after the arrival of Europeans. What nature rough-hewed with the violence of volcanic eruption and the patient building of coral, humans moulded and refined into the islands we see today, creating an environment where human input and natural forces are inseparably fused.

CHAPTER 1

MAJESTIC FORCES OF NATURE

Their wide geographical dispersal – the 25 000 Pacific islands are scattered across an ocean that covers a third of the planet – is echoed in the variety of landscapes found on the islands. Micronesia and Polynesia are characterised by steep-sided volcanoes, coral atolls and lagoons, Melanesia by its rugged nature. In many places, the two extraordinary, contrasting island-building forces of volcanoes and coral reefs can be seen together. And all the islands share the fate of lying in an ocean with its own self-contained regime of weather and currents.

Volcanic cliffs in the Na Pali Coast State Park, on the island of Kauai, Hawaii.

A *world of winds and currents*

The islands of the Pacific are in thrall to the regular but temperamental winds and currents that pass in perpetual motion across this vast oceanic basin.

Stretching for more than 10 000 miles (16 000 km) from north to south and east to west, the Pacific Ocean covers about one-third of the Earth's surface, and accounts for half of the total area of the world covered by water. Because of its immense depth, averaging 14 000 ft (4270 m), greater than any other ocean, the Pacific contains more than half of the world's sea water.

The sheer scale of the Pacific Ocean has a direct bearing on its currents and winds, but their strength and regularity derive from other factors. With its considerable temperature differences across the latitudes, which run from one polar region to the other, the Pacific is like a huge energy-recycling machine, of which the currents and winds are the product. In addition, the ocean is virtually surrounded by land, with an almost complete barrier reinforced by high mountains on the eastern side, and narrow links to adjacent oceans. This makes it a giant self-contained pool, where the currents have no other option but to circulate.

Purpose-built   Coconut palms – here on Rangiroa, in the Tuamotu chain – are well adapted to the buffeting of the trade winds.

***Onshore breeze**   South-east trades, known locally as **maraamu**, constantly brush the shores of Polynesia.*

Trade winds and westerlies

The trade winds are linked to the rotation of the Earth. They flow from areas of tropical high pressure towards a low-pressure band caused by rising hot air along the equator. There are two systems. In the Northern Hemisphere, the trade winds spring from the subtropical high-pressure zones beyond 30° of latitude north, notably from an anticyclone (area of high pressure) that sits to the northeast of Hawaii. Blowing from the north-east towards the southwest, they are called north-east trades. In the Southern Hemisphere, the trade winds form in a vast band of subtropical high pressure beyond 30° of latitude south and blow from south-east to northwest (south-east trades). The trade winds are relatively cool and moderate, with speeds of 10-40 mph (20-60 km/h). The two systems converge near the equator along a seasonally shifting line, the intertropical convergence zone. Here, the weather is humid and unstable, with unpredictable winds, and sometimes large areas of calm – the doldrums.

The temperate zones north and south of the areas of subtropical high pressure are brushed by an incessant flow of winds moving towards the poles from west to east, the westerlies. They generate the variable weather that characterises the maritime climates of the mid-latitudes.

Travelling on the trades

The winds and currents of the Pacific have played a key role in the history of the islands, pushing Polynesian canoes and the ships of the early European explorers before them. In 1565, the Spanish navigator and priest Andrés de Urdaneta was the first European to discover how to use the winds to cross the Pacific. To reach the islands, navigators followed the trade winds which blow from the east towards the equator. To continue homewards, de Urdaneta found it was necessary to sail south from the equator towards the South Pole, and catch the westerly winds of lower latitudes.

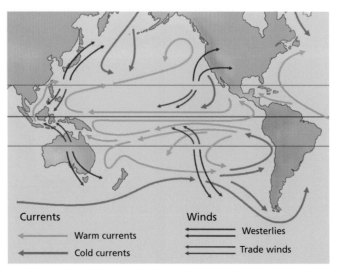

Currents	Winds
← Warm currents	← Westerlies
← Cold currents	← Trade winds

Setting a course *Pacific islanders use their knowledge of the currents and winds to sail their outrigger canoes.*

the western Pacific. This water converges and flows back eastwards along a line just to the north of the equator, forming the Equatorial Counter Current, which spans the Pacific from the Philippines to Colombia and separates the North and South Equatorial Currents.

The circular movement of vast quantities of water across the Pacific also draws in cold water from the polar regions on the eastern flank. In the Northern Hemisphere, the cold California Current cools the west coast of the USA as it is drawn southwards; in the Southern Hemisphere the cold Humboldt Current sweeps northwards along the west coast of South America. These currents can cause major disturbance to the patterns of weather across a wide area. The periodic eastward shift of warm surface water in the western Pacific, a phenomenon called El Niño, brings drought to Australasia and Indonesia and torrential rain to the Americas.

Spiral of life *This mass of phytoplankton, twisted by the ocean currents, was photographed off the South Island of New Zealand.*

Wind patterns

The atmosphere of the Northern Hemisphere is more changeable than that of the southern one due to the greater ratio of land to sea. But the open seas of the Southern Hemisphere give rise to very high winds between 40° and 50° of latitude south, known by sailors travelling around the Cape of Good Hope and Cape Horn, and south of New Zealand, as the 'Roaring Forties'.

The general system of winds is also affected by the monsoons in the western Pacific. These are powerful seasonal winds caused by the large temperature variations between the continental landmass of Asia – hot in summer, cold in winter – and the vast areas of ocean adjacent to it, where temperatures remain more stable. In summer the intertropical convergence zone shifts northwards over the landmass of Asia, and its line passes through the islands of the western Pacific. Having crossed the ocean from the south, the moisture-laden air carried by summer monsoon winds precipitates as heavy rainfall. During winter, when the intertropical convergence zone shifts southwards generally, and to the south of the western Pacific islands, the winter monsoon winds come from the north-east and are generally drier and fresher.

The flow of currents

Trade winds have an effect on the surface water of the Pacific. In the Northern Hemisphere, they move it westwards along the equator in the North Equatorial Current, which then turns in a clockwise direction and heads towards Japan in a warm current called the Kuro Shiro. In the Southern Hemisphere, the trade winds also blow the surface water westwards as the warm South Equatorial Current, which turns anticlockwise to circulate around eastern Australia and New Zealand. A proportion of both currents is deflected in the opposite direction as they meet the landmasses of

The tropical climate

Almost all the islands of the Pacific are situated in the tropics. Pitcairn and Easter Island are exceptions, lying to the south of the Tropic of Capricorn. In general, the islands have a warm, humid climate, freshened by the trade winds. French Polynesia, lying at the heart of the Pacific, has what might be considered typical Pacific weather. There are two distinct seasons. In winter (May to October) temperatures are 25-28°C (77-82°F), with clear skies and just the occasional shower. In summer (November to April) the weather is wet and oppressive. Temperatures rise to 27-30°C (81-86° F), the air is saturated with humidity, and there are numerous heavy downpours. Hurricanes and severe tropical storms may occur at any time during the summer.

One ocean, 25 000 islands

The Pacific Ocean encompasses a huge number of islands, islets and atolls, many barely larger than a tennis court. Some are the remains of an ancient continental landmass, but most have been driven up from the ocean floor on the crest of volcanic activity.

The vast Pacific basin has a dual personality: much of it is very stable, but many parts are subject to violent movement and convulsion. In fact, the whole of the ocean floor is on the move, propelled by the phenomenon known as plate tectonics: bit by bit, the ocean floor is being renewed along the line of the East Pacific Ridge and thrust outwards towards the adjacent continents.

Plate tectonics

The surface of the Earth is made up of a series of superimposed layers around a hot central core. The thin outer layer, the crust, is broken up into large plates that slot together like a jigsaw. These rest

A necklace of islands   *Rangiroa, in the Tuamotus, French Polynesia, consists of 240 islets forming a chain around the rim of a lagoon.*

on the more solid layer of the mantle, and together they form the lithosphere. Under this fairly rigid outer coating, about 60 miles (100 km) down, is the more volatile, semi-molten asthenosphere, on which the lithosphere 'floats'. Like pieces of armour, the plates can move, giving the Earth's crust the flexibility needed to accommodate the instability of the asthenosphere and the rest of the molten mantle beneath it.

In some places, the plates are moving apart (divergent plates) and elsewhere they are colliding (convergent plates). Because an oceanic plate is heavier and more solid, it pushes

beneath the lighter continental plates that form the land-masses: in the western Pacific, the Pacific Plate is being driven down (subducted) beneath the lighter Eurasian and Indo-Australian Plates. The immense pressure at these subduction zones creates deep trenches, and pushes up mountains on the continental plate. The fault lines running along the boundaries between the convergent plates are the source of seismic activity as the plates rub together, a process that also generates great heat and molten rock, or magma. Under pressure from the mantle, magma forces its way up through the fault to form the chain of volcanoes around the Pacific known as the 'Ring of Fire'. Many of the Pacific islands are the progeny of this volcanic activity.

This clash of plates is caused by the Pacific basin expanding. In the eastern Pacific, the Pacific Plate is pulling away from the Nazca Plate (off western South America), creating a divergent rift. Here, too, magma rises, filling the rift, forming the mountains and volcanoes of the East Pacific Ridge, and pushing the adjacent plates away. This divergent movement is relatively fast by geological standards – about 6 in (15 cm) a year – enough to produce a shift of 950 miles (1500 km) over 10 million years. However, although some 4000 miles (6400 km) long, there is little to see of the East Pacific Ridge, for most of the mountains are under the sea. A rare exception is Easter Island.

Hot spots

The Pacific islands that lie on the Indo-Australian Plate are continental in nature. These are the comparatively high and massive Melanesian islands, including Papua New Guinea's Bismarck archipelago, the Solomons and New Caledonia, which were largely formed by the folding and mountain-building caused by convergent plates. By contrast, the islands in mid-ocean owe their origins entirely to volcanic activity, having been pushed up from the ocean floor. Some are, or were, on plate boundaries. But others, notably

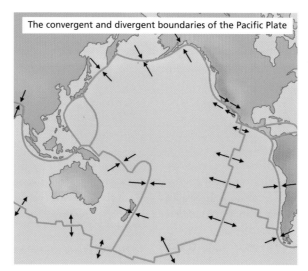

The convergent and divergent boundaries of the Pacific Plate

Volcanic heritage *Parts of the Hawaiian island of Kauai still have a raw look, even though the island is about 5.1 million years old. It was thrust up from the ocean floor by a 'hot spot' in the Pacific Plate.*

False impression *Coconut palms on a* motu *(flat reef islet) off Bora Bora in French Polynesia give a false impression of fertile soil.*

the Hawaiian islands, are in mid ocean, many miles away from any plate boundary. They owe their origin to a 'hot spot', an isolated point in the middle of a plate where, for reasons not fully understood, a concentration of magma rises from the mantle and pierces the lithosphere.

Geologically, however, the distinction between continental and volcanic islands is not always clear-cut. Many of the continental islands, being on the plate margin, are also volcanic. And an additional geological feature affects both categories: the presence of coral. Reefs have formed around continental islands (such as New Caledonia) and around volcanic islands (such as the Society Islands of French Polynesia and the Cook Islands). The atolls consist entirely of a ring-shaped coral reef, where the original volcano has

disappeared. To complicate the picture further, in some places – for example the Solomon Islands – volcanic activity has thrust up ancient banks of coral from the seabed.

Deceptive soil

The first European explorers believed that most of the Pacific islands were highly fertile. But this was an illusion cast by the lush vegetation that grows on them. In the moist, tropical climate, volcanic soil is able to generate profuse growth, but it is also vulnerable to rapid degradation from storms and any agricultural development, which quickly exhausts its nutrients. Atolls are even less promising: their soils are poor and dominated by lime, which makes them highly porous. In fact, only the bigger continental islands, with their high content of sedimentary rock, are really suited to agriculture.

The truth is that most of the islands of the Pacific are handicapped by fragile ecosystems, prone as they are to cyclones, droughts, floods, volcanic eruption and global environmental problems. One factor in their favour is a comparatively small population: with the exception of Papua New Guinea, these islands have always been lightly populated.

Colonising plant *Because coconuts float, coconut palms can colonise islands. Their root structure then helps to stabilise the sandy soil.*

The gift of volcanoes

In the extreme heat and pressure of the mantle beneath the Earth's crust, rock is kept in a state of molten turbulence, ready to push up through the crust wherever a weakness develops. The resulting volcanoes may never break the surface of the ocean, but those that do become islands.

Fuming *Mount Yasur, on Tanna in Vanuatu.*

In January 1960, an unusual eruption took place on the flanks of Kilauea, the most active volcano on Hawaii. The rising magma caused subterranean water to vaporise, and the resulting steam shot molten lava and rocks 1500 ft (460 m) into the air. It was just one of the many moods of volcanic activity – spectacular, unpredictable and life-threatening.

The Pacific has two distinct types of volcano, which relate to their geological history and their location. There are about 1000 volcanoes in the 'Ring of Fire' around the perimeter of the ocean, and some 40 of them will erupt in any given year. They are all related to the subduction zones, where the Pacific Plate is pushing beneath the lighter continental plates. They may erupt in island chains, or on the continental plates; others, appearing in the centre of the ocean, are the product of hot spots.

Islands in the Ring of Fire

The clash of tectonic plates on the western shores of the Pacific has produced some major volcanoes, and is responsible for shaping much of the landscape. A number of high peaks in New Guinea and its islands have volcanic origins, including Mount Lamington (5512 ft/1680 m) on the mainland, Mount Ulawun (7657 ft/2334 m) on the island of New Britain, and Mount Bagana (5730 ft/1746 m) on Bougainville.

Volcanoes lining the Pacific Plate's boundaries with the Indo-Australian Plate and Philippine Plate have created a string of mountains in the ocean following a serpentine path stretching from the Marianas in the north to New Zealand in the south. Many of these – off Vanuatu and Tonga, for instance – have remained submerged. Others form the backbone of the Melanesian archipelagoes, and some rise to considerable heights, notably: Mount Karakomba (8028 ft/2447 m) on Guadalcanal in the Solomons; Mount Lombenden (4908 ft/1496 m) on Ambae, and Mount Marum (4167 ft/1270 m) on Ambrym, both in Vanuatu; Mount Tomanivi (4340 ft/1323 m) in Fiji; and Kao island (3379 ft/1030 m) in the Ha'apai archipelago of Tonga.

Mid-ocean islands

Only 5 per cent of volcanoes on the planet are located in the centre of oceanic plates. The classic example is the Hawaiian chain, part of the Hawaiian Ridge, which has a total of 82 volcanoes – active, dormant, but mainly extinct – and extends into the Emperor Seamounts to the north. This chain represents the pathway of the Pacific Plate over some 44 million years. At the lead end, at the far south-east of the chain, is the island of Hawaii, still under construction. Its active volcanoes of Kilauea and Mauna Loa mark the site of a hot spot in the Earth's crust.

Hot spots are like wells of magma that settle beneath the lithosphere at fixed points relative to the Earth's core. Their island-building process begins when magma pushes up through the Earth's crust on the seabed and spills out around the vent, slowly creating a cone that will eventually reach the surface. Over long periods of geological time, hot spots remain virtually stationary, while the tectonic plates are constantly on the move. Hence, a volcano forms over the hot spot, but as the oceanic plate moves, the volcano moves too, and so is gradually disconnected from the source of heat, and dies. The hot spot by this time will have begun building a new volcano. One day Hawaii, or at least Kilauea and Mauna Loa, will lose their place on the hot spot to the Loihi Seamount, which currently lies about 20 miles (32 km) offshore to the south-east and is still about 3180 ft (970 m) below sea level. But Loihi is not expected to break the surface for another 60 000 years.

Volcanoes without an active core gradually collapse into themselves and are eroded away by the elements. The result is a chain of islands of decreasing size. Thus Hawaii, currently standing over the hot spot, is the largest island in the chain; geologically older and smaller islands lie towards the north-west, leading out to a series of small islands and pinnacles, many preserved from total submersion only by coral reefs growing on their flanks. The

From volcano to atoll: the Society Islands

The island chains of French Polynesia provide examples of hot-spot generated archipelagoes. Like the Hawaiian islands, they all have a south-east to north-west orientation. The Society Islands provide a good example: they consist of nine large volcanic islands, rising to more than 16 000 ft (4875 m) above the ocean floor, as well as a number of submerged volcanoes and atolls. Mehetia, the youngest island, is the only one with an active volcano. Three relatively quiescent submerged volcanoes lie off its western flank. Tahiti, in the centre of the archipelago, has two young but extinct volcanoes. The highest, Mount Orohena, rises to 7352 ft (2241 m). The strange landscape of Moorea, the island to the west of Tahiti, was formed by the collapse of a volcano around a caldera. Its highest peak

Young cone *Mehetia is the exposed summit of an active volcano.*

rises to 3937 ft (1200 m), and the island is rimmed with reefs. To the west lies Bora Bora, where the remains of a collapsed volcano is surrounded by a lagoon and coral reefs. Farther west still the chain drops away in a series of pure coral atolls, with no volcanic remains visible above the surface.

Chain reaction *As an oceanic plate carries a volcano away from its hot spot or point of origin, it becomes inactive and eventually collapses.*

orientation of the Hawaiian islands, south-east to north-west, corresponds to the direction in which the Pacific Plate is moving away from the divergent boundary marked by the East Pacific Ridge. The Midway Islands and Kure, both of which are low-lying coral atolls, form the far end of the Hawaiian chain, about 1000 miles (1600 km) from Hawaii. One day, the Hawaiian islands may look more like the Midway group, but not for about another 27 million years.

The theory of hot spots was proposed in 1963 by the Canadian geophysicist J. Tuzo Wilson, a pioneer of the theory of plate tectonics. It fits the observed facts well, but a great mystery still remains. Why do hot spots remain stationary, when all else moves?

Young giants

Volcanic islands that are active or dormant are said to be 'young'. They are a few million years old or less – Hawaii is only about 400 000 years old. The largest mid-ocean volcano, Mauna Kea, on Hawaii, rises to 13 796 ft (4505 m) above sea level. But this is less than half its total height. Measured from the ocean floor it rises to almost 32 000 ft (9750 m) – taller than Mount Everest. Because they consist largely of piles of cinders and ash, and other loose debris, volcanoes are much more vulnerable to erosion than other mountains – once their youth has past.

Bloom of youth *Mount Haleakala (left), on Maui, Hawaii's biggest neighbour, is 800 000 years old and rises to 10 023 ft (3055 m) at the Red Hill. Although it has not erupted since 1790, it is dormant, not extinct.*

Crater lake *Rano Kau is one of the main craters of Easter Island, which was thrust up from the East Pacific Ridge.*

Nature's cauldrons

A caldera is a large, circular volcanic crater, usually formed by the collapse of the volcano following a massive eruption that empties out its magma chamber. Low-lying calderas may become inundated by the sea and form massive natural bays, such as that of Rabaul in New Britain, the largest island off Papua New Guinea. The Kilauea caldera in Hawaii is 2.5 miles (4 km) across and still erupting, with several simmering lakes of molten lava.

Islands built by living creatures

Strung out like pearls in a necklace, coral islands are fragile oases of land often barely rising above the lagoons and sea that surround them. Sometimes numbering dozens in a single cluster, they are the by-product of coral polyps, working in their billions over thousands of years.

Motif *Coral isles typify the south Pacific.*

The vision of atolls, with their soft white sand, turquoise lagoons and fringes of coconut palms, forms a central part of the south Pacific dream. But behind their charmed physical beauty lies the yet more magical tale of their creation by fragile and minuscule animals – the very same animals that also construct the spectacular marine worlds of the coral reefs.

Heads above the water

It was Charles Darwin (1809-92), the celebrated British naturalist, who first suggested how atolls are formed. Colonies of tiny coral polyps collect in the shallows around the flanks of a volcanic island, producing the hard lime secretions that protect their soft bodies. Over the years, these secretions build up as coral stands and then form reefs, which create a barrier to the surrounding ocean. Meanwhile, the volcano becomes inactive and begins to collapse; through erosion it gradually drops back into the sea. But the coral polyps can match the speed of this collapse – about 0.5 in (1 cm) per year – by building upwards to stay close to the ocean's surface, where they can make full use of the sun's energy.

The result of this process is a circular coral reef set around a diminishing volcanic core, which is gradually replaced by a lagoon. When the volcanic core disappears completely, the reef and its lagoon is called an atoll. After many thousands of years, the volcanic foundations on which the reef was built may be hundreds of feet below the surface of the ocean: by this time the atoll is resting on high walls of coral.

Geological core-sampling in the Tuamotu chain, in French Polynesia, shows how these coral walls build up progressively. In the youngest islands at the south-eastern end of the chain (closest to

Biggest lagoon, biggest atoll

Stretching 1000 miles (1600 km) in all, the coral reef encircling Grande Terre, the largest island of New Caledonia, is the second longest in the world after Australia's Great Barrier Reef. Separating the island's coasts from the reef is a huge lagoon. Its total area of 9070 sq miles (23 500 km²) makes it the world's largest. Kwajalein, in the Marshall Islands, is the world's largest atoll. It has 90 islands in a chain 80 miles (130 km) long and 18 miles (30 km) wide, set around a lagoon with a surface area of 660 sq miles (1700 km²).

In the path of mighty forces

Some islands consist of ancient coral atolls that have been thrust upwards from the seabed by geological movement – by volcanic action or by the folding that occurs where tectonic plates collide. Thus slabs of ancient coral may end up above sea level as limestone plateaus. A spectacular example of this is the northern part of Guam, which rises to nearly 1000 ft (300 m). Elsewhere, uplifted atolls have formed the islands of Rota, Tinian and Saipan in the Marianas, the Lau islands of Fiji, Vava'u and Tongatapu in Tonga, Makatea in the Tuamotu islands of French Polynesia, and Lifou and Maré in New Caledonia. Typically, raised atolls are fronted by vertical cliffs and terraces that drop down to the sea, and are riddled with caves. Some inland caves retain rainwater, which can provide favourable conditions for gowing particular crops, such as the lychees and avocados of Maré, or the vanilla of Lifou.

the hot spot), the coral is about 1150 ft (350 m) high. At Hao, near the centre of the chain, it is 1970 ft (600 m) high and 3280 ft (1000 m) high at Rangiroa in the far north-west. The Enewetak atoll in the Marshall Islands stands on a coral pedestal 4156 ft (1267 m) high.

Atolls tend to be either circular or crescent-shaped. Sand, made up largely of crushed coral, accumulates in the protective embrace of the reefs, creating shallows. The resulting lagoons of calm water can range in scale from tens of feet to 30 miles (50 km) in diameter. Only rarely are they completely enclosed: often the reef is broken on the leeward side, permitting the constant exchange of water, nutrients and wildlife that is a feature of lagoon ecology.

Sand also accumulates over reef-heads exposed to the air, which quickly amass debris brought in on the tides and winds, as well as plant and animal life. This is the start of the island-building process, creating the characteristic flat reef islets known as *motus*.

In the image of their makers

Most atolls are low-lying, rarely rising to a height of more than 20 ft (6 m) above sea level. They are constantly at risk from the fury of the sea, and also under threat from global warming, which may cause the sea level to rise. If the average global air temperature

Niche dwellers   Atoll plants are specialists. They have to be salt-tolerant, and capable of surviving long periods with little or no rain.

increases by 5 °C (9 °F) by the year 2100, as some predict it might, sea levels could rise by over 3 ft (1 m).

The soil on coral atolls, dominated by lime, is poor in nutrients, and retains little moisture. Rainfall is usually the only source of fresh water. In such conditions, vegetation tends to be neither dense nor very diverse. In other words, atolls are very fragile – just like the tiny coral polyps that created them.

***Birth of an atoll**   First the volcano rises from the seabed. Coral colonises the shallows around its shores and continues to build as the volcano subsides, eventually forming a ring of islands.*

***Building site**   Exposed coral (left) provides the foundation blocks for island-building.*

Melanesia: the big islands

Papua New Guinea and New Caledonia make up a chain of continental islands that has piled up at the interface between the Pacific and Indo-Australian Plates. Their landscapes are dominated by high mountains created by the buckling of rocks at the interface and by volcanoes.

Home-grown *Gardens are essential to the pattern of life in Melanesia.*

Riches and fragility

The Melanesian islands have the richest resources of the Pacific. The geological strata contain valuable minerals: copper, silver, gold, chrome in Papua New Guinea; nickel, chrome, zinc, cobalt, iron in New Caledonia. The fertile and well-watered soil of the river valleys permits intensive agriculture and subsistence gardening. Today, much of the land has been given over to commercial farming, but such development is often undermined by the natural disasters that blight the region.

The large islands of Melanesia lie on the Indo-Australian Plate, and are the result of the folding and lifting process caused by the impact of the heavier Pacific Plate. Rising from a base on the sea floor at a depth of about 6500 ft (2000 m), they are composed primarily of sedimentary rock laid down in the far distant past – in contrast to the more recent basalt of the volcanic islands. Indeed, most of the islands of Melanesia correspond to this basic structure, complicated by the intrusion of volcanoes.

Mountains and volcanoes

The mountains rise to 8200 ft (2500 m) in the Solomons; 5900 ft (1800 m) in Vanuatu; 4300 ft (1300 m) in Fiji; 3300 ft (1000 m) in Tonga. Grande Terre, in New Caledonia, is divided by a mountain range called La Chaîne which culminates at Mounts Panié (5341 ft/ 1628 m) and Humboldt (5308 ft/1618 m).

With the exception of New Caledonia, all these islands are prone to seismic activity, which has resulted in not one but two chains of volcanoes, adding further drama to the high relief of the landscape. The highest mountains are in the volcanic ranges of mainland Papua New Guinea: the Owen Stanley Range in the south-east rises to 13 363 ft (4073 m) at Mount Victoria, while Mount Wilhelm in the Bismarck Range, in

Snaking path *A flat-bottomed river valley on the east coast of New Caledonia provides valuable agricultural land.*

the centre of the country, reaches 14 790 ft (4508 m). These ranges represent the older, more stable chain, thrust upwards 1.6-1.9 million years ago. The entire northern coast of Papua New Guinea and the neighbouring archipelagoes are dotted with younger volcanoes, of which about 40 are active.

River islands

The larger Melanesian islands are the only ones in the Pacific with extensive river systems. In New Guinea, the central mountain chain feeds two large systems. The one in the north includes the Sepik River, navigable for most of its 683 miles (1100 km) and the Ramu River which is 397 miles (640 km) long. The main river of the southern system is the Fly River – 683 miles (1100 km) in length. On Grande Terre of New Caledonia, the rivers flowing from the Chaîne range are comparatively short – the longest is the Diahot River (56 miles/90 km) – but they provide vital irrigation for the fertile valleys.

Spectacular entry *An underground river emerges in a waterfall in the forest of Papua New Guinea.*

Heaven and hell

The Pacific can produce glimpses of paradise and hell at the same time. On the one hand there are the perfect atolls of the Society Islands, on the other the tortured volcanic wastelands of Hawaii, or Vanuatu's Ambrym.

In tourist brochures, the Pacific islands appear as a tropical Eden. The key elements that contribute to this image are the azure-blue clarity of the ocean, the exuberance of the lush vegetation, and the coral-fringed shores. Add to these the warm sea breezes rustling the palm fronds, the scent of frangipani blossom, soft white sand, lagoons dotted with *motu* islets, iridescent birds among the hibiscus and bougainvillea – and it becomes the stuff of dreams.

Pacific dream
A hammock slung from coconut palms, white sand, blue sky and a warm lagoon.

Beyond the brochure

The reality is far more complex. Ambrym, a spectacular volcanic island in Vanuatu, presents a contrasting image: beaches on the south side of the island are not white but black, while at its heart is a volcanic wasteland – beautiful only in its awesome magnificence. The volcanic centre is accessed from the south-west by means of a path cut along a dry river bed. It passes first through a lush area of palms and ferns, moss-draped trees and wild sugar cane, their deep greens contrasting with the dark soil. With flying foxes (large bats) flitting overhead, the scene becomes ever stranger, evoking medieval paintings of purgatory. The plant life comes to a halt as the path enters the utter desolation of the lava field, a sterile world of twisted black rock, grey ash and cinders.

In the distance, the massive silhouettes of the active volcanoes, Mounts Marum (4166 ft/1270 m) and Benbow (3802 ft/1159 m), crowd the horizon. It is several hours' walk yet to Marum's crater from here, following a path over crumbly tephra (volcanic debris) and lava flows, frozen in mid-motion into ankle-twisting bumps and potholes. The volcanoes sit on the rim of a large caldera, 7 miles (12 km) across, originally formed 2000 years ago and still highly active. Over the past 200 years there have been eight major eruptions in which lava has spilled out into the surrounding landscape, the last in 1929. The caldera remains a blast-zone, virtually devoid of life. Rumblings can be heard deep below the ground, and Benbow occasionally belches plumes of ash, while the fumaroles that pierce the crater flanks exude a hellish, sulphurous breath.

'Like nowhere else on Earth'

Recently a team of explorers spent several days in the caldera on the island of Ambrym. Several of them were lowered into the craters of Marum and Benbow, to positions close to lava lakes simmering and spluttering at 1204°C (2200°F) some 1200 ft (365 m) below the rim. The volcanoes ejected globules of lava and exhaled noxious fumes so acidic that they corroded camera casings and spectacles. Progress was then frustrated by torrential rains and quarrels with their local porters. Reporting in an article entitled 'To Hell' (*National Geographic*, November 2000), Donovan Webster described how he was awe-struck by the power of the volcano, yet mesmerised by its beauty. 'It is like nowhere else on Earth,' he said.

Dark side *Ambrym's volcanic landscape is a complete contrast to the brochure images of the Pacific islands.*

Off the beaten track *Hawaii's long coastline has many wild and unspoilt corners, havens of peace and beauty.*

CHAPTER 2

PACIFIC IN NAME, VIOLENT IN NATURE

The name 'pacific' was chosen by the Portuguese navigator Ferdinand Magellan when his ships were marooned in an agonising calm on the first European crossing of the ocean. But far from being peaceful, the region is very violent – regularly battered by an annual round of typhoons and deluges, and frequently laid waste by volcanic eruptions, earthquakes and tsunamis. Even clear skies can present a danger, presaging, as they may, prolonged and devastating droughts which turn the soil to dust or make it concrete-hard. And all the while the level of the sea is rising, threatening to drown the coastal land where 90 per cent of the population of the islands of the Pacific live.

A glowing eye of molten lava on Kilauea, on Hawaii, one of the world's most active volcanoes.

In the path of cyclones

About 20 cyclones sweep the Pacific Ocean each year, hitting especially the western sector. Winds reaching speeds of 185 mph (300 km/h) are accompanied by deluges that bring flooding and landslides in their wake. These terrifying storms cause widespread destruction to the islands.

Cyclones are called hurricanes in the Americas and in the north-eastern region of the Pacific. In East Asia they are often called typhoons – a word that seems to come from the Chinese *tai fung* (great wind) and was used for the first time by the English adventurer William Dampier in 1687. In statistical terms, if a wind exceeds 30 mph (48 km/h) it is classed as a tropical storm; if it then increases to 75 mph (120 km/h) – 12 or more on the Beaufort scale – it becomes a tropical cyclone. Like hurricanes, cyclones are assigned names, the first each year starts with the letter 'A'.

Storm bath
The island and motus of Maupiti in the Society Islands of French Polynesia were devastated by cyclone Oséa in November 1997.

Storm damage
Many houses on Maupiti lost their roofs.

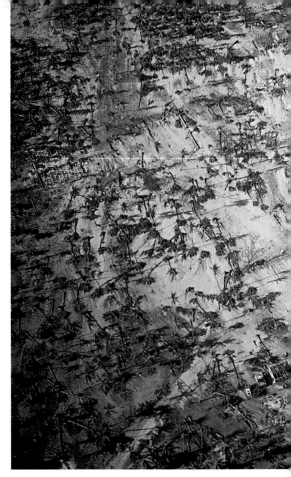

Atmospheric monster

Cyclones are large and violent whirlwinds of hot and humid air, measuring 185-500 miles (300-800 km) across and rising to a height of about 6 miles (10 km). Turning on a vertical axis, they spin clockwise in the Southern Hemisphere and anti-clockwise in the Northern Hemisphere. The result of the Earth's rotation, this phenomenon is known as the Coriolis effect. As with hurricanes, there is a circular area of calm, the 'eye', at the centre of the storm, with clear skies and extreme low pressure. The eye acts as a kind of chimney, so the winds are not simply surging around the vortex, but racing upwards in an intense updraft, drawing more air into the lower atmosphere at ground level. Outside the eye, winds can reach speeds of 185 mph (300 km/h). Cyclones with windspeeds of over 150 mph (241 km/h), often labelled 'super typhoons', can flatten whole villages and rip the heads off coconut palms. Weak cyclones are sometimes referred to as 'banana typhoons', because they can do no worse than flatten banana trees.

As the hot and humid air rises from the base of a cyclone to high altitudes, it cools and condenses into clouds capable of unloading 24 in (600 mm) of torrential rain in 24 hours – about as much as London receives in an entire year. It has been calculated that 15 billion tons of water may fall on French Polynesia in a single day – 250 million tons on Tahiti alone. In one second, the energy discharged is the equivalent of Tahiti's electrical consumption over 40 days. Meanwhile, the low atmospheric pressure may cause the sea to swell and rise by up to 10 ft (3 m) – the so-called 'storm surge' that can inundate coastal regions.

These cataclysms usually coincide with the hot season. In the south-west of the Pacific region, 90 per cent of cyclones take place between December and April. In the north-west, most cyclones occur between August and December, but they may strike at any time of the year.

Statistically dangerous

Every year between 30 and 100 tropical storms and 45 cyclones occur around the world. Almost half of these form over the Pacific, most of them off Southeast Asia (which has 30 per cent of the world's storms), the remainder in the south-west Pacific (between Polynesia and Australia), and along the coasts of Central America and Mexico.

Meteorologists have identified five main areas where cyclones build up around the world, all between 5° and 10° of latitude on each side of the equator, where the spiralling caused by the Coriolis effect is at its most intense. Three of these areas are in the Pacific, two in the Northern

Tower of strength *Churches, more robustly built than houses, survived Oséa virtually intact.*

Hemisphere and one in the Southern Hemisphere. The most productive source of cyclones is around the western Caroline Islands in the Federated States of Micronesia.

The life cycle of a cyclone

The regions where cyclones originate have a combination of the perfect conditions to set them in motion and develop their full potential. First, warm and highly unstable air, which, because of the Coriolis effect, forms into huge rising spirals in areas of initial calm. This creates areas of low pressure that draw in air from the surrounding region. Second, the warmth of the sea – more than 27°C (80°F) – which causes rapid evaporation and boosts humidity. As this water vapour rises and condenses into rain, it releases energy that heats the air, increasing its instability. It is this second condition that, over a period of a few days, accelerates a simple spiralling motion into a furious and devastating cyclone.

Once triggered, cyclones move away from their place of origin. The trade winds push them, sometimes for thousands of miles, along a curving path towards the tropics and their final destinations, usually between 15° and 30° of latitude. The swirling winds may reach very high speeds, but the eye itself moves at a fairly leisurely pace of 10-20 mph (20-30 km/h). The lifespan of a cyclone can vary from a few hours to ten days, but eventually it will peter out when it meets more stable conditions or cooler latitudes, or runs into land and is no longer fuelled by moisture from the sea.

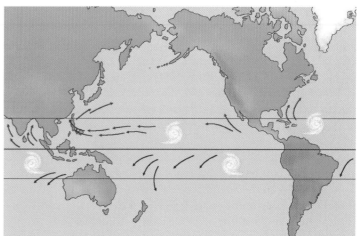

Wind direction *Cyclones begin close to the equator and follow divergent paths in the Northern Hemisphere (red) and Southern Hemisphere (blue).*

Cyclone alert

Satellite images enable meteorologists to detect the cloud formation that might develop into a cyclone. The telltale sign is the formation of a distinct eye. As soon as a developing cyclone is identified, information is transmitted to meteorological stations across the Pacific, which monitor its path and strength, and attempt to predict where it will go. By broadcasting warnings, they are able to alert the inhabitants of threatened islands.

Eye of the storm *This cyclone over the south Pacific was photographed from the space shuttle Discovery.*

When the Earth moves

Volcanic eruptions, earthquakes, tsunamis – the Pacific region is painfully vulnerable to all these manifestations of geological violence. Most of this action is concentrated around the rim of the ocean, on the margins of the tectonic plates, and in Hawaii at the centre.

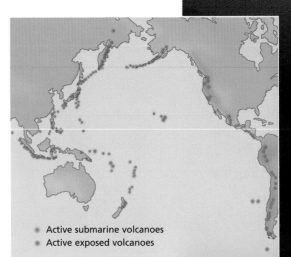

- Active submarine volcanoes
- Active exposed volcanoes

The majority of active volcanoes in the Pacific region are found on the periphery of the ocean, where the Pacific Plate and the Philippines Plate collide with the continental plates. These margins form the 'Ring of Fire'. Many of these volcanoes are 'orogenic' – that is, they are linked to the grinding geological process of mountain building that occurs at plate margins. The glaring exceptions to this pattern are the mid-ocean volcanoes, relating to the 'hot spots' that pierce the centre of the Pacific Plate, but these likewise suffer from all the dangers associated with the instability of the Earth's crust.

On the western flank

Volcanic activity at the interface between the Pacific and Philippines Plates has given rise to the Marianas chain of islands. But the only active volcanoes in the region, indeed in all of Micronesia, are in the Northern Marianas, the most famous of which is on Pagan, an island that lies 200 miles (322 km) north of Saipan – itself the site of five dormant volcanoes. Pagan's volcano has erupted 19 times in the past 500 years. When it erupted in 1981, a section of its peak was blasted away and a fountain of fire and rocks soared 12 miles (20 km) into the sky. Half the island's arable land was destroyed and the population had to be evacuated. There was another eruption in 1988 and the island has only been partially re-inhabited.

Melanesia, lining the margin between the Pacific and Indo-Australian plates, has also had long experience of volcanic activity. Its archipelagoes – with the notable exception of New Caledonia – have suffered every kind of disaster associated with seismic and volcanic activity: eruptions, earthquakes, earth tremors and tsunamis (or tidal waves). There are 40 active volcanoes in New Guinea and neighbouring island groups.

Rulers of the deep These submarine volcanoes in the South Fiji Basin are known as the Three Kings. They rise 6500 ft (2000 m) above the seabed.

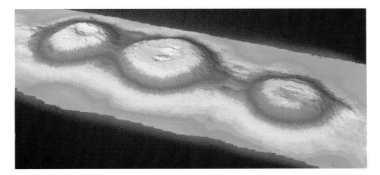

Hawaii Volcanoes National Park

Founded in 1916, this park encompasses two volcanoes: Mauna Loa (13 679 ft/4170 m) and Kilauea (4078 ft/1423 m). A two-day walk along a hiker's path leads up to the still-active crater of Mauna Loa. Kilauea is one of the world's most active volcanoes, offering a constant display of pyrotechnics. Visitors can tour the crater by car, using an 11 mile (18 km) road that passes lava flows and fiery fountains, pools of molten lava, hissing jets of vapour, crumpled lava fields, jungles of giant ferns, and the remains of vegetation burnt to a crisp by recent eruptions. Hawaii's other famous volcano is Mauna Kea, 20 miles (32 km) to the north of the park. Rising to 13 796 ft (4205 m), but now extinct, it is crowned with a leading astronomical observatory.

Quake awareness

Vanuatu is on the fault line where the Indo-Australian Plate is slipping beneath the Pacific Plate, an effect that pushes the islands 4 in (10 cm) to the north-west every year. A study is being conducted in Vanuatu to assess the dangers that earthquakes and tremors pose to the capital, Port-Vila, and Luganville on the island of Espiritu Santo. The aim is to minimise risk by identifying the most vulnerable zones.

Rivers of fire Mauna Loa, on Hawaii, still erupts from time to time, producing spectacular flows of molten lava.

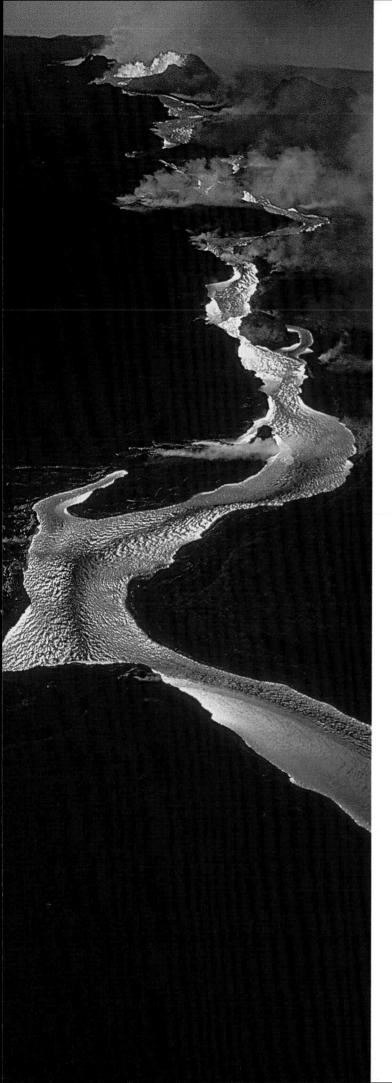

The island of Manam, lying close to the northern coast of New Guinea, in Madang Province, is a classic volcanic cone, rising to 6000 ft (1829 m) and extending to 6 miles (10 km) in diameter. Eruptions on Manam have increased in frequency since 1974. That of December 1996 caused 13 deaths; another major eruption occurred in October 1998. The inhabitants of five villages were evacuated but have since been permitted to return to their homes.

Volcanic island *Tanna Island in Vanuatu is constantly active.*

Two other volcanoes in the area have also been more active in recent years. Mount Lamington (5512 ft/1680 m) reawoke suddenly in 1951, killing 3000 people, and set in motion a series of mudflows that lasted until 1956. The volcano on the island of Bam (2247 ft/ 685 m) has erupted 16 times since 1872, most recently in 1960.

On New Britain, a large island to the east of mainland New Guinea, the principal manifestation of volcanism centres on its capital, Rabaul, and its extraordinary natural harbour in Blanche

Giant crater *Calderas are formed when a spent volcano collapses in upon itself, as was the case with the volcano of Ambrym, in Vanuatu.*

Bay. The bay is a huge flooded caldera, 5 miles (8 km) wide by 9 miles (14 km) long, and still has a number of active craters on its rim. The eruption that created the bay of Rabaul occurred about 1400 years ago – comparatively recently in geological terms. After a dormant period lasting 101 years, on the morning of September 19, 1994, the two craters of Vulcan and Tuvurvur re-erupted, blasting ash to a height of 18 miles (30 km) over the city and harbour. Happily, seismologists had predicted this eruption and the population of Rabaul had been evacuated. Nonetheless, the eruption all-but destroyed Rabaul, once one of Papua's most beautiful cities, and cast a blight over the region from which it has not yet recovered. Vulcan ceased activity after a few days, but Tuvurvur poses a continuing threat.

Bougainville, the largest island of the North Solomons Province of Papua New Guinea, has seven volcanoes that have been active for the past 10 000 years. The largest of these, Mount Bagana (5741 ft/1750 m), has erupted 22 times since its first recorded bout of activity in 1842. Most of its eruptions are exceptionally violent and explosive, accompanied by heavy ashfall and *nuées ardentes* – lethal clouds of searing gas.

55

Deadly power Kanangio, on the island of Karkar off northern Papua New Guinea, claimed the lives of two vulcanologists when it erupted in 1979.

Approach with care A vulcanologist wearing breathing apparatus measures gas temperatures in a sulphur spring on Vanua Lava, in the Banks Islands of Vanuatu.

On the southern flank

In the Solomon Islands, the activity of the steaming, cone-shaped island of Savo (1591 ft/485 m) was noted by the Spanish navigator Álvaro de Mendaña de Neira and his pilot Hernando Gallego in 1568. There was a series of eruptions between 1835 and 1850. Kavachi, a submarine volcano, has erupted 24 times since 1939, and on eight of these occasions it thrust up temporary islands that were later washed away by the waves.

In Vanuatu, nine of the 13 main islands have active volcanoes. Yasur (1184 ft/361 m), on the island of Tanna, has been active for at least two centuries: Captain Cook remarked on it in 1774. Usually it does little more than emit smoke and sulphur fumes, and a plume of ash that rises to 6500 ft (2000 m), but sometimes it ejects a hail of large volcanic 'bombs' that claim casualties: two tourists and a local guide were killed in this way in 1995. The biggest active volcano in Vanuatu is on the island of Ambrym (4377 ft/1334 m). This is a complex island formation, with a set of volcanic cones rising from a caldera 5.5 miles (9 km) by 7.5 miles (12 km) across. The island has erupted 18 times since 1774, most recently in 1991, and on 15 of these occasions the volcano produced lava flows.

The volcanoes on Taveuni in Fiji were held to be dormant until recently. Now they are thought likely to recommence activity at any moment. The island has been inhabited for 2000 years and has

erupted at least 20 times over that period, but the last eruption was in the 17th century.

Farther east still lie the Samoan islands, where the margin between the Pacific Plate and the Indo-Australian Plate takes a dog-leg turn before heading south towards New Zealand. Mount Silisili (6099 ft/1859 m) on the Samoan island of Savai'i – the largest island of Polynesia after those of Hawaii – began erupting in 1911. The eruption of Mount Matavanu (1318 ft/402 m) at around the same period laid waste the agricultural lands of the north coast.

The 150 islands and islets of Tonga were forged by a double line of volcanoes, and the western line (which includes Fonuafo'ou, Tofua, Lateiki, Fonualei and Niuafo'ou) are all active, if currently calm. There are also a number of submerged active volcanoes in the sea around the archipelago. During its regular eruptions, the Metis Shoal, first mapped in 1851, pushes up cinder cones that rise briefly above the surface of the sea.

Hot spots and earthquakes

Much of Polynesia has been formed by the work of volcanic hot spots. The Hawaiian islands are the most celebrated example of this phenomenon. The five active volcanoes on Hawaii itself (the biggest island) are the most recent in the chain – less than half a million years old. Most active are Mauna Loa (13 679 ft/4170 m),

Kilauea and the Loihi Seamount, which is gradually rising from the ocean floor. On the island of Kauai to the north-west, the volcanoes are about 5 million years old, and have now been severed from the hot spot. Farther north-west still the archipelago has dropped back into the sea in the form of a submerged chain of extinct cones called the Emperor Seamounts. The volcanoes of French Polynesia that have become detached from their hot spot are similarly extinct.

Earthquakes are another feature of the clash of tectonic plates, and of hot spots, too. In Oceania the worst-affected regions are New Zealand (which records some 14 000 earth tremors every year), Hawaii, and the islands of Melanesia. Despite – or rather because of – the frequency of their occurrence, this seismic activity is comparatively moderate in its violence, and rarely causes much damage, although an earthquake in Papua New Guinea in 1970 claimed 165 lives in the province of Madang.

Killer waves

A tsunami, often called a tidal wave, is a vast wave triggered by seismic activity or a submarine landslide. The shockwaves are transferred to the water and move swiftly across great distances, creating a swell that contains many millions of tons of water. On contact with a coast, this vast volume of water suddenly converts into a towering wall 30-50 ft (10-15 m) high. When it breaks over the coastline it causes widespread devastation. In 1883 the eruption of Krakatoa, between Java and Sumatra in Indonesia, unleashed a tsunami that killed 36 000 people on the adjacent coasts; it then travelled around the globe creating unusual wave patterns that were widely recorded. Since the beginning of the 20th century, Hawaii has been hit by 13 giant waves; in 1946 a tsunami with waves more than 50 ft (15 m) high devastated Honolulu and killed 173 people. Northern Papua New Guinea has similarly suffered from tsunamis. One hit the island of Umboi in 1888, killing 3000.

On Friday July 17, 1998, at about 7 pm, a fisherman in the lagoon of Sissano on the northern coast of mainland Papua New Guinea, in West Sepik Province, saw what he described as a 'wave of fire' on the horizon. 'I thought the end of the world had come!' he recalled. It was not an illusion: four gigantic and strangely luminous waves were indeed heading towards the coast. According to this witness, the phenomenon lasted for about six minutes, then the sea became quite calm again. But during this time the villages and coconut palms that once lined 12 miles (20 km) of beach separating the sea from the lagoon were razed to the ground. Some 2200 people died or disappeared, thousands more were injured, and the villagers all lost their homes and possessions.

Lucky escape *Surviving villagers of Sissano, Papua New Guinea, survey the damage following the tsunami that struck in July 1998.*

Flattened *Damage caused by the same wave farther along the coast in West Sepik Province.*

The survivors remember hearing a huge bang 'like a clap of thunder'. Then they saw the sea withdraw, leaving fish hopping about on the seabed. Other witnesses spoke of a low roar 'as if an aeroplane was flying over very low'. From the evidence, it would appear that this was a doubly extraordinary tsunami. First, there was its strange luminescence, which might be explained as reflections of the setting sun, or perhaps as the result of heightened activity by the kinds of marine organisms that emit phosphorescence when disturbed. Second, there was its sheer force. The source of the wave, according to the geological observatory of Port Moresby, was probably the two earthquakes that occurred that day, measuring 7.1 on the Richter scale. Several conditions coincided to produce such a devastating effect. The first was the proximity of the epicentres of the earthquakes, which converted all their energy into the shockwave. A second was the fracture of the seabed, which sent a shudder through the water, accentuating the shock. A third was the presence of submarine cliffs close to the coast, which converted a deep-water swell into a high wave as colossal volumes of water suddenly encountered shallows.

Shock wave *Seismic energy released in mid ocean is converted into waves that assume huge and devastating proportions as they run into coasts.*

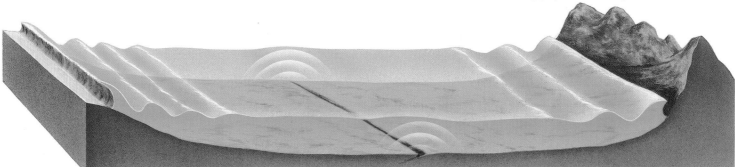

When the ocean misbehaves

All the world is affected by global warming, and by the climatic seesawing of El Niño, but the Pacific is in the front line. It is here that the climate appears to be behaving most out of character, and where rising sea levels are having the most critical impact.

Power of the ocean
Waves pound the coral reefs with a ferocious energy.

Invasion force *A tidal surge flooded this road and coconut plantation on one of the Tuamotu islands.*

According to the World Meteorological Organisation, average temperatures on the surface of the globe rose by nearly 0.5 °C (1 °F) between 1961 and 1990. Evidence of this warming can be seen in the melting of the polar ice caps and the retreat of glaciers around the world. The resulting rise in sea levels poses a real danger to many of the islands of the Pacific.

In addition, an increase in climatic turbulence linked to the phenomenon called El Niño has recently had a dramatic effect across the entire Pacific basin, causing a succession of droughts on the one hand and catastrophic flooding on the other. The occurrence and duration of El Niño appears to be becoming ever less predictable, with a knock-on effect on the old patterns of wet and dry seasons, and the cyclone seasons.

Are these two events linked? This remains the subject of controversy among researchers. Some are not convinced, arguing that the increase in temperature and the swelling of the oceans are relatively recent phenomena, while El Niño has existed since time immemorial. Others believe that, even if they have independent causes, these phenomena now interact and combine to produce even more disquieting effects.

The boy spells trouble

For hundreds of years – even before recorded observations began in 1567 – South American fishermen noticed the periodic arrival of warmer water in the eastern Pacific, along the coasts of Ecuador and Peru, and consequent increases in their catch. This phenomenon usually occurred at intervals of three to seven years, and

as it appeared at around Christmas time, it was named El Niño ('the boy-child') after the boy-Jesus. For many years El Niño was thought to be a local maritime curiosity. Now, however, its full implications, as a complex meteorological mechanism with very wide, and often catastrophic, consequences, are better understood.

When El Niño appears, the climates of the eastern and western Pacific seem to become inverted. The most notable inversions take place in sea temperatures (the cold water of the east becomes warmer, and the warm waters of the west become colder); in atmospheric pressure (the generally higher pressure of the east falls, and the lower pressure of the west rises); and in rainfall (the dry regime of the east turns to deluges; the wet monsoons of the west turn dry). The normal circulation of the trade winds also changes. Usually these winds blow towards the west, pushing warm surface water with them; now they weaken, and may even change direction. Warm currents thus reach the coast of South America, unloading the warmth and humidity of their accompanying air onto Peru, Ecuador and Central America, and causing storms and torrential rain across the Americas – as happened in 1998.

Bringing frost to coffee plantations

Meanwhile, El Niño brings inverse disruption to the other side of the Pacific. The warm and humid ocean air that normally bathes the western coasts of the ocean now turns cool and dry; rain becomes scarce; the landscape becomes desiccated; and sometimes the weather becomes distinctly chilly. Between 1995 and 1998, an unusual period of aridity struck the western Pacific, from New Zealand to Indonesia. In the Marshall Islands the United States had to install desalination plants to produce emergency supplies of fresh water.

In 1997 and 1998, cool, dry winds associated with El Niño hit New Guinea. Harvests failed, plantations withered, fires raged in the forests, grasslands and cultivated fields. Coffee and cocoa plantations at a height of 7200 ft (2200 m) were devastated by frost – a phenomenon without parallel. Nearly a million people suffered from famine, while the lack of safe drinking water accentuated

The United Nations mobilises; the United States demurs

The problem of rising sea levels provokes heated exchanges at environmental conferences. To many Pacific islanders threatened by flooding, the industrial nations seem infuriatingly complacent. In November 1998, delegates from 180 nations met at Buenos Aires for the fourth international conference on climate change. The aim was to thrash out the practicalities of limiting emissions of carbon dioxide, the principal greenhouse gas, in the light of the plan negotiated by 38 industrialised countries at Kyoto in 1997. At Kyoto, it was agreed that by 2012 emissions should be reduced to 5.2 per cent below 1990 levels.

The USA, which alone is responsible for 36.1 per cent of this pollution, refused to agree to this accord. In 1998, delegates from the island nations of the Pacific exhorted the international community and leading industrial countries to put concrete measures in place, and urgently. US president Bill Clinton signed the Kyoto Agreement, but the US Senate delayed ratification. Then in 2001, the new US president George W. Bush rejected the Kyoto Agreement, arguing that it would hamper the development of US domestic industries. Fifty-five other countries, including Britain, also failed to ratify it.

Tracking El Niño The movement of El Niño (in red and white) along the equator was recorded from space in 1997, and transcribed in a series of thermal images (reading from left to right).

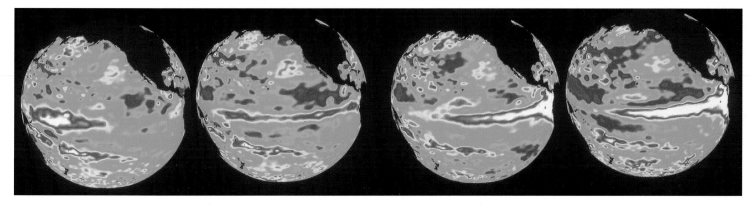

problems of hygiene and caused a rise in cases of diarrhoea and infectious diseases.

El Niño is now seen as one half of a large-scale cycle, of which the counterpart, christened La Niña ('the girl-child') has a converse, cooling effect. This observation has been confirmed by statistics gathered by the Franco-American satellite Topex-Poseidon, which observes the changes in the surface of the ocean caused by currents. During La Niña, the ocean along the South American coast can be seen to cool, while the warmer waters concentrate in a large area of the western Pacific. This has the effect of increasing precipitation and the frequency of cyclones in the western and central zones of the Pacific. In early 1999, the Fijian islands, having just emerged from a prolonged drought caused by El Niño, were deluged by rain unleashed by La Niña.

The effects of El Niño and La Niña appear to be becoming more severe and less predictable. During the El Niño episode of 1997-8, an uncharacteristic series of cyclones struck the Cook Islands and French Polynesia, and Tuvalu was hit by a cyclone in June 1997, well outside the usual cyclone season of November to April.

The threat of submersion

This behaviour may be due to global warming. Temperatures have increased in recent decades and whether the cause is man-made or a natural cycle, the implications are worrying. If, as some predict, air temperatures increase by 5°C (9°F) during the present century, sea levels will rise by 3 ft (1 m) by 2100 – enough to submerge much of Tuvalu, most of whose 96 000 inhabitants live less than 6 ft (2 m) above sea level. Most islands will be dramatically reduced in land area; some will disappear. Tuvalu has already made contingency plans for evacuating its population should this happen. Rising water levels have already begun. Several *motus* (small islets) in Kiribati have sunk beneath the waves. Other side effects include the contamination of subterranean fresh-water by sea water, increased coastal erosion and the loss of low-lying agricultural land. If the current trend continues, governments face the considerable expense of building sea defences.

Rain does not stop play A downpour adds a new dimension to a game of football at Okaiboma in Papua New Guinea.

CHAPTER 3
FLORA AND FAUNA

The deep green tropical vegetation of the Pacific islands suggests an equivalent richness in wildlife. But the reality is different: only in the west of the region, notably in New Guinea, is this expectation realised. Here the forests contain rich collections of giant tropical trees, draped with lianas, ferns, lichens and orchids, and harbouring a host of unusual animals. These include many of the species found in neighbouring Australia, such as wallabies, tree kangaroos and crocodiles, as well as giant butterflies and birds of paradise. But elsewhere, many of the islands are too isolated, too small and too infertile to support a comparable density and variety of plant and animal life. But there is a fabulously rich range of wildlife beneath the sea, concentrated into the highly complex ecosystems of coral reefs, or out in the ocean, where whales, sharks and turtles roam.

The beauty of a coral reef is the product of an intensely competitive food chain.

Paradise of birds

The large islands of Melanesia are home to an extraordinary number of birds, in dizzying diversity. The Polynesian islands, by contrast, are markedly less rich, but they play a key role as destinations for migrating species. Meanwhile, frigate birds and terns sail nonchalantly across the huge expanses of ocean.

Spared of competition from predatory monkeys, squirrels and other mammals, many of the birds in the great tropical forests of the region have been left in peace to evolve in remarkable ways. The huge tracts of forest in New Guinea are an ornithologist's paradise, with nearly 700 species. For instance, there are dozens of parrots of all sizes and colours, ranging from tiny pygmy parrots to the large grey-feathered palm cockatoo. They also include the colourful rainbow lorikeets, which fly around in noisy flocks numbering thousands, feeding on flower nectar and pollen. There are also flycatchers, kingfishers, swifts, nectar-feeding honeyeaters, and black and golden starlings. One of the oddest birds is the hornbill or kokomos, named after its hefty ivory-coloured beak; in flight, it clatters over the treetops with the noise of a train. The female uses her droppings to wall herself into a hollow tree trunk: here she sits on her eggs while her companion passes her food through a narrow slit.

The western archipelagoes of the Pacific are also home to birds of prey, such as the harpy and crested eagles of New Guinea, and the rare peregrine falcon of New Caledonia, which can dive through the air at a speed of 220 mph (350 km/h).

Flightless wonders

Because of the lack of predators, several species of birds found in the islands of the Pacific became ground-dwellers, and lost the power of flight. The flightless kagu of New Caledonia, with its elegant grey plumage and orange-red beak and legs, still holds out its white and brown wings when pursued. Its cry resembles a gentle kind of barking. Like many flightless birds, it is mainly nocturnal, emerging after dark to forage for insects, worms and snails. The female lays one egg per year, on the ground. Such habits made the kagu easy prey for dogs brought by Europeans, and it came close to extinction. It is now a protected species.

The cassowary, a relative of the Australian emu, lives in the tropical rain forests of New Guinea and adjacent islands. Growing to a height of 6.5 ft (1.9 m) and weighing 130 lb (60 kg), it has a large horny casque, which supposedly protects its head when dashing through the undergrowth. It has no feathers on its neck, revealing skin

Fast food *The fish or sea eagle is a skilful hunter, able to use its powerful claws to snatch and lift prey exceeding its own weight.*

The incubator bird

The megapode is a flightless bird found in New Guinea, Tonga, the Solomons, Vanuatu and Palau. The female does not sit on her eggs, but places them in the base of holes that she digs with her extra-large feet in warm places such as sand, piles of decaying plant material or volcanic ash. With the task of incubation taken care of, a process that lasts for about 40 days, the parents are free to go about their daily business. The young take care of themselves after hatching and can fly within hours.

Defenceless *The crested kagu (Rhynochetos jubatus) is a native bird of New Caledonia. Because it is flightless, its population has been decimated by imported animals, especially dogs.*

Long-haul flight *Sooty terns (Sterna fuscata) spend months flying over the ocean to reach their winter quarters, in this case the Marquesas Islands in French Polynesia.*

Streamers *The red-tailed tropic bird (Phaethon rubicauda) is distinguished by its tail feathers, which are as long as its body. Tropic birds dive to catch fish and squid.*

that is coloured brilliant blue, and wattles (folds of loose skin around the throat) that are bright orange, yellow and red. The cassowary has long been hunted by indigenous people for both its meat and its tail feathers, which are used to make ceremonial head-dresses. The bones are carved into sharp arrowheads and tools. When attacked, cassowaries defend themselves vigorously: their sharp spurs are capable of disembowelling the aggressor. The female lays her eggs on the ground and the male incubates them and helps to raise the offspring after they have hatched.

Coloured adornments and elaborate nests

The most common native birds across the Pacific are the pigeons, with some 50 species found in the region. Some are brilliantly coloured fruit-eaters, which spend their days in the high branches of trees. Others are ground-dwelling foragers, and tend to be darker coloured. The imperial pigeon of New Guinea, with its green body, is one of the most beautiful examples of the fruit-eaters. The crowned pigeon of New Guinea is the largest pigeon in the world, measuring 30 in (80 cm) in height – almost the size of a turkey. It has blue-grey feathers and bears a graceful fan-like crown of white tipped feathers.

As with other animal species, the ostentatious appearance of many of these birds relates to reproduction and the need to attract the opposite sex. The birds of paradise have taken this concept to extremes. But there are exceptions to this pattern: the male bower-bird, for example, does not display its feathers to attract a mate, but

Birds of paradise

Emblem of Papua New Guinea, the birds of paradise owe their name to Magellan, who thought that creatures bearing such lavish plumage must have heavenly origins. Of the 43 known species, 38 are found in Papua New Guinea, where they live in the forests. These remarkable birds have been given grand names to match their splendour, such as Count Raggi's bird of paradise (*Paradisea apoda raggiana*), pictured left. The males use their gaudy display feathers to court the females in elaborate mating rituals. While spreading their plumes, they sway, strike postures and hang upside-down, emitting a variety of calls that include whispers, piercing whistles, clucking and buzzing.

Extreme insects

The forests of Oro Province in eastern New Guinea harbour the world's largest butterflies, including the Queen Alexandra birdwing (*Ornithoptera alexandrae*), with a wingspan of nearly 12 in (30 cm). For protection, it lays its eggs in a poisonous vine, and is itself poisonous. But these natural defences do not protect it from loss of habitat to oil palm plantations, and it is now a protected species. New Guinea also has the world's biggest moth: the Hercules moth (*Coscinoscera hercules*), with a wingspan of 10 in (25 cm). One of the most beautiful insects of the tropical forest is the green scarab beetle, whose iridescence makes it sought after for jewellery. New Guinean stick insects may be more than 12 in (30 cm) long. Large scolopendra centipedes can deliver a severe bite, but this is not fatal to healthy adults.

Flower feeder
Lories are found on many of the islands. Among the most colourful members of the parrot family, they all have brush-tipped tongues to feed on nectar and pollen.

rather creates elaborate and meticulously decorated constructions. Using fern fronds and twigs, it builds a kind of house, often with a roof and entrance, which it surrounds with a carpet of moss and adorns with coloured or sparkling objects, such as flowers, fruits, stones and lichen. Despite all the work that goes into these love-nests, three-quarters of the males – and particularly the young ones – fail to win a female, while some of the older, more experienced males attract dozens of partners.

Red breast *The male frigate bird is identifiable by its bright red throat sac, which it inflates to advertise its chosen nest site during courtship.*

Residents and visitors

A large number of birds overwinter in the Pacific islands. Most breed during the summer in Alaska or Siberia, and then fly south towards the end of August, returning north for the Northern Hemisphere's spring. Others make just a brief stopover before heading on to their final destination in Australia or New Zealand. Among these migrants are several species of sandpiper and snipe, the golden plover, which nests in the north of Siberia, and the threatened bristle-thighed or Tahitian curlew, which breeds in Alaska. Albatrosses tend to prefer the high latitudes, though three species regularly migrate to the Hawaiian islands, where they breed.

Several sea birds are an essential part of the Pacific landscape. Notable among these are the terns: the white tern, the Arctic tern, the noddy tern and the sooty tern, which has a white body and a black head. Gannets, petrels, puffins and boobies are also fairly common. The most graceful, perhaps, is the frigate bird. With its wide wingspan

of 6.5 ft (1.9 m) and forked tail, the frigate bird can glide and manoeuvre with ease. Because its feathers are not water-repellent, a frigate bird cannot land in the sea.

Imported species

Dozens of species of birds have been brought to the islands by settlers over the centuries. The ancient Polynesians often travelled with chickens; the Europeans introduced the turtle dove and the eagle owl. The Indian mynah bird (*Acridotheres tristis*), imported towards the end of the 19th century to eradicate insect pests in coconut and citrus plantations, has now spread throughout the Pacific region, and its raucous cry and aggressive habits, its dark, iridescent feathers and yellow beak have become familiar features of the island landscape. Indeed, mynah birds have reproduced with such success that in some places they have themselves become a pest, and have usurped the habitat of many local species, such as the finches and blue-tinged doves of Tahiti.

The geographical isolation of the Pacific islands has fostered the evolution of unique species, but it has also been responsible for the extinction of several of them. Human settlers brought with them the first predators, in particular the rat, to fatal effect. The introduction of other animals to control the rats, such as cats and birds of prey, simply aggravated the problem. As a result, the region has the distinction of being the one with the most birds under threat of extinction. On Guam, nine out of the 11 native species were exterminated by the accidental importation of the brown tree snake, a native of the Solomon Islands, with military cargo during the Second World War. The US government has spent considerable sums of money trying to ensure that it does not find its way to other islands in the Marianas.

Odd bird *The cassowary of New Guinea is not only flightless; its plumage looks more like hair than feathers.*

The plight of native animals

The smaller Pacific islands have very few indigenous mammals. Only one type is widespread across the region: the bat. New Guinea, by contrast, is far better endowed, with a rich and diverse range of fauna throughout its extensive grasslands and forests.

Night prowler *A native of the forests of Melanesia, the marsupial cuscus moves slowly around the branches of trees, emerging mainly at night to feed.*

Rich diversity *Only New Guinea can boast an extensive variety of wildlife, with such species as this amphibious agama lizard.*

In the company of geckos

There are several hundred types of gecko living in the region. Unlike most lizards, they are nocturnal (they have no eyelids). Thanks to adhesive toe pads, geckos can walk up walls and across ceilings, and often spend the night hunting insects attracted by the lights in houses. They can also change colour to match their background.

Until they were brought by human settlers, few mammals colonised the islands of the Pacific – with the exception of bats. Most of these are fruit-eating bats, although a few species are insectivorous. In New Caledonia they are a cherished source of food. In Tonga, bats are considered sacred, and only members of the royal family are permitted to hunt them.

Strange native beasts

Marsupials are not found only in Australia. New Guinea has 18 marsupials, most of which live in the treetops. Australia and New Guinea share a large number of animals, such as the echidna, or spiny anteater. This is a marsupial monotreme – a mammal that lays an egg into a pouch, where it is incubated. Another example is the quoll, a marsupial 'native cat', and one of the region's most ferocious predators, attacking birds, insects and small reptiles. The cuscus is found in New Guinea and eastwards to the Solomon Islands. This monkey-like marsupial, with a body length of up to 2 ft (60 cm) excluding the long tail, lives in trees, feeding on fruits, berries and leaves. It is fairly common and found even around the towns.

There are many kinds of reptile in the islands, such as lizards, geckos, skunks, snakes and crocodiles. The saltwater crocodile, which is found in New Guinea and the Solomon Islands as well as

Little devil *The dasyure quoll is a small carnivorous marsupial, related to the Tasmanian devil. Although shy, it can also be ferocious.*

Winging their way *Bats, such as the flying foxes, are the only mammals that have spread through the Pacific islands without help from humans.*

Australia and Southeast Asia, is the largest crocodile in the world, measuring as much as 20 ft (6 m) in length. It sometimes travels far up rivers, but generally lives in the sea, and has been found swimming hundreds of miles from the coast, returning to land only to lay eggs.

The vast majority of the larger land-dwelling animals of the Pacific islands – pigs, dogs, cats, goats, horses, cattle, deer – have been imported during the successive waves of immigration, and the result has frequently been disastrous for the local native fauna.

Virgin forests and tropical gardens

The image of luxuriant growth in the Pacific islands is misleading. For every tropical forest, there is also an atoll where plants struggle to survive. But here human input has played its part by coaxing the land to greater productivity, and has done much to shape the island ecology that we see today.

Most Pacific plants come originally from Southeast Asia. They have colonised the lands to the east by natural propagation, or by accompanying human migration. Hence, as a general rule, the farther east you travel across the ocean, the less variety there is among the plantlife. The rich luxuriance of the rain forests in New Guinea, with their 9000 plant species, contrasts with the relative poverty of the Polynesian islands, with 1000 species on larger islands such as Tahiti, and fewer than 100 on the atolls.

Much of this contrast is attributable to the soil conditions. The well-watered mountain landscapes of the large volcanic islands of Melanesia have a rich soil that encourages the proliferation of plantlife. The lime-dominated atolls, by contrast, have a thin soil that is low in nutrients and retains little moisture.

Primitive plants

In the western Pacific, the forests – heirs to the primitive vegetation of the ancient continent called Gondwanaland of 150 million years ago – are dense and rich. In New Guinea, they include nutmeg trees, ironwood, ebony and mahogany – trees that sometimes reach heights of 260 ft (80 m), trailing thick lianas from their branches. The majority of these plant species are indigenous: of the 3250 catalogued plants of New Caledonia, three-quarters are native species. As everywhere else in the world, the rain forests of the Pacific islands are under threat, mainly from logging – notably in the Solomon Islands and New Caledonia.

Sacred plants

The *Araucaria columnaris* or candelabra pine of New Caledonia grows to 150 ft (45 m) in a characteristic cylindrical shape. According to Kanak tradition, it is the king of plants, a symbol of virility. The cordyline is cherished for its striking red and green, tongue-like foliage. The ancient Polynesians planted it near to their *marae* (open-air temples), and its leaves were used in religious ceremonies. It is also used by the Kanaks to mark the entrance to places of ritual importance. The banyan – a massive tree with aerial roots – is thought to be the resting place of dead ancestors and spirits.

Burning bright The Marianas are noted for their profusion of flame trees, which burst into colour in summer with thousands of flowers that all but cover the green foliage.

Under water Heavy rainfall creates areas of swampland where water-loving plants thrive. Ferns, palms and lilies are anchored in the mud by spreading roots.

Dry plains and coastal wetlands

The drier plains are carpeted in grassland savannah, dotted with tough, shrubby trees such as the niaouli (*Melaleuca quinquernervia*), which has virtually fireproof bark from which an antiseptic oil is made; or the gaïac (*Acacia spirorbis*), which has an extremely hard wood that is used by the Kanaks to make weapons and tools.

The coasts are delineated by ranks of red mangroves, with their tangle of roots anchored into the mud. A large number of plants and animals, such as crabs and shellfish, inhabit the ecosystem created by mangroves. Once despised as invasive and mosquito-ridden, mangroves are now appreciated for the rich habitat they provide, and for the work they do in stabilising the coastline.

Rank profusion *The tropical forest that cloaks the Torricelli mountains in West Sepik Province, northern Papua New Guinea, contains many of New Guinea's 9000 plant species.*

Food source *The breadfruit tree was imported from Asia by early settlers. HMS Bounty was carrying saplings from Tahiti to the Caribbean when the mutiny took place.*

Atolls are generally capable of supporting only rather specialised plants that can adapt to their impoverished, drought-prone, saline conditions. Some, such as the palm-like pandanus or screw pine, have very long roots that improve their ability to collect water; others have tiny, compact leaves that restrict the loss of water through transpiration. Despite the unpromising conditions, plants quickly colonise new islets or *motus* soon after they appear. Vegetation may propagate itself by passing from one island to another. In the case of the pandanus, coconut palm and casuarina tree, the seeds can float in the sea and germinate on the beach, even after several months in the water. Birds can also disseminate plants by eating their seeds, then depositing them on another island in their droppings. And the spores of some plants, such as ferns, may be carried many hundreds of miles on the wind.

Breadfruit, taro, yam and pandanus

A large number of island plants have been introduced by the various waves of settlers. The first Polynesians travelled with plants essential for their survival: coconut palms, breadfruit trees, banana trees, yams and taro for food; the pepper shrub (*Piper methysticum*) to produce their sacred drink, kava; the paper mulberry tree to make matting and clothes. They also travelled with sugar cane, which has been grown on New Guinea for thousands of years, and may even have originated there. The ancient peoples of the Pacific islands also introduced most of the flowering plants that adorn the gardens of the region today: frangipani, bougainvillea, hibiscus, flame trees (*royal poinciana*), and poinsettias.

There is one major exception to this rule: the famous *tiare Tahiti* (*Gardenia tahitensis*), a native plant. Its richly scented white flower is the national flower of Tahiti. The Polynesians use this to perfume the ointment called *monoï*, made from coconut

Heirs of Gondwanaland

Among the rich flora of New Caledonia are a number of plants that might be described as living fossils. They are descendants of plants that once grew on the early continental landmass, Gondwanaland, which 150 million years ago contained Africa, South America, the Antarctic, India, Australia, New Zealand and New Caledonia, before continental drift pushed them apart. The islands of New Caledonia have 44 of the world's 600 gymnosperms, the plant group that includes conifers and that flourished at the time of the dinosaurs. There are 13 species of araucaria, including the huge kauri, a giant of the forest, and the candelabra pine (*Araucaria columnaris*), which grows to a height of 150 ft (45 m) on a trunk 6.5 ft (1.9 m) in diameter. Other survivors include the false or southern beeches (*Nothofagus*); the cycas, with unbranched trunks and fern-like crowns that resemble palm trees; and the giant ferns, such as the arborescent *Cyathea intermedia*, which can grow up to 65 ft (20 m) high.

Fragmentation *The pandanus bears large fruits that break into segments as they hit the ground.*

Tropical symbols Bougainvillea and the sweet-scented, white blossom of the frangipani tree are part and parcel of the popular image of the islands.

Breadfruit for **popoï**, mulberry for **tapa**

The breadfruit tree is well adapted to island life. Growing to a height of 50-65 ft (15-20 m), it bears massive fruits weighing up to 11 lb (5 kg), which are rich in starch and vitamins A and B. In good conditions, a breadfruit tree is capable of producing 1000 fruits a year for half a century, and it thus holds a place as one of the key sources of nutrition on the islands. When baked, the fruit has a pleasant, nutty taste, reminiscent of chestnuts. The ancient Polynesians used breadfruit to make a fermented paste called *popoï*, which could be preserved for months. The bark of the breadfruit tree is used to make fabric; its wood is carved into dugout boats; its sticky sap is used in bird traps.

The paper mulberry tree (*Broussonetia papyrifera*) is the source of the distinctive fabric called *tapa*, used to make clothing and ceremonial mats. The bark of the tree is separated from the trunk, softened in water, then flattened into fine sheets with a mallet. To make a very large *tapa*, the sheets are glued together with manioc juice. Once dry, the material is decorated with motifs, painted with natural plant dyes, made for example from casuarina sap, or the roots of the nono plant (*Morinda citrifolia*). For some time now, *tapas* have been largely replaced by imported cloth, but they still play an important social role in the exchange of gifts.

oil, and to make garlands. Traditionally, this flower, or a hibiscus, is worn behind the right ear to indicate that you are unattached, and behind the left ear to show that you are spoken for.

After the coconut palm, the pandanus is the second most useful tree. Its stilt-like aerial roots permit it to survive in the poor and salty soils of the islands. Its bitter-tasting fruits were once an important food source in the less habitable atolls. The leaves can be used to make roofs, twine, sails, loincloths and hats, and a variety of useful domestic articles such as mats and baskets. The hard peel of the fruits, which turns a bright red, is used by the islanders to fashion festive necklaces, while the thick sap makes a powerful alcoholic drink.

Colour blast The flowers of hibiscus bushes unfurl to display a pollen-laden spike.

Medicine tree The niaouli tree of New Caledonia produces an oil used in the pharmaceutical industry.

The sweet potato mystery

The sweet potato and manioc are the only plants of the region that come from South America. We do not know how they were introduced, but contact between South America and the Polynesian islands before the European era has not been ruled out. It seems more likely, though, that the sweet potato was brought by Spanish explorers in the 17th century. Certainly it appears to have reached New Guinea at about that time, and has since become the staple food of the New Guinea Highlands.

Healing nono

Certain of the region's plants are of great interest to international pharmaceutical companies and health food manufacturers. Used by the islanders for centuries to beneficial effect, they are now being studied to discover their active ingredients. For example, the mamala tree, a medicinal plant used in Samoa, may have a valuable application in the treatment of AIDS. The nono (or noni) plant, the fruit and leaves of which have long been used in poultices by Tahitian healers, has now become one of the prime export products of French Polynesia. Its juice, said to be good for treating cardiovascular conditions, arthritis and diabetes, has become a fashionable health drink in the USA.

The Europeans brought a broad range of new plants to the region: fruiting trees such as mango, papaya, tamarind, avocado, soursop, mangosteen, carambola; and, for export, coffee, cocoa and vanilla. The introduction of new plants was not always a success, however: the miconia, a broad-leaved shrub imported from South America in the 1930s, has spread at such speed in the uplands of Tahiti that it is now considered as much of a pest as lantana, which has taken over some valleys and grown into impenetrable thickets. The miconia has also gained a foothold in Hawaii, and is posing a threat to native forests there.

The multipurpose coconut palm

Coconut palms accompanied all the Pacific migrations, and have now colonised even the smallest and most remote atolls. For the islands, this palm is an important source of food and drink, building materials, and cash.

To Europeans, the coconut palm is a symbol of tropical islands, conjuring up images of white sand, turquoise seas and holiday indolence. To Pacific islanders the tree is an essential part of life, and every part is put to use.

First, the coconut itself. Growing in clusters among the fronds at the top of the tree, it has to be harvested if it is to be used in prime condition. When opened with a machete blow, it yields its cool, pure and slightly sweet juice, or 'water'. The solid 'flesh' of the coconut adheres to the wall of the shell: in a young, green coconut this is a transparent jelly that is prized as a safe, nutritious baby food. The harder

Sun-dried *Traditionally, coconut flesh is dried in the sun to make copra.*

white flesh of more mature coconuts is grated, steeped in boiling water and then squeezed to make coconut milk, which is a key ingredient in numerous local dishes. The meat can also be dried to make copra, which is pressed to produce coconut oil. Scented with floral essences or the oil of sandalwood, it is the main ingredient of *monoï*, which Tahitians use to keep their hair lustrous, and to moisturise their skin and protect it from the sun.

Empty coconut shells are used to make containers, plant pots, percussion instruments, and even – thanks to the ingenuity of missionaries – bras for performers of the Polynesian *tamure* dance. The shells and husks are also a good source of fuel. Plaited coconut

Hidden danger *Coconut palms produce about 100 coconuts a year. They may fall to the ground at any moment – a well-known hazard.*

fibres and the husks of green coconuts are used to make rope. Young coconut shoots are often used in cooking: the flowers produce a sap that is collected to make a wine or a toddy called tuba. The fronds are made into roofs, matting, hats, baskets and brushes. The trunks provide timber, fencing posts and a material for carving, and the roots are used in a variety of medicinal preparations.

Copra: industrial coconuts

Copra was one of the first export crops to be developed by European colonists. Plantations were introduced to boost production. Coconut palms are well suited to this kind of exploitation: they give their first crop after five or six years, and then produce coconuts for the next 60 years. The fruits are allowed to mature on the tree and are collected when they fall to the ground. They are husked, split into two or three pieces and the flesh is dried in the sun or in a kiln. The dried copra is then exported and mechanically pressed to extract the oil, which is used to make shampoo, soap, detergent and margarine. The residue is turned into livestock feed. Copra-production plays an important part in the economy of New Guinea and Vanuatu, as well as some of the smaller Pacific states, notably Tuvalu and Kiribati.

Oil fields *Coconut groves have become a familiar part of the island landscape. Used in copra production, they can provide a modest but steady income.*

Timeless wonders of the sea

With its reefs and other marine habitats, currents, and vast expanses of deep ocean, the Pacific supports a rich sea life. Fish, molluscs, crustaceans, sea mammals… all clamour for a place in a complex web of coexistence.

Gentle giant   Despite its huge size, the whale shark is not dangerous. It lives off plankton, which it hoovers up in its slit-like mouth.

In the more temperate zones of the Pacific, millions of fish gather in shoals, feeding on heavy concentrations of plankton. Peruvian anchovies and Japanese sardines, both members of the herring family, share such feeding grounds with six species of tuna, and – in the north – five species of salmon. The tropical zones have an even greater variety of life, notably in the western sector, around the larger islands of Melanesia. Some of the world's richest coral reefs are found here, where there are six times more species of fish than in the Caribbean.

Some of the larger fish have an awesome reputation, not always deserved. The reef shark is one of the few sharks to inhabit the shallow waters of lagoons, where it thrives on easy pickings from the abundant marine life. Although 5 ft (1.5 m) long, it is shy and poses no threat to humans. This is not the case with the larger tiger shark, so named because of its stripes, which hunts at night in the channels connecting the lagoons to the sea, ambushing fish that move in or out as the tide changes. Tiger sharks are voracious, and will eat jellyfish, turtles, sea snakes and sea birds – even driftwood and tin cans.

The bigger, man-eating sharks live in the open ocean, outside the reefs: these include the blue shark and the hammerhead shark, with its curious T-shaped head, both of which grow to about 13 ft (4 m) in length. The great white shark, the largest predatory fish in the world, can be double this size. It is capable of eating seals whole, and mashing prey with its seven rows of teeth. Great whites are constantly on the move and may travel 300 miles (480 km) in a day.

The biggest shark of all, indeed the biggest fish in any ocean, is the whale shark, which can grow to 43 ft (13 m), but lives entirely on plankton, which it filters through sieves called 'gill-rakers' located in its gill openings.

Polynesians occasionally catch the smaller sharks for food. They also use sharkskin to make drums, and their teeth to make ceremonial adornments.

Ancient survivor   The nautilus has an ancestry that goes back 100 million years, as witnessed in its fossil record.

Shells and molluscs

Molluscs play a vital role in the ecosystem of reefs. The Pacific contains more than 1000 species, including the numerous bivalves and gastropods whose shells fill the display tables of the tourist markets – such as the spotted cowries, with their shiny, porcelain-like surface, and the delicately pronged murex shells. Many are under threat of extinction, for example the marine conch, a large gastropod which the Polynesians used as a kind of trumpet. The giant clam (*Tridacna gigas*) is similarly threatened in the wild, but is now farmed commercially for its meat.

The top shell, a large, cone-shaped gastropod is collected for its meat and its shell. The shell used to be a key source of mother-of-pearl, and for a long while it was a major income-earner in many of the islands, before natural mother-of-pearl was usurped by synthetic materials. The nautilus is a cephalopod, like squids and octopuses. It swims by adjusting the gases in the spiralling chambers of its shell, which is also collected and sold as a souvenir.

Turtles

Like their cousins the tortoises, turtles were once land animals, but they have adapted to life in water and are quite at home in the open sea. The females return to land to lay their eggs on the beach, but they spend the rest of their lives at sea. Turtles have been

Sea cucumbers

During the 19th century a vibrant trade grew up around the sea cucumber. This strange-looking invertebrate, related to sea urchins and starfish, was much prized by the Chinese, not only as a food, but also for its tonic properties. Sea cucumbers loll on the bottom of lagoons, feeding on plankton and other organic particles. Easily collected, they were cleaned and dried or smoked, and then turned into a valuable trade commodity known as trepang or *bêche-de-mer*. So widespread was this trade that the term *bêche-de-mer* became the name of a pidgin language used to facilitate exchange.

Tightly packed   Even before they end up crammed side-by-side in a tin, anchovies appear to like living in tightly packed shoals.

hunted since time immemorial for their meat. In the 19th century, however, commercial hunting – primarily for their shells, which were used to make spectacle frames, fountain pens, furniture inlay and knick-knacks – brought them close to extinction. There are several species of turtle in the Pacific: the leatherback, the largest, can grow to 7 ft (2.1 m) in length and weigh 1200 lb (540 kg). Most remain perilously close to extinction.

Female turtles reach maturity at about 20 years of age and return to the coast where they were born. They drag themselves up the beach, dig a hole in the sand with their flippers, and lay about 100 eggs the size and shape of a ping-pong ball, which they then bury. If they are not found by poachers, these will hatch, and the baby turtles will head instinctively for the relative safety of the sea, running the gauntlet of sea birds and other predators who wait along the shore for this traditional feast. But only one in every thousand young turtles has to survive to adulthood to ensure the survival of the species.

Deep-sea volcanic vents

In 1977 the ocean deep yielded a surprising secret. At a depth of 8500 ft (2600 m), scientists on board the mini-submarine *Alvin* found volcanic hydrothermal vents – like underwater geysers – while searching for evidence of diverging tectonic plates on the East Pacific Rise. This alone was good news, but even more extraordinary was the discovery of a number of marine creatures, living in the darkness and the warm water around the vents.

They included giant clams, mussels, tube worms, blind crabs, fish, shrimps and octopuses. These creatures had adapted to a unique way of life based on a food chain that depended on the chemical nutrients emitted from the vent. It suggested that life on Earth may not necessarily have begun with photosynthesis from sunlight, as previously thought: it may have been triggered by synthesis from minerals – or 'chemosynthesis'.

Mysteries of the deep

There is life at every level of the ocean, even in the deepest, darkest recesses of the Marianas Trench, where the ocean bed lies at 36 200 ft (11 034 m), the lowest point on Earth. This is the haunt of strange fish that illuminate the darkness with their natural bioluminescence – but it remains largely unexplored.

Under pressure *Turtles have been exploited by humans for their meat, shell and eggs. Other predators feed on their eggs and young. These combined threats have brought Pacific turtles to the brink of extinction.*

Dangerous creatures

It is not just the sharks that pose life-threatening dangers to the unwary. One of the most vicious creatures in the shallows is the innocuous-looking cone shell, which is capable of injecting a lethal poison by means of a dart. Humans have been known to die within five hours of being stung. The blue-ringed octopus, although just 2 in (5 cm) long, possesses enough venom to kill ten men, and anyone who has been bitten is liable to collapse in paralysis within ten minutes.

A number of sea snakes hunt in lagoons. Like turtles, these were once land animals that have taken to the sea, and they can stay under water for an hour before coming up for breath. Most species of sea snake are poisonous.

The Portuguese man-of-war, a jellyfish of the *physalia* genus, has a formidable reputation: its long filaments can inflict very painful stings, but these seldom kill. Far more threatening is the much smaller box jellyfish, which delivers burn-like stings, and in a case of multiple stings, can kill. The stonefish is perhaps the most dangerous stinging fish in the world. It lurks on the sea floor in the shallows, well camouflaged, as its name suggests. A spine on its dorsal fin delivers a sting charged with powerful myotoxins that can quickly lead to heart failure.

Whales, the giants of the Pacific

The Pacific Ocean is home to a number of marine mammals, including whales and dolphins. They roam its vast spaces, following age-old patterns of migration, moving from the cold and nutrient-rich polar regions to breeding grounds in the tropics.

Fellow mammal *Monk seals share the waters around Hawaii with the whales.*

At the beginning of winter, in both hemispheres, thousands of whales leave the icy feeding grounds around the poles and head for the warm waters of the region, where the females give birth. Here they bring up their young for several months, as they develop the thick layer of blubber that they need to protect their internal organs from the Arctic or Antarctic cold. During this long summer period the adults barely eat, but live on reserves built up over the winter months.

Several species migrate from the poles to the central Pacific each year, but the groups from each hemisphere remain quite separate and do not intermingle. At the end of the season the whales return north or south from where they came.

Queen of the ocean

The blue whale is the biggest animal in the world – in fact it is the largest animal that has ever lived. An adult can grow to 100 ft (30 m), and weigh as much as 170 tons. Despite its huge size, it eats only small prey, mainly tiny, shrimp-like krill and plankton, which it sieves through the baleen in its mouth, along with a daily intake of 3 tons of water. The calves, which weigh 7 tons at birth, drink 130 gallons (600 litres) of milk a day, growing strong on a liquid that has a 42 per cent fat content. With fewer than 1000 blue whales left in the Southern Hemisphere, the species is under threat of extinction.

Humpback whales are also baleen (filter-feeder) whales, and they grow to about 50 ft (15 m). Found in all the oceans of the world, they also have separate northern and southern populations. Humpbacks have extremely long pectoral fins – up to 20 ft (6 m) long – which make them exceptionally mobile. They seem to revel in leaping out of the sea, sometimes doing a half-somersault, and are very talkative, performing 'songs' that may last for more than half an hour. Humpback whales have been a protected species since the 1960s.

The sei whale, another baleen whale, measuring about 50 ft (15 m) and weighing 30 tons, is similarly threatened. Sei whales tend to live in small groups, mainly in temperate zones and deep water. During the 1960s they were killed in large numbers in the Southern Hemisphere, but a ban on hunting has allowed the population to stabilise and grow to around 37 000 – although they once numbered 100 000.

Coming up for air *As with all the whale species, sperm whales surface from time to time to breath air through the 'blowholes' on top of their head.*

Smallest family members

Dolphins are cetaceans – members of the same family that includes whales. In fact, bottle-nose whales and killer whales (orcas) are classed as dolphins, albeit much larger than the others. The most widely distributed species of dolphin in the Pacific are the common dolphin, the bottle-nose dolphin, the rough-toothed dolphin and Risso's dolphin. All feed mainly on small fish, as well as shrimps and squid, and live in groups of about 20 individuals. Because they pursue tuna, dolphins were often caught in fishing nets, a fate that befell thousands every year. Following an international campaign, fishing practices were adjusted, and most tuna in the Pacific is now caught by methods that spare the dolphins.

lion whales were killed in the southern Pacific and Antarctic region.

With a public outcry over the threatened extinction of whales, and the looming crisis in the industry as whale stocks fell well below sustainability, a moratorium on whaling was introduced in 1986. All commercial whaling was banned. Japan, however, still continues to hunt whales, 'for scientific research'. In 1998, on the initiative of Australia, the countries of the south Pacific proclaimed the region a sanctuary for whales. Despite these initiatives, eight of the 11 main species of large whales are still threatened.

Whale tourism

'Whale watching' has now become a major attraction in certain parts of the Pacific. Tour operators in Hawaii, Niue and Tonga offer trips that take guests close to the whales, using specially adapted boats with viewing platforms and 'hydrophones' to pick up and broadcast the mating calls. In New Caledonia, in August and September, it is possible to see humpback whales arriving from the Antarctic. Schools of humpbacks similarly arrive in Hawaii on their 3700 mile (6000 km) journey south from Alaska, to take up winter quarters around the island of Maui. A whaling museum has been set up at Lahaina on Maui, in a former whaling station.

The International Whaling Commission keeps an eye on these modern whaling activities, checking that sea tours have minimal impact on the whales. Cetaceans have a highly developed sense of hearing and are easily disturbed by the sound of boat engines.

Sperm whales

The sperm whale, or cachalot, is a toothed whale that can grow to 60 ft (18 m) long and weigh 60 tons. It has been extensively hunted in the past for its spermaceti, a thick waxy oil found in large quantities in the head of the whale that was used to make candles, cosmetics, ointments and lubricants. The intestines also contain a valuable substance called ambergris, which was widely used to fix the scent in perfumes. The sperm whale swims to impressive depths, and can stay under water for 90 minutes before surfacing to breathe. Another toothed whale, the pilot whale, is one of the smallest at 20 ft (6 m) long. It stays all year in the southern Pacific, and can be seen, for instance, around the Cook Islands.

Industrial whaling

Because of the high market price of whale oil, in the 19th century whaling was a lucrative industry. Another valuable product was 'whalebone' (baleen), which, before the days of plastic, provided flexible, strong strips of material to make corset stays, umbrella ribs and riding crops. In the Pacific, whaling tended to centre on the eastern sector, pursued in particular by American whaling ships from the east-coast port of Nantucket. In 1840 there were some 500 American whaling ships, and the result was a dramatic reduction in whale stocks. But the slaughter continued, and during the 20th century, when harpooning techniques became more effective, and factory ships speeded up the processing of carcasses, some 1.5 mil-

The dugong

The dugong, or seacow, is a large herbivorous marine mammal that lives in the coastal waters and estuaries of the western Pacific. A distant relative of the elephant, it can grow to 10 ft (3 m) in length, weigh 880 lb (400 kg) and live for 70 years. After a gestation period lasting 13 months, the female gives birth to one calf, which she suckles in the water. Placid in temperament, eating nothing but seagrass, dugongs have always been easy prey for hunters in pursuit of their meat and their blubber. They are now a protected species.

Nature and nurture   This tiny coral island, or motu, has emerged from the lagoon of Bora Bora, behind the protective barrier of the reef.

Unit of exchange   The cowries are a large family of marine molluscs, many of which have glossy, brightly marked shells like this one. In some parts of the region, cowrie shells are used as money.

Dangerous exposure
This conch is extending its foot, with the aid of which it can turn itself over and take up a new position on the sand.

Empire builders   Tiny and delicate coral polyps extract their food by siphoning sea water, and secrete the lime that creates the coral, which serves as a kind of external skeleton.

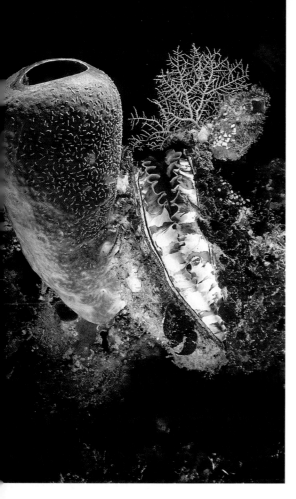

Food processor *Sponges continually filter water to extract nutrition from the organic particles suspended in it.*

At the heart of the coral reef

Flying over the tropical islands of the Pacific is a visual treat. The coasts are rimmed by coral reefs, and their lagoons present a painter's palette of colours, from blue and green to pristine white and all the shades in between. The different blues speak not only of the depth of the water, but also of its clarity. Divers can see up to 100 ft (30 m), a factor that brings a sparkling clarity to the extraordinary diversity of reef life. Coral reefs are the largest constructions made by living creatures on Earth – a remarkable feat given the minuscule size of the builders, the coral polyps. Over the millennia they have been able to create the walls of coral that are the foundation blocks of countless islands. Indeed, coral can be credited for initiating the processes on which much of the life of the Pacific now depends. Living coral reefs are like cities, inhabited by thousands of different organisms, each with its own habitat, food preferences and lifestyle. Seaweeds, shellfish, marine worms, urchins, sea anemones, fish, crabs, sea snakes and octopuses play out their roles in an endless ballet, illuminated by sunlight during the day, and by bioluminescence at night. Comparable in biodiversity to tropical forests, these coral reefs present some of the richest habitats in the world, and the relations between the many species within them are both complex and delicate. Small changes can upset the entire edifice. The increase of human activity, and the rise in sea temperatures with global warming, poses a serious threat to the health of reefs. But so far those of the Pacific have coped better than many others around the world.

Shaped to fit *The shapes of coral reflect the prevailing conditions. In calm waters, it can take more delicate, branch-like forms.*

Notorious hunters *Barracudas are armed with impressive, flesh-tearing teeth that command the wary respect of divers. The young tend to move around in shoals, which are, paradoxically, less menacing than a lone, large barracuda.*

Spare parts *The brittle star moves along on its five legs, which grow back if it loses any. It feeds on marine detritus using its mouth on the underside of the central disc.*

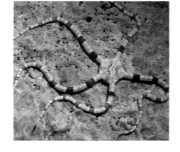

Island life

1. Tropical forests cloak the higher altitudes. Fed by copious rains, they are a rich mass of giant ferns and moss-laden trees.

2. Steep-walled crater lakes in the interior are surrounded by dense plantlife. Some of these lakes are home to large eels that grow to more than 5 ft (1.5 m) long.

3. Strong currents surge through the channels between the reef islands, carrying a daily exchange of sea water that refreshes the lagoon.

4. The coconut crab, or robber crab, has pincers strong enough to break a coconut. It lives in a burrow, and the female lays her eggs in the sea.

5. Mangroves create dense thickets along the coasts. Their strong aerial roots are salt-tolerant, and supremely adapted to this rigorous environment.

6. In bays fed by rivers, the water is brackish and laden with soil particles. Rich in nutrients, it provides a fertile habitat for marine life.

7. Coconut palms take root above the high-tide mark, providing firm footholds and protection for a ground-cover of shrubs and grasses.

8. In inland valleys, plants like the yellow-flowering alamanda vine grow like weeds. Their woody stems and tough root structures enable them to cope with the long periods of drought.

9. The Indian mynah bird, an introduced species, has invaded most of the region and colonised the lowlands to the detriment of native species.

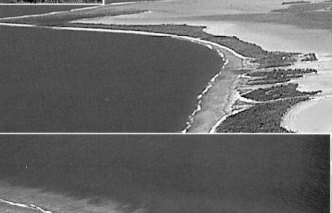

8

7

6

5

Multicoloured *Many species of small shrimp are decorated with exuberant colours and markings.*

Taking the strain *Coral located on the seaward side of a reef tends to be more compact, to parry the pounding of the waves.*

1. The puffer fish can blow itself up to the size of a football if threatened, by taking in a large quantity of water. This also has the effect of raising the sharp spines that cover its body.

2. The moray eel lies in wait for its prey, with its head projecting from its lair. It grips its victims with its sharp teeth, and locks its body into the hole to prevent it being dislodged.

3. The octopus usually leaves its home only at night, when it goes in search of crabs and shells, which it can open with its strong 'beak'. It can move by using its arms, or shoot backwards by 'jet propulsion'.

4. The giant clam has a brightly coloured mantle lining the rim of its shell. Microscopic algae living in its tissue give it a startling iridescence.

5. The surgeonfish owes its name to the extendable blades located at the base of its tail. Sharp as scalpels, they serve as an effective defence mechanism.

6. The crown of thorns starfish destroys living coral by everting its stomach and ingesting the polyps. When populations grow unchecked by predators, these star fish pose a major threat to coral reefs.

7. Lobsters hide in holes in the coral reef during the day and come out at night to feed on dead fish, dying invertebrates, and vegetable detritus.

8. The slate pencil urchin is covered with thick spines 5 in (12.5 cm) long, which provide excellent protection against predators while it slowly makes its way across rocks and coral, feeding on algae.

9. Sharks may come into the lagoon through the surge channels. Rather than hunting aggressively, they tend to feed on dying and wounded fish, providing a kind of cleaning service.

10. The top shell, a cone-shaped gastropod, is so named because it resembles a spinning top. It is collected for its pearly shell, and also for its flesh.

11. The Napoleon wrasse moves with majestic ease around the coral reef. Weighing sometimes more than 220 lb (100 kg), it has few predators.

Self-advertisement *Clownfish can live among stinging tentacles, being immune to them. This strategy of defence allows them the luxury of vivid colours and high visibility.*

Killer shell *The cone shell kills its prey by injecting them with its poisoned dart. The poison can cause serious injury, even death, to swimmers and divers.*

Animal, vegetable or fruit? *The pineapple sea cucumber moves slowly across the seabed, swallowing and regurgitating sand, from which it extracts organic matter.*

Quicksilver *Jacks of the carangid family are noted for their 'lightning movement': flashes of light from the metallic sheen of their body reflect through the water.*

Which way? *Butterflyfish flutter around the reef in a way that their name suggests, picking off coral polyps and invertebrates. Their markings are similar front and rear, to confuse predators.*

Eat or be eaten *This red-spotted crab feeds on organic detritus. In turn, it is much appreciated by human gourmets.*

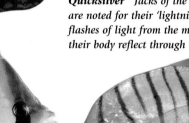

Quick on the draw *Triggerfish are ferocious hunters. The 'trigger' is a defensive spine that can be raised and locked into position on the fish's back.*

Smooth glider A manta ray, with a 'wingspan' of perhaps 20 ft (6 m), glides majestically over lumps of coral, feeding on plankton and small fish.

Red alert The reef-dwelling lionfish has highly visible flag-like spines, which serve as a warning that they are armed with a virulent poison. It feeds on small fish and invertebrates.

Hidden danger The bizarre-looking stonefish is superbly camouflaged to hide among the weeds and coral stands, from which it can gulp prey that unsuspectingly passes by. Its dorsal spine is charged with a highly toxic poison.

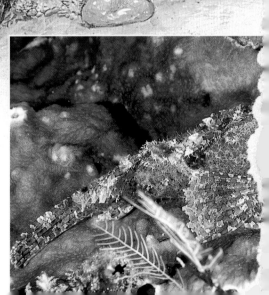

CHAPTER 4
PEOPLE AND RESOURCES

For centuries, the people of the south Pacific were sustained by the produce of their gardens, forests and lagoons, sometimes trading fish, fruit and vegetables between the islands. European traders found the region a source of valuable products, such as sandalwood, pearls and sea cucumber, while colonists brought new plantation crops to the larger islands – sugar cane to Fiji, pineapples to Hawaii and coffee to New Guinea. The old ways of subsistence agriculture and fishing are now complemented by export production. Some nations have leased their fishing rights to foreign, industrialised operators. New Guinea, New Caledonia and several of the other islands have rich resources in minerals and forest timber, but their extraction takes a heavy toll on the environment. And one growing industry depends upon the Pacific islands remaining pristine and idyllic: tourism.

Islanders still use traditional methods to reap the natural bounty of the sea.

Fishing: dugouts and tuna fleets

The coral reefs and coastal waters of the south Pacific provide seafood for the islanders, who collect it by snorkelling and from canoes. Out of sight of the islands, rather less delicate methods are used to harvest tuna.

Traditional ways *Small-scale fishing, using outrigger canoes and nets, provides a livelihood for many islanders across the region.*

For the islanders of the south Pacific, the ocean has always been a source of food. The daily rhythms of life revolve around the departure and return of the outrigger canoes (the traditional craft of the fishermen) or the crackle and purr of outboard motors on the aluminium boats that have in part replaced them.

Parrotfish, wrasse, bonito and top shells

Having negotiated a path through the coral strands within the lagoon, the boats move out into the ocean, carried through the channels in the reef by the descending tide. It is on the outer fringes of the reefs that the most prized catches lurk: grouper, wrasse, sea-perch, snapper, parrotfish, triggerfish. But at the right time of year, in the four months before the onslaught of the cyclone season, the boats venture farther out into the ocean to seek larger prey: bonito, jacks, shark, barracuda and the much-cherished dorado – also called Pacific dolphinfish and known locally as *mahimahi*.

The island women also harvest the seas. Usually accompanied by their children, they scour the seabed and tide pools at low tide for top shells, clams, crabs, prawns and octopus.

The shark-callers of New Ireland

Every island has its own fishing traditions. In some Polynesian islands, fishermen create a huge semicircle out of outrigger canoes, then drive the fish towards the shore by hitting the water with stones attached to lengths of rope. In the islands of Papua New Guinea, most famously in Kontu and other villages on the western coast of New Ireland, individual fishermen practise the remark-able art of 'shark-calling'. By shouting out sacred incantations from their canoes and shaking a rattle of coconut shells in the water, they manage to lure sharks of up to 10 ft (3 m) in length into a handheld noose, and then bludgeon them to death with staves.

In Fiji and Samoa, gentler methods are used to catch the *palolo* or *balolo* worms (*Eunice viridis*) – segmented marine worms that nor-mally live deep within fissures in the coral reefs. Twice a year, on precise days in the lunar calendar (the last quarter of the moon in October and November), they come to the surface to reproduce. On the nights when the worms appear, the islanders wait patiently until dawn, then pull them out by the basketload, filling their boats. The worms are a great delicacy, and are nicknamed 'caviar of the Pacific'.

Popular sport *Specially equipped boats operate from the ports of resort islands, offering the thrill of grappling with large fish guaranteed to put up a fight, such as shark, swordfish and tuna.*

Beware the ciguatera

Ciguatera is a type of human food poisoning caused by microscopic algae (*Gambierdiscus toxicus*) that produce toxins in fish. When coral dies, these algae rise from the depths and invade the reefs and lagoons. They are consumed by small herbivorous fish, which are in turn eaten by larger carnivores, such as wrasse, snappers and groupers. The toxins thus progress up the food chain, eventually reaching human beings. The symptoms of ciguatera are rashes, vomiting, and aches and pains in muscles and joints. French Polynesia has the highest incidence in the region, giving rise to speculation that nuclear testing may also have caused the kind of disruption that triggers the release of the algae.

Walls of death

Until 1989, vast drift nets were towed behind fishing vessels to catch tuna. These 'walls of death' also caught dolphins, sharks and turtles, provoking such outrage among ecological organisations that a moratorium was imposed on their use. Now floating long-lines have come under the spotlight. According to ecologists, these cause the deaths of thousands of sea birds each year. Attracted by the bait (usually small fish), the birds dive, become snagged on the hooks and are drowned. Nearly 100 000 birds, particularly albatrosses and petrels, are killed in this way every year. Ecologists also cite another evil: the use of cyanide to kill reef fishes, usually destined for Asian restaurants. This poison renders the biggest fish senseless and easy to catch, but it also indiscriminately wipes out coral polyps and smaller fish of no commercial value.

Hung out to dry *Large catches of fish are preserved by salting fillets and drying them in the sun, or smoking the fish over slow-burning fires.*

their prey. There are various methods of catching tuna: semicircular purse-seine nets account for 80 per cent of the yield, but long-lines (lines up to 100 miles/160 km in length, bristling with as many as 3000 baited hooks) and rod and line are also used.

The fish are frozen on the ships, then taken to canneries in Thailand, Indonesia, Pago Pago in American Samoa, Levuka in Fiji, and Noro in the Solomon Islands. Most of the catch is skipjack tuna and yellowfin, but the most prized specimens are the longfin tunny or albacore, which are usually caught by long-lines. These are handled with great care, preserved in refrigerated sea water, then flown to markets specialising in *sashimi* – the preparations of raw fish prized in Japan, and now also in other parts of the world.

The tuna industry

The Pacific is one of the world's prime industrial fishing zones, not because it is particularly rich in variety – outside the coral reefs the water is comparatively low in nutrients and marine creatures generally – but because it is the haunt of one of the most important commercial fish: tuna. In fact, the south Pacific is the world's most productive zone for tuna, with annual catches of 1 million tons, representing a value of about £1 billion. The Pacific provides more than 50 per cent of the world's tinned tuna.

Some 1300 ships, mainly American and Asian, armed with the latest electronic shoal-detection equipment, scour the ocean for

Poachers and gamekeepers

To protect tuna stocks in the long term, the countries of the region have introduced licensing and quota systems in their Exclusive Economic Zones (EEZs), under treaties negotiated with the main countries involved – the USA, South Korea, Taiwan, Japan and the Philippines. In exchange, they receive royalties to the value of some £30 million a year. Despite this, some tuna stocks are running perilously low: there is concern that populations of bigeye tuna and southern bluefin have both fallen beneath sustainable levels.

It is not an easy task for the island nations to police their vast maritime territories. The Fisheries' Agency of the Pacific Islands Forum – a group representing 16 independent and semi-independent countries – has to cover a surface area of 11.5 million sq miles (30 million km²). To combat under-reporting of catches and poaching by foreign, non-licensed fleets, the agency has stipulated that all tuna boats must be equipped with satellite surveillance systems. With these instruments, every boat can be identified and its movements charted. Such information is used to check that the ships respect the terms of their licence. Any vessel suspected of infraction may be intercepted and inspected by naval patrol boats, and risks heavy penalties.

The black pearls of Tuamotu

For generations, shell divers in the Tuamotu islands in French Polynesia collected mother-of-pearl from oysters on the seabed, at depths of up to 130 ft (40 m). But since the 1960s the islands have produced a more precious commodity. The native giant blacklipped oysters (*Pinctada margaritifera*) are seeded with a piece of Mississippi River mussel. After three years of intensive care, the oysters are opened to reveal their treasures – pearls in a variety of colours from dark grey to iridescent green. Cultivated by hundreds of farms, the pearls are sold at auction to French and Japanese jewellers and are now one of the main sources of income for French Polynesia, second only to tourism.

Turning silver into gold *Huge shoals of Pacific tuna are plundered every year to satisfy the demands of the lucrative international tuna market. The catches are tipped into the holds of the fishing vessels, and are then taken to land-based canneries.*

Yam, taro and sugar cane

Most of the people of the Pacific islands work on the land and live on fruits and vegetables they grow themselves. Industrial-scale agriculture is comparatively rare.

Continuing a way of life that is hundreds of years old, many islanders live by subsistence farming, growing the same varieties of vegetables and rearing the same kinds of livestock that their ancestors brought with them on their great voyages of exploration, discovery and settlement. Tuberous plants such as taro, yam, cassava (manioc) and sweet potato form the staple foods of the south Pacific. They are grown in vegetable gardens in the fertile valleys, while in steep terrain the land is often terraced. As the range of crops is limited, farmers are wary of soil exhaustion and practise crop rotation, regularly allowing plots to lie fallow for a year. They supplement their diet with fruit: coconuts, breadfruit, papaya (pawpaw), bananas, mangoes and citrus fruits. Every household keeps poultry and pigs, which are highly prized, are allowed to range freely on many islands and slaughtered only for special occasions.

Sugar cane, pineapples and coffee

Since the colonial era, some of the better land has been given over to export crops. A significant legacy of this trend is the ethnic divide in Fiji. Between 1879 and 1916, some 60 000 Indians were brought to Fiji to work in the sugar plantations established by the British. Their descendants today make up half of the population of the archipelago. Some 23 000 of them still work in the cane fields, which are often rented by individual families from the landowners, who are all native Fijians. The crop is sold to the Fiji Sugar Corporation and transported to the mills via a network of narrow-gauge railways which stretches over 370 miles (600 km). Sugar accounts for around one-fifth of Fiji's exports, mainly to the UK, Malaysia and Japan.

Home-grown Islanders produce much of their fruit and vegetables in their own gardens. Surplus crops are sold in the markets. Above left: Pigs are an integral part of village life and are sometimes treated as pets.

Truck and train Transporting the harvested sugar cane in Fiji.

Hawaii has developed a sizable sugar industry and is the world's largest producer of pineapples. Other plantation crops have been introduced elsewhere: coffee is grown in Papua New Guinea and on a smaller scale in New Caledonia; oil palms are grown in the Solomons; copra plantations are found across the region.

Vanilla and spices

The isolation of the islands and the difficulties this poses for transport explains the moderate levels of export-oriented farming in the region. Cattle ranching in New Caledonia, Vanuatu and Papua New Guinea serves little more than local demand. The islands are now focusing on export products with high added value. Tonga grows pumpkins for export to Japan, as well as vanilla and spices. *Kava*, an intoxicating liquor made from the fermented root of the pepper shrub, is produced for export in Vanuatu and Fiji, for use by the pharmaceutical industry in the production of tranquillisers. The Solomons, Vanuatu and Papua New Guinea are sources of ngali nuts, a food source that is now also used to make oil for soaps and shampoos.

Yam, the sacred tuber

Yams are a staple food and their cultivation plays a key role in the pattern of agricultural activity throughout the year. Each phase of cultivation is accompanied by a ritual: preparation of the ground in July; planting a month later; erecting the supports from September to December; then harvest around March and April. In New Caledonia the 'master of the gardens', having dug up the first yams from a sacred field and assured himself that they are ready to eat, gives the signal that the harvest and the festivities can begin. The yam holds an almost sacred position in society. It is much prized in the ritual exchange of gifts at marriages and funerals, and is also a symbol of virility: the yam festivals on some islands are notoriously hedonistic occasions.

Stripping away the virgin forests

In the 19th century the forests of the South Pacific were plundered for their sweet-smelling sandalwood; now they are used to supply timber and plywood. Over-exploitation has resulted in serious ecological damage, and the Pacific islands have had to take action to protect their forest heritage.

Looking to the future *To manage the forests in a sustainable way, governments are promoting practices such as selective felling.*

I took just 50 years to wipe out the sandalwood trees of the South Pacific. Felling began in Fiji in 1819, then shifted to the other archipelagoes as each reserve in turn was exhausted: to Vanuatu in the 1820s, then to New Caledonia in 1840. By 1865, the sandalwood trade in the south Pacific had come to an end.

Forest clearance, erosion and pollution

Today, the tropical forests of the Pacific still attract foreign companies, mainly from Asia, and from Malaysia in particular. Dozens of these companies have obtained concessions that allow them to cut swathes out of one of the last regions where there is virgin forest – in the Solomon Islands, New Caledonia, Vanuatu, Fiji and Samoa. Their practice of clear-felling – removing all the trees in the area being worked – leads to soil erosion and river pollution, as rainwater drains across the land unrestrained. Meanwhile, this export-oriented exploitation goes on largely unregulated – and often illicitly as the number of trees removed exceeds the quantities declared. International organisations have drawn attention to the serious consequences of such practices, and island governments have responded by tightening controls and imposing quotas. They have also demanded that the companies process a proportion of the timber on the islands, to stimulate the local economy.

Today processed timber – plywood and veneers – ranks first among the exported manufactured products of Papua New Guinea. However, the post-1997 Far Eastern financial crisis and the recent drop in international timber prices have resulted in a slowdown in production, and sales of wood, formerly the prime source of foreign exchange for the Solomons, have dropped by 80 per cent.

Mini sawmills

The Solomon Islanders are experimenting with portable sawmills. These produce sawn timber rather than massive logs, and can be operated by just two people. Selective felling using this method allows the forest to regenerate, and the wood is sold by the villagers on their own behalf. Revenues and the jobs created have a direct impact on local communities. For example, the inhabitants of Big Nggela (Nggela Sule) in the Solomon Islands, horrified by the intensive logging on the nearby Pavuvu Islands carried out by a Malaysian company, have begun to use portable sawmills to export their timber direct to New Zealand.

Factory scene *Forestry has created a springboard for establishing associated industries.*

Tree nursery *In Fiji, where major forest clearance has seriously compromised the nation's forestry resources, a major replanting programme is under way, primarily of pines.*

Buried treasure

The large western islands of the Pacific comprise one of the richest mining regions on Earth: New Caledonia has nickel; Papua New Guinea has gold, silver, copper and oil. But the future of the mining industry in the Pacific appears to lie on the ocean bed.

Nickel, the treasure of New Caledonia, was discovered in the 19th century and since then its rich supply has been found to represent one-third of the world's total known reserves. Extraction is performed by opencast or 'strip' mining. Machines dig giant gashes into the central mountain chain of Grande Terre, New Caledonia's biggest island. Two-thirds of the ore is dispatched to Japan; the remainder is processed at the smelting works in Nouméa.

The riches of Papua New Guinea

Geologists have identified rich mineral seams on the mainland and islands of Papua New Guinea, one of the largest reserves on the planet. Several large mines are now in operation: the gold and copper mine of Ok Tedi, in Western Province; the gold and silver mine of Porgera, in the Highlands; the silver mines on Misima Island; and the gold mine on Lihir Island, which in 1997 began to tackle one of the largest concentrations of gold in the world.

Under guard *Bougainville, part of Papua New Guinea, has only recently emerged from a civil war provoked by the Panguna copper mine.*

The price of phosphate

Three islands in the south Pacific have been left drained by the exploitation of phosphate, fertiliser derived from ancient accumulations of seabird droppings. The island of Makatea, in French Polynesia, now lies almost deserted. On Banaba in the Kiribati archipelago, the local chiefs ceded exploitation rights to a British company in 1900. The islands received some compensation in the 1960s, but the phosphate was finally exhausted in 1979. On Nauru, it was extracted by a consortium from Australia, New Zealand and Britain. Following independence, extraction brought wealth to the islands, but now the supplies have been exhausted and the landscape has been left disfigured.

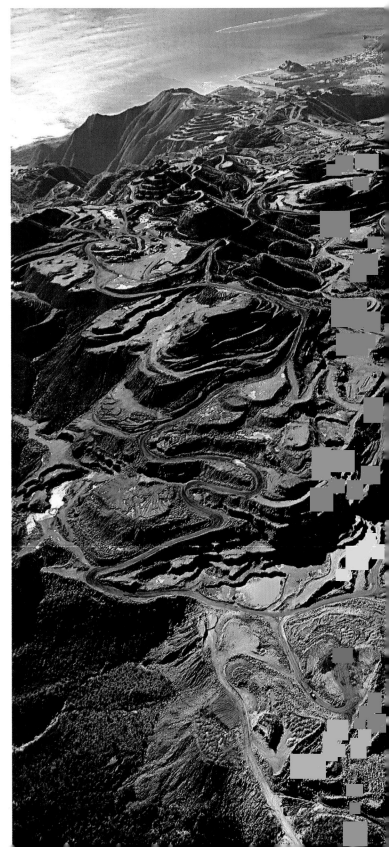

Tax havens and passports

Vanuatu, the Cook Islands, Tonga, Samoa and Niue are tax havens. In return for a fee, companies can register in these countries and so avoid taxes when investing in other countries. These offshore financial centres have recently attracted the attention of Interpol, who suspect the Russian Mafia of using them to launder criminal profits. Vanuatu also offers flags of convenience to international shipping companies: 500 ships sail under the Vanuatu flag, taking advantage of the more relaxed working conditions, safety and environmental regulations.

At the end of the 1980s Tonga decided to sell passports. Several thousand foreign nationals, notably Hong Kong Chinese, each paid about £12 000 to acquire one. But many countries have refused to recognise the passports as valid.

High income *The relatively high wages paid in mining have helped the economy to develop.*

Fossil resources

Papua New Guinea also has huge reserves of oil and natural gas, notably at Kutubu in the Southern Highlands. Oil is exported but, because of the lack of a local market, 175 million cu ft (5 million m³) of natural gas are returned to the wells each day. A gas pipeline 1550 miles (2500 km) long to take the gas to aluminium refineries in Queensland – both from Kutubu and from Hides, also in the Southern Highlands, where reserves are estimated at 8 828 billion cu ft (250 billion m³) – has been suggested.

Prospecting in the undersea volcanic domes in the Manus Basin, which also lies within Papua's territorial waters, has revealed abundant reserves of zinc, copper, silver and gold. But it is the polymetallic nodules, found on the seabed around several of the island groups that excite most interest. The size of a potato, these concretions have a high metal content of manganese, cobalt, nickel and copper and could supply the needs of the entire planet for thousands of years. They lie, however, at depths of 13 000-16 500 ft (4000-5000 m) and, as yet, the techniques available to bring them to the surface are too costly. Two UN agencies, the International Seabed Authority and the South Pacific Applied Geoscience Commission, have begun to draw up maps and are helping to coordinate the work of industrialised nations anxious to draw on this resource.

Pollution and abuses

The mines may be the treasure houses of the Pacific islands, but their exploitation has had lamentable consequences for the environment and for traditional societies. Extraction operations have polluted rivers, and waste carried by the rains into the ocean has destroyed coral reefs and killed creatures living near the coast. The valuable seams have also become the focus of political and social conflicts. For example, disputes over environmental damage and the lack of local benefit from the copper mine at Panguna, on the island Bougainville in Papua New Guinea, triggered a nine-year civil war which ended in 1998, having claimed more than 15 000 victims. In mainland Papua New Guinea, the enormous opencast mines have created vast scars in the landscape, while the sudden arrival of large sums of money upsets social equilibrium. Besides which, these huge worksites actually employ very few local people.

Carrying the burden *Mining has major logistical implications, heavier traffic being a major one. Local people are more likely to suffer pollution than to reap the benefits.*

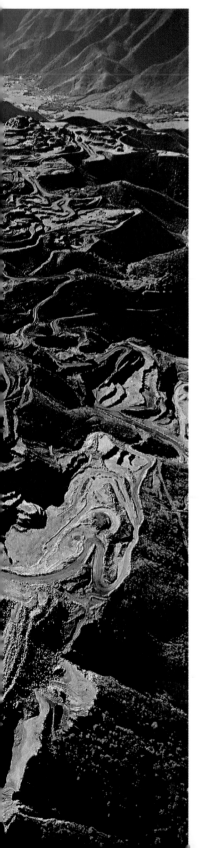

Landscaping *New Caledonia is the fourth-largest producer of nickel in the world, and this brings in most of the territory's earnings. Its extraction has ravaged the landscape around Thio, on the eastern coast of Grande Terre.*

Tourism: a new approach

Picture postcard perfect: a tropical climate, coral reefs and harlequin-coloured fish promise the fulfilment of desert island fantasies. The Pacific islands are a tourist's dream, and tourism is the region's most promising development sector.

Rooms with a view *Luxury hotels are spectacularly sited on the Fijian islands Viti Levu and Vanua Levu.*

For French Polynesia, the Cook Islands, Tonga, Samoa, Fiji and Vanuatu, tourism is the primary economic activity and main foreign income earner, but otherwise the Pacific remains largely undiscovered. While some islands are well-equipped to welcome foreign visitors, others remain under-developed – though facilities are constantly improving. Numerous aeroplanes now fly between the islands, giving access to all the archipelagoes. Luxury hotels, exclusive hideaways, village resorts and casinos are multiplying, thanks to investment from France, Asia, the USA, Australia and Japan. International organisations are helping to fund road construction and upgrade airports, but investment is intermittent and vulnerable to economic cycles.

Backpackers' Pacific

Adventurous backpackers can roam the Pacific using local inter-island ferries, buses and trucks. There are plenty of low-cost hotels on the main islands; elsewhere, travellers can arrange to sleep in the homes of villagers. Sometimes this is organised in the form of semi-official 'homestays', but in more remote villages assistance from the local chief may be needed. Visitors can drink *kava* with the locals, learn to split a coconut with a machete, visit the markets, listen to the fulsome Sunday singing in the missionary churches, and watch the rituals of yam cultivation. For those in search of the spirit of Joseph Conrad, Robert Louis Stevenson and Captain Cook, this is the only way to visit the islands.

Dream home *A bungalow on stilts provides an idyllic holiday home for visitors to Huahine, in French Polynesia.*

The Pacific à la carte

For many decades the Pacific rested on its laurels, happy to sell itself on its white-sand beaches, palm trees and lagoons; its bungalow hotels; its ukuleles, *tamure* dances, frangipani garlands and sarong-like pareos. But now, to meet competition from other destinations, the Pacific is developing new attractions, better targeted towards tourists – who for the most part come from Australia, New Zealand, the USA, Japan, France, the UK, Germany and Canada. New activities focus on nature, sport and the discovery of the Pacific's historic heritage. Today's visitors can partake in activity-based ecotourism, and there are off-the-beaten track adventures for backpackers – giving them closer, more sympathetic access to local people and their traditions.

The choice of destination is dazzling – encompassing not only the archipelagoes, but all the islands within them. Some islands are extremely touristic, notably Hawaii, Guam and Fiji. Hawaii is the market leader, receiving ten times more visitors each year than all the rest of the south Pacific. The Japanese and Australians fly in to do their shopping in the malls of Hawaii and Guam.

Some islands, such as Saipan (Northern Marianas), Tahiti, Viti Levu (Fiji) and the Cook Islands, receive large numbers of visitors and are highly commercialised, while Papua New Guinea, the Solomon Islands, Vanuatu and the Federated States of Micronesia are low key, unspoilt and authentic. Others, such as Kiribati, Tuvalu, Pitcairn, Wallis and Futuna, Niue, Raiatea, Taha'a, Huahine, Rangiroa, Tikehau – to name but a handful – remain undiscovered. The more difficult the access, the more likely it is that an island or region will have retained a traditional way of life – as is the case with the east coast of Grande Terre and the Loyalty Islands of New Caledonia, the Marquesas and the Austral Islands in French Polynesia, and the Ha'apai Group in Tonga.

Meet the people

Lagoons, watersports and lazy days on the beach are the big attractions of the clubs and resort hotels of Bora Bora and Moorea in French Polynesia, of Waikiki Beach on Oahu, the Coral Coast of Fiji, and Isle of Pines of New Caledonia. Here the big hotels and shopping galleries offer a taste of local culture through local products, such as craftwork. More extensive exposure to local customs is now being actively promoted by the cultural centres, museums and reconstructed villages, such as the Tjibaou cultural centre at Nouméa, Te Fare Tahiti Nui cultural centre in Papeete, the Polynesian cultural centre on Oahu, the Robert Louis Stevenson museum near Apia on Samoa, and the Fiji museum in Suva.

Aloha! *It's party time in Hawaii, where old traditions are liberally interpreted for tourists.*

There are a growing number of nature reserves, sanctuaries for reef fish, migratory birds and whales. On land there are superb walking trails, traversing jungles and mountains. Some lead up to the craters of active or quiescent volcanoes: Haleakala on Maui, the

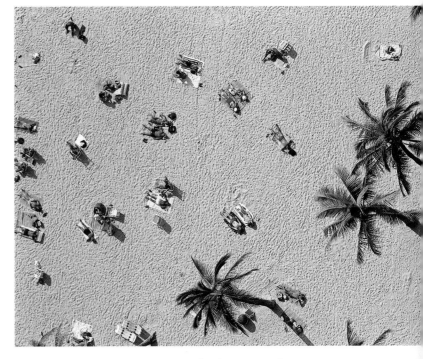

Flat out *Waikiki is famous among surfers for its waves, but the beach also attracts less energetic pleasure-seekers.*

Masks and stone statues

Going up the Sepik River in Papua New Guinea is one of the great experiences of Oceania. Visitors can witness a living but ancient culture that stretches back for thousands of years, and buy the local wares – sculpture, carved masks and string bags. Similar experiences can be found in the Tari Basin (PNG), in Vanuatu, the Solomons and New Caledonia. The south Pacific is rich in archaeological sites: there are *marae* (outdoor temples) throughout Polynesia; Lelu in the Federated States of Micronesia has a ruined royal city dating back to around 1400; Tonga has its *langi* royal tombs and the 13th-century megalithic arch of Ha'amonga 'a Maui on Tongatapu; and there are the unique and extraordinary statues of Easter Island.

Hawaii Volcanoes National Park on Hawaii, Yasur and Ambrym in Vanuatu, Mount Lamington and Rabaul in Papua New Guinea, Savo and Tinakula in the Solomons.

Scuba diving is a growth industry. Visitors can dive with experienced guides to admire the underwater beauty or to view the wreckage of the Pacific War, scattered across a number of lagoons. The most spectacular sunken cemeteries are in Micronesia, for example on Chuuk in the Federated States of Micronesia, and on Palau.

With such choice and variety, the future looks bright for tourism in the South Pacific, but it will be marked by a clearly defined trend: to involve more local people at ground level and give them greater access to the revenue generated by tourism, 60 per cent of which currently flows out of the islands to foreign owners, operators and suppliers.

CHAPTER 5

ISLAND LIFE

To the first European navigators in the south Pacific, the islanders were 'Indians'. French colonists called the people of New Caledonia Kanaks, from a Polynesian word meaning 'human'. In the early 19th century, the French explorer Dumont d'Urville classified the thousands of islands and cultures of the southern Pacific into three groups: Melanesia, the black islands; Polynesia, the many islands; Micronesia, the little islands. These classifications are a broad brush with which to paint the subtle variations across this vast region, and at the time they meant nothing to the inhabitants themselves. For them, the essential symbols of identity were the village, clan or tribe. Even so, Dumont d'Urville's labels stuck and gained acceptance, so that today the peoples of the region see themselves as Melanesian, Polynesian or Micronesian.

Boats have always had a central role in island life, as here in the Trobriand Islands, Papua New Guinea.

Melanesia

The islands of Melanesia are the most naturally rich in the region, and their inhabitants – a mix of coastal and interior tribes – the most culturally diverse.

Gift of the gods *The ease with which yams grow in the rich volcanic soil has played a fundamental role in the development of Melanesian culture.*

The western islands of the Pacific are the largest, and the richest in resources, of all the islands of the region. Ancient splinters of the proto-continent Gondwana, all these islands, with the exception of New Caledonia, are still regularly shaken by the volcanic activity that has also given them their abundantly fertile soil. Mountainous, well-watered by rain, and fringed by atolls, they have the richest flora and fauna in the region.

There are four independent countries in Melanesia – the Solomons, Fiji, Vanuatu and Papua New Guinea – while New Caledonia remains a French territorial collectivity. Some 6.8 million people now live on these islands. By the standards of the South Pacific, they are densely populated. The presence of high, forest-clad mountains and the distances between the islands has led to a multitude of autonomous tribes and clans, with numerous and diverse cultures, many with long historic roots. Papua New Guinea has been inhabited for perhaps 40 000 years; the other islands for

up to 5000 years. The coastal peoples are traders, exposed to outside influences, and their cultures have been shaped differently from those of peoples living in the remote and isolated mountains of the interiors. This combination of factors has led to a plethora of local languages – Papua New Guinea alone is said to have 500. To bridge the problem, the Melanesians have developed the *lingua franca* called pidgin, a family of trading languages based on English. The pidgin (*pisin*) of Papua New Guinea, Vanuatu and the Solomons share many common features.

Common traditions

All the more remarkable, then, are the common strands that unite the Melanesians. They grow yams, taro, sweet potatoes and sago. Wealth, traditionally, is judged in pigs – an animal to which elaborate rituals are attached. Social organisation is based on the clan or tribe, led by a chief or headman, and much of the land is held in communal ownership. As a consequence, many neighbouring villages are in a permanent state of conflict or dispute, which is sublimated in ceremonies, festivals, exchanges of gifts, and sometimes battle, ritual or otherwise. Traditional religion, where it has survived the work of missionaries, centres upon ancestors, who are celebrated in daily life by various rites and propitiatory practices.

The impact of colonisation

A reputation for head-hunting and cannibalism initially deterred colonisation of the bigger islands. Parts of Papua are so inaccessible that remote tribes have made contact with the outside world only in the past few decades. The effect of colonisation on Papua New Guinea, the Solomons and Vanuatu has been limited: the populations are still predominantly Melanesian. In Fiji, by contrast, the influx of labour from India had a huge impact, and in New Caledonia the Kanaks now account for just 40-45 per cent of the population.

Favourite sport *On the Trobriand Islands of Papua New Guinea, football is as popular as anywhere else in the world.*

Nouméa, resort city

Of all the capitals of French territorial collectivities, Nouméa is the farthest from Paris. Enriched by nickel, the city has become a commercial and administrative centre, with an up-beat, cosmopolitan feel. The mix of urban comfort and holiday nonchalance has made this 'Paris of the Pacific' into a popular tourist destination, a couple of hours' flight from Australia.

Vibrant city   Founded in 1854, Nouméa rose to prominence in the Second World War, when it became the US base for the Solomons campaign, directed from Anse Vata (in the foreground).

New Caledonia: reluctant cohabitation

In New Caledonia, the European population has monopolised the island's riches. But under pressure from the Kanaks and the French government, it now acknowledges that it will have to share.

'If we have to kill to get our claim taken seriously, then we will kill.' This statement by a militant separatist Kanak just before the tragic turn of events of 1984-8 bore witness to the determination and resentment of a people who had suffered the sharp end of colonialism for over a century. Inspired by the newly won independence of other nations across the South Pacific, and promises of self-determination from the French government, Kanak militants proclaimed independence in 1984. They were challenged by equally determined anti-independent Calédoniens, mainly French settlers, who feared the economic and social consequences of severing links with France. As tensions mounted, the anti-independence militants took up arms and precipitated a violent conflict.

A particularly bloody episode on the island of Ouvéa in 1988 brought the conflict to world attention. A large-scale kidnap of gendarmes by Kanaks was punished by the slaughter of all the kidnappers by French special forces – an episode that convinced the French government of the urgent need to put an end to the crisis. Under the 1988 peace agreement, called the Matignon Accords, political power was redistributed more equitably and the Kanak community was offered better prospects of integration, with the assistance of a massive aid programme. In 1998, the Nouméa Accord renewed the principle of 'cohabitation' between the two main communities, extended New Caledonia's autonomy and postponed any final decision about independence for at least 15 years.

Melting pot   Most of Nouméa's population are non-Kanak: European, Polynesian, Asian.

A cosmopolitan world

The French colonists set up churches, ranches and plantations, and dug mines in the nickel-rich mountains. They brought in labour from Asia, notably from Java and Vietnam. The result is a cosmopolitan population now totalling 211 000, but the new arrivals have tended to stay in the urban centres of Grande Terre, notably in the capital, Nouméa. In the outlying villages, traditional life remains little changed. Here, children play in streams running past the terraced taro gardens, while old men relax beneath the banyan trees and women prepare food in the shade of open pandanus-roofed shelters. This is the true New Caledonia – an image that bears little resemblance to the scenes of violence splashed across the pages of the world's press in recent decades.

The Loyalty Islands: custom preserved

The inhabitants of the Loyalty Islands – Lifou, Maré, Tiga and Ouvéa – have suffered far less intrusion from European domination. In 1899 the French government declared the islands a Kanak reserve, where traditional customs are maintained and the people still own their ancestral lands.

How's that?   In New Caledonia, cricket is predominantly a sport played by women.

Vanuatu: shaking off a Franco-British legacy

For 74 years, the flags of Britain and France flew side by side in the New Hebrides. Now independent, the country still bears some marks of this dual influence. But the inhabitants see themselves, above all, as ni-Vanuatu.

Ancient rhythms *The Small Nambas of Malakula keep alive their time-honoured traditions, or* **kastom**.

Leading light *The rebellion of Jimmy Stevens (centre) roused fears elsewhere.*

The story used to go that the people of Vanuatu believed that the queen of England and the president of France were husband and wife, as they were the joint rulers of these islands. In fact, the joke was on their colonial masters: the people believed no such thing, but saw it as a humorous jibe at the expense of the Europeans. The annexation of the islands in 1906 was dictated by strategic considerations. To oppose the territorial advances of the Germans in the region, the French and the British divided this archipelago of 4706 sq miles (12 190 km²) and ruled it as a condominium. This unusual hybrid status lasted until 1980, when Vanuatu ('Land Eternal') won its independence.

The Santo rebellion

Vanuatu did not have a very auspicious start to its independent life. Eight weeks before independence in 1980, a 58-year-old activist called Jimmy Stevens declared the unilateral secession for Espiritu Santo, the largest island of the archipelago. Of mixed descent, part Tongan, part Scottish, Stevens was an ardent defender of Melanesian culture. The new government of Vanuatu had to face down this revolt, and brought the rebels to heel, with military assistance from Papua New Guinea – a regional power that similarly feared secession by its constituent islands. Jimmy Stevens was arrested, tried and imprisoned. He died in 1991, three years after being freed under an amnesty.

Despite these divisions, the common Melanesian identity of the archipelago remains strong. Their 202 200 citizens call themselves ni-Vanuatu (people of Vanuatu) and share a pidgin *lingua franca* called bislama or beach-la-mar (from the old trade in sea cucumber, *bêche-de-mer*). English and French are still official languages, but the fact that there are more than 100 local languages illustrates the diversity of cultural origins in the 68 inhabited islands.

Size matters

The ancestral lands of the Big Nambas lie on a plateau in the north-east of the island of Malakula. These people owe their name to the size of the penis sheath (*namba*) that the men wore as their only form of apparel. Their reputation for hostility towards outsiders protected them from intrusion for many years, but in the 1930s the community was decimated by a viral disease, precipitating the collapse of their culture. The Big Nambas were subsequently converted to Christianity, and many left to live on the coast.

The Small Nambas, who wear penis sheaths of more modest proportions, live in the forested lands to the south. Their culture has remained better preserved, but is under threat as new generations adopt Western ways and drift towards the coastal settlements.

Time passing *Far removed from the bustle of the capital, Port Vila, village life is tranquil, as here on Oyster Island.*

Meeting point *Market day at Uru Harbor, on the east coast of Malaita Island, provides an opportunity to socialise.*

Kastom and the surveyor

Some 87 per cent of all land in the Solomon Islands is owned according to *kastom* (customary rules). Families own their garden plots, which are passed down from generation to generation, while the remainder is owned as communal land. Colonisation distorted this practice, but now, more than 20 years after independence, the government has begun a survey to establish a land registry along traditional, ancestral lines, to help settle disputes over ownership. Following public consultation, verbal agreements on boundaries will be formally committed to paper.

The Solomon Islands: unspoilt beauty

There are nearly 1000 islands in the Solomon archipelago, but only a third of them are inhabited. Visitors are immediately struck by their tranquil pace and easy, uncomplicated charm.

Dozens of sailing canoes ply the waters of Lau Lagoon in the north of Malaita island. The women are heading for the coast to sell freshly caught fish, coming in from the 60 tiny islands that rise from the shallows farther out to sea. The islands have been hand-built by dumping rocks, stones and blocks of coral in the sea and pouring huge quantities of sand on top. Coconut palms help to bind the foundations and provide shade and a food supply. Some of the artificial islands look like fortresses set on the sea; others are so small they can accommodate just one house, set on stilts to protect it from the waves. The islanders live by fishing, and operate a mutually beneficial exchange with the families who cultivate gardens on the mainland.

The milk round

The Solomon Islanders have succeeded in preserving their culture, even through the period of British colonial rule (1884-1978). Having repulsed various invasions by the Tongans between the 14th and 18th centuries, they were able to put up resistance against the Europeans during much of the 19th century, which gave them a reputation for being inhospitable. In fact they are nothing of the sort, as anyone who has spent time on the islands and witnessed the subtle culture of a society that has evolved over some 6000 years will testify.

Traditional craft *The women make mats from coconut fibres.*

The Solomon Islands today have a population of some 432 200, mainly Melanesians, scattered over a total land area of 10 640 sq miles (27 557 km^2). The archipelago stretches over 1000 miles (1600 km) from end to end. There is no better way to appreciate its geography than to take the inter-island air service on what local pilots call the 'milk round', so frequent are the stops. The 9 or 18-seater planes buzz over hundreds of forest-clad volcanic islands, each ringed by a lagoon. This topography largely explains why the Solomon Islands seem in many respects pleasantly disconnected from the world at large. However, although activity is laid-back, it covers the fact that the economy is slowly recovering from 5 years of ethnic unrest, and in 2003 the beautiful islands stood on the brink of civil war.

Water bus *On a lagoon, a canoe is the ideal means to transport people and goods.*

Papua New Guinea: at the outer limits of travel

The largest of the Pacific countries has preserved a landscape that has been barely touched by modern times. In its remote hills and valleys, isolated village communities continue traditions handed down over thousands of years.

The natural look *This makeover consists of mud and flowers.*

Party clothes *Sing-sings, the traditional festivals of the Highlands, offer an opportunity to reinforce a unique culture with vigour.*

Adugout canoe slides over the muddy waters of the Sepik River in the north-east of the huge island of New Guinea. As the guide punts the boat with masterly skill, he points at a piece of land that divides the water in the middle of the river. It is a piece of the riverbank, as big as a garden, which has become detached by the strong current and still carries on it some shrubs and a couple of herons. Nearby, crocodiles watch placidly as this hefty piece of flotsam passes. The boat pulls into the shore and disgorges its camera-wielding passengers, who head for a village set a little way back from the riverside. Thatched houses on stilts jut out over patches of grass, in the shadow of some coconut palms. The largest of the buildings, with soaring peaks at either end, is richly adorned with paintings and intricate ceremonial sculptures – of the kind now produced for sale up and down the river. This is the *haus tambaran*, the spirit house, a male preserve, scene of initiation rites. Its presence reinforces the memory of ancestors and the traditional rules that operate here. The bigman, the village chief, takes the group to admire his garden. Chewing on betel nut, he tells a young boy to fetch a coconut. He opens it with deft skill and offers the milk to the visitors to drink. It is a simple, elemental gesture, but it is also a moment that will stay in the mind forever, the kind of unique and rich experience offered by Papua New Guinea – the last frontier for travellers in search of somewhere unspoilt.

The prosperous Highlands

From the idyllic beaches on the coasts to the dense tropical forests inland and the Highland plateaus in the central mountains, Papua New Guinea gives a sense of grandiose space. Five million people occupy the total land area of 178 472 sq miles (462 243 km^2). Papua New Guinea has a complex geography: composed of part of one of the world's largest islands, shared with Indonesia's Irian Jaya, plus the three large islands of New Britain, New Ireland and Bougainville, and scores of tiny islands.

The cultures are immensely diverse, each clan or *wantok* (from 'one-talk', a language community) having adapted its way of life according to its surroundings. The comparatively cool Highlands, where a third of the nation lives, is a rich agricultural region. Its inaccessibility for long provided an obstacle even to the most tenacious missionaries. When it was eventually discovered by Europeans in the 1930s, the first encounters thrilled social anthropologists keen to study the relationship between these ancient tribal societies and their environment, and the social links that bound them together. They found refined and complex art, a remarkable mastery of agriculture, and highly ritualised ways of making war.

An easy adaptation

Western civilisation came swiftly to the Highlands along the roads that soon followed the first Europeans. Coffee plantations created jobs and brought money into circulation. Then discoveries of gold

Port Moresby, capital with an edge

Port Moresby is named after Captain John Moresby, the first European to visit the land of the Motu in 1873. Missionaries settled near the village of Hanuabada, and in their wake came traders and the notorious 'blackbirders' in search of cheap indentured labourers. The town grew as the capital of British New Guinea, and shot to prominence in the Second World War, as the base from which the anti-Japanese campaign was conducted. Today, this sprawling city of 300 000 people is tainted by a reputation for violent crime.

Modern materials *Hanuabada, destroyed in the Second World War, has been rebuilt with cement and corrugated iron.*

and oil brought more wealth, and the inhabitants integrated with the new economic order with remarkable speed and good humour. The old cultural traditions remain strong, however, found, for example, in the social organisation of the clans, which remain staunchly loyal to their allies of the past.

It is at the Highland sing-sings, the colourful festivals that combine music and dance, that the dynamism of Papuan culture is most in evidence. Participants turn out in full regalia: dresses, body paints, beads, shells, feather headdresses and improvised adornments made out of anything that glitters. Some arrive in jeeps, stand under umbrellas, carry golf clubs – here the modern world joins hands with the extravagance of the human imagination.

National identity

The Highland communities are keenly aware of the special quality of their surroundings and their unique heritage. This pride feeds the flames of rivalry with their compatriots from the coast and the islands. There were many pessimists when this unwieldy country took independence from Australia in 1975. Against the odds it has survived, in an era of rapid global change.

How can a country so diverse achieve a sense of national identity? Pidgin helps, spoken by the majority of inhabitants. Also, the existence of a central government, a parliamentary democracy, brings a unity to the nation. The shared values of a communal life in touch with nature is perhaps the strongest unifying force – values that are found throughout the islands of the Pacific.

Feast day *Independence Day, a national holiday, is celebrated in the Trobriand Islands by communal feasts.*

Papua

The island of New Guinea is divided in two by a straight line down the middle: to the west lies Papua (formerly Irian Jaya). When Indonesia was granted independence in 1949, the Dutch decided to hang on to this possession. But President Sukarno of Indonesia laid claim to it, as part of the former Dutch East Indies. In 1961 he sent in troops and the UN put pressure on the Netherlands to withdraw. Thus Papua was dragged into the Indonesian orbit. Autonomy was officially granted to Papua in January 2002.

In the clouds *The uplands of Morobe Province, in the north-east, shows how nature still dominates the landscape of Papua New Guinea.*

Fiji: India in the south Pacific

In the islands of Fiji, an influential and economically powerful Indian population contests the supremacy of the native Melanesians. The antagonism between the two communities undermines any concept of national identity, but does not entirely preclude peaceful cohabitation.

The heat is on *Preparing the ground for fire-walking, on Mbengga.*

On May 21, 2000, Fiji hit the world's headlines. A group of armed men led by a Melanesian Fijian businessman, George Speight, stormed the parliament building in Suva and seized Mahendra Chaudhry, the first Fijian Indian to take the post of prime minister, together with other members of the government. For more than eight weeks Speight held them hostage at gunpoint while tense negotiations took place with the army and the Great Council of Chiefs. The crisis ended with the release of the politicians, and Speight's arrest for treason. But the cause of the dispute remains: to what extent should Fijian Indians be allowed political influence at the expense of the native Fijians.

This archipelago of 320 islands was once the exclusive territory of Speight's forebears, who came to live here 4000 years ago. But in the 19th century their birthright was thrown into jeopardy when the British imported thousands of Indians to work in the sugar plantations. Now the island population is split almost 50-50 between Indians and native Fijians, raising problems in a parliamentary democracy where votes are cast largely along ethnic lines.

The Indians want not only representation, but political acknowledgment for the key role they play in the economy. The Melanesian Fijians may remain the predominant landowners, but it is largely the Indian community that works the cane fields and other plantations, and runs most of the key businesses.

A harmonious nation

Crises apart, politics have only marginal impact on the harmony that generally reigns over the land. Fiji receives about 400 000 tourists a year, who enjoy the friendly, relaxed atmosphere, the beautiful landscape and the numerous well-equipped beach resorts and hideaway hotels. The Fijian nation is unusual in Melanesia in the extent to which it has adopted Western ways, but traditional life still thrives in the interior of the large islands and on the small islands. On the island of Mbengga, for example, the inhabitants practise the custom of fire-walking.

Fijian style *The uniform for the presidential guard and the police consists of a tunic, skirt and sandals.*

Suva, the capital

In 1884 the British made Suva the seat of government and built a port, which became the vital link with the world outside. By 1920 the capital was a flourishing trading centre: some of the architecture bears witness to this age. Today, Suva is the hub of the tourist industry, the biggest industry in Fiji, and the atmosphere is cosmopolitan. The modernity of the city is symbolised by the parliament building, opened in 1992, which marries traditional Fijian architecture with the latest construction techniques. With 196 000 inhabitants, Suva is one of the largest towns in the South Pacific. It is also the seat of the University of the South Pacific, which has more than 2000 students, many from neighbouring countries.

British legacy *In Fiji, vehicles drive on the left, as here on Viti Levu.*

Heavenly view   Bora Bora is often cited as the classic Pacific island.

Colonial legacy   In the Marquesas Islands schooling is in French.

Polynesia

The early Polynesian navigators conquered a vast maritime empire and established their villages and gardens in dozens of archipelagoes and islands across the centre of the Pacific. Their distinctive culture – tenacious and socially oriented – was subtly altered by colonial rule, but remains strong.

Of Dumont d'Urville's three island divisions, Polynesia is the most uniform. As its name suggests, it encompasses 'many islands': a dozen big archipelagoes and hundreds of islands, atolls, and *motus*. But the one million inhabitants of these scattered lands share a common ancestry, culture and language.

The last lands to be settled

The Polynesian world covers an area about the size of Africa, defined by a triangle with sides 4350 miles (7000 km) long. The three corners are formed by Hawaii, Easter Island and New Zealand. The archipelagoes consist of volcanic islands and coral atolls. Near the equator they have a tropical climate, but Easter Island is more temperate. These lands were among the last in the

Pacific – and indeed in the world – to be settled by humans, between 1500 BC and AD 1000. With their ocean-going outrigger canoes, the Polynesians accomplished astonishing feats of navigation without the aid of instruments. Once settled in their new homes, they set about moulding them to their needs. While the sea gave them fish and shellfish, they coaxed the poor soils into yielding their staple foods: taro, yams, coconuts and breadfruit. From these and other organic raw materials they created houses, tools, clothing, jewellery – the artefacts of their civilisation.

Mana and tabu

Traditional Polynesia society is hierarchical and conservative. Power is vested in an aristocracy that draws its legitimacy from a legendary genealogy. All community organisation, as well as social, political and religious practices, are founded on explanations closely linked to a canon of legends and myths. Although ancestor cults have been widely displaced by Christianity, many aspects of the old religion survive. People, animals and things all possess a sacred supernatural power called *mana*, seen as a positive force, while access to certain places is forbidden: they are *tabu*, a negative force, and the origin of our word taboo.

Colonisation and Polynesian revival

Polynesia was one of the last regions of the world to be explored, colonised – and decolonised. The influence of missionaries was a key factor in this process, and in the remoter islands often had a greater impact and continuity than the colonial administrations. The effect on local cultures varied greatly from island to island. Hawaii is now a mini-America in the Pacific, where Polynesians make up a small minority. By contrast, Samoa and Tonga are proud Polynesian kingdoms. Today Polynesian culture is undergoing something of a renaissance.

Natural fibre   Tapa, traditional cloth, is made by beating the bark of the paper mulberry tree.

French Polynesia: a fragile Eden

European explorers were entranced by Tahiti and its people. Today, the islands retain much of their original magic, despite a hazardous ride through history and the brutal dilemmas of the modern world.

The 118 islands of French Polynesia are spread over an area equivalent to the whole of Europe. They take two forms: either they are very low-lying, virtually at sea level, as coral atolls; or they rise high above the sea, the exposed peaks of long-dormant volcanoes, their sharp-angled ridges encrusted with vegetation.

The New Cythera

Early European visitors were enraptured by this visually stunning paradise inhabited by handsome dark-skinned women who offered their favours freely. The French navigator Louis de Bougainville declared the island a New Cythera, the island of Aphrodite, Greek goddess of love. He also compared it to Eden. 'Everywhere we encounter hospitality, ease, a gentle joy and all the evidence of happiness. This large population rejoices in the treasures which nature has heaped upon it.' The crew of the *Bounty* were so taken by Tahiti that they mutinied in the vain hope of making new lives for themselves there. Even the cool-headed scientists on Cook's expeditions fell under its spell.

Fresh produce *Where the French go, markets soon follow. The one in Papeete, capital of Tahiti and French Polynesia as a whole, dates from 1847.*

Land of contrasts *On the volcanic island of Moorea, the steep mountains rise abruptly from a narrow coastal strip.*

Eden abused

However, reality was less gilded. The island chiefs, even during these early encounters, knew that their visitors represented formidable rivals with the power to grab by force whatever they coveted. And so they did: Bougainville claimed Tahiti for France in 1768 and the tribal chiefs were persuaded to accept the status of a French protectorate in 1848. The last Tahitian king, Pomare V, gave up his throne in 1880 and within a decade the French had imposed colonial control throughout the islands.

French Polynesia has suffered the tragic paradox of becoming a tainted Eden through the activities of the very people who so admired its beauty. Smallpox, syphilis and opium devastated the population. Tahiti today has its riots, slums, youth unemployment,

Mountain retreat   Tahiti is famous for its beaches, but its interior, clothed in lush vegetation, also has a wild beauty.

an unsustainable and heavily subsidised economy, and an inflated cost of living. On the political front, the French military's nuclear tests at its site on Mururoa have created ripples of opposition spreading far beyond the region.

Maupiti, a case in point

Maupiti is a tiny island in the far north of the Society Islands. It has been virtually ignored by tourism, while its neighbour Bora Bora attracts all the attention. To reach the interior of its lagoon, boats have to run the gauntlet of a perilous channel, which for many years discouraged outsiders. The main island rises like a tower assaulted by green undergrowth and is surrounded by a belt of white-sand *motus*. On this silvery perimeter watermelons are grown.

But there the idyll ends. The watermelons, sold in the markets of Papeete, are the source of the islanders' wealth, but it is hard won. First, the islanders had to transport hundreds of sacks of earth to the *motus* in their canoes. To water their crop, they dug deep holes in the rocky island soil to reach brackish water, filtered by the coral.

In this modern world, the ancient gods of Maupiti have fallen silent. Like much of the islanders' traditional culture, they were

Sunday best   The weekly service, conducted in Tahitian, is an occasion to turn out in hats and fill the church with rousing hymns.

first silenced by the missionaries of three different churches, who bitterly contested the several hundred souls on the island, then they were forgotten as the new money was converted into cement, corrugated iron and videos, which painted vivid images of a different, beckoning world beyond Maupiti's limited horizons. To add to their woes, in 1997 the island was devastated by hurricane Oséa. The young, for their part, get bored, and dream of the neon attractions of Papeete. Some, seeing their island as a prison, have committed suicide by swallowing weedkiller.

A dream come true

Such troubles are not unique to French Polynesia, or indeed to the south Pacific – but they seem more poignant in such a beautiful setting, which so beguiled the early European visitors and still remains a dream come true for French Polynesia's numerous tourists. About 180 000 holiday-makers come to these islands each year: among destinations in the south Pacific, only Fiji has more. Much of the tourist trade is conducted by big international hotel chains – but the islanders are wary of allowing this kind of development to go unchecked and have blocked a string of luxury resort proposals. For themselves, they prefer the virtues of a low-key communal life, which still sparkles with characteristic touches, such as wearing flowers in the hair.

The three kings of Wallis and Futuna

Wallis and Futuna, three small islands totalling 98 sq miles (255 km²), is a land of kings – the only kings within the republic of France. The 'Tuisigave' and the 'Tuiagaifo' rule Futuna, and the 'Lavelua' rules Wallis. They are working kings in the pay of France and are not hereditary; they can even be dismissed. The islands, in the possession of France since 1887, were upgraded to the status of a French territory on July 29, 1961. Since then the kings have shown unswerving loyalty to France, but they have been known to overstep their authority and encroach upon the prerogatives of the French state. In 1992 the kings of Futuna decided that Sunday should be reserved exclusively for God – an extension of a rule that applies to many islands of the Christianised Pacific, where little happens on Sunday except church services. To reassert the secular law so central to the French constitution, the French authorities had to dispatch *gendarmes* from Nouméa, and the kings backed down.

A few facts and figures

French Polynesia occupies 1.5 million sq miles (4 million km²) of ocean, but just 1522 sq miles (3941 km²) of land. This is parcelled out to 118 islands in five archipelagoes: Marquesas, Tuamotu, Gambier, Society (which include Tahiti and the capital, Papeete) and Tubuai (or Austral). The French annexed them in the middle of the 19th century and in 1903 the colony took the name French Establishments of Oceania. This became a *territoire d'outremer* (overseas territory) under the name French Polynesia in 1947. Today, its Territorial Assembly commands considerable autonomy. French Polynesia has some 262 000 inhabitants, of whom 100 000 live in or around Papeete. Polynesians and mixed race people make up 80 per cent of the total, Europeans 12 per cent and Chinese 5 per cent. Wallis and Futuna constitutes a separate territory, lying well to the west between Samoa and Fiji. The third island of the group, Alofi, lies close to Futuna.

Hawaii: paradise 'made in the USA'

The 50th state of the Union, the Hawaiian islands have been almost totally Americanised, for better (economic conditions are far superior to those of the rest of the Pacific) or for worse (the cost of living is high and Polynesian culture has been smothered).

Front line *Hawaii plays a key strategic role in the USA's presence in the Pacific.*

Hawaii, an archipelago of 122 islands, of which 14 are inhabited, constitutes the northernmost point of the Polynesian triangle. It was settled comparatively recently, between the 4th and the 11th centuries, by people from the Marquesas. The first European to reach the islands was Captain Cook, who landed on January 18, 1778 and baptised his new discovery the Sandwich Islands, after his patron Lord Sandwich.

A kingdom, then a US state

The islands were united by the warrior king Kamehameha I in 1782. He and his descendants ran them as a constitutional monarchy. Missionaries and whalers arrived in the 1820s, and in their wake came American sugar and pineapple planters, who imported labour from Asia: Chinese, Japanese, Filipino. All the while, the native population was being decimated by introduced diseases. In 1887 the Americans obtained exclusive ownership of the base at Pearl Harbor. Then in 1893 foreign residents, led by sugar planters, deposed Queen Liliuokalani, and the following year they proclaimed a republic. The archipelago was annexed by the United States in 1898 and became an American territory in 1900. On December 7, 1941, the Japanese bombed Pearl Harbor, drawing the United States into the Second World War.

President Eisenhower proclaimed Hawaii the 50th state of the Union on August 21, 1959. Today, the islands are a key military and nuclear base, the command centre for US strategic interests in the Pacific. The military and federal government play a central role in the islands' activities. Honolulu, the state capital, on Oahu, is the political, economic and educational hub. Tourism has become the principal source of revenue

This American state has its share of problems. Honolulu is one of the most expensive cities in the USA, as nearly everything has to be imported. And there is an undercurrent of resentment, expressed politically by various Polynesian nationalist movements, who have laid claim to ancestral lands, and are pressing for some kind of sovereignty. But this can also be seen as an expression of the broader revival in Polynesian cultural identity and pride.

Quiet days *Parts of Honolulu have retained the exotic charm of a provincial island capital.*

Know your Hawaiians: hapa, haole and Japanese

There were 300 000 Polynesians living on these islands before the arrival of European settlers. By 1853 there were apparently just 71 019 'indigenous people' and 1856 foreigners. Today, the population stands at 1.2 million, of which 20 per cent have mixed, part-Hawaiian origins (*hapa* in Polynesian); 25 per cent are Caucasian (*haole*); 22 per cent are Japanese; 15 per cent Filipino; 6 per cent Chinese; 12 per cent other (African Americans, Koreans, Samoans). Only about 9000 are held to be pure Hawaiians. All these figures are dwarfed by the tourist statistics: 7 million visitors come to the islands every year.

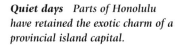

Mass production *Taro, usually grown in family gardens, is here cultivated on an industrial scale.*

Far-flung Polynesia

There are tiny, remote archipelagoes and islands scattered throughout Polynesia. Easter Island, Pitcairn, and some of the Cook and Marquesas Islands lie well off the main tourist beat.

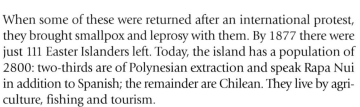

On the shore *Sail boats beached at Aitutaki lagoon, in the Cook Islands.*

Hidden refuge *Pitcairn was selected by the* **Bounty** *mutineers for its isolation.*

The tiny atolls and islands of Polynesia were settled during the last wave of migrations. Their size and isolation explains their political status today, linked to larger powers. Easter Island has been a part of Chile since 1888. Pitcairn is administered by Britain. The Cook Islands and Niue, annexed by New Zealand in 1901, are self-governing territories in free association with that country.

Unsurpassed beauty

The bizarre statues, the *moai*, of Easter Island are famous the world over. This volcanic island of 63 sq miles (163 km²) is one of the most isolated in the Pacific. Its Polynesian settlers called it Rapa Nui or Te Pito o Te Henua, 'navel of the world'. The name by which we know it derives from its discovery by Dutch navigator Jacob Roggeveen on Easter Day in 1722. Before colonisation the island had a population of about 4000, and in the more distant past may have sustained some 10 000. In 1862 Peruvian 'blackbirders' came here to seize slaves, who were put to work on mainland plantations and on the guano islands.

Community spirit *The market at Hanga Roa, capital of Easter Island, is a favourite gathering place.*

When some of these were returned after an international protest, they brought smallpox and leprosy with them. By 1877 there were just 111 Easter Islanders left. Today, the island has a population of 2800: two-thirds are of Polynesian extraction and speak Rapa Nui in addition to Spanish; the remainder are Chilean. They live by agriculture, fishing and tourism.

Situated at the heart of the Polynesian triangle, the Cook-Rarotonga archipelago was explored by Cook in 1773. Around 20 000 people live on the islands today, and there are 30 000 Cook Islanders in New Zealand. Many of the traditional shacks have been replaced by neat cottages surrounded by flower gardens and lawns. Niue was discovered by Cook in 1774. He called it Savage Island, because of the hostile reception he received. It has 2500 inhabitants, but 2000 of their fellow islanders now live in Sydney, Australia, and 12 000 live in New Zealand.

Pitcairn, and the mutiny on the *Bounty*

Pitcairn was discovered in 1767 by the English navigator Philip Carteret. Just 1.8 sq miles (2.8 km²) in area, it is so small and isolated that subsequent ships could not find it again. This is why in 1790 it seemed ideal to Fletcher Christian and his eight fellow mutineers on board HMS *Bounty*, as they sought refuge from the British navy.

Together with some Tahitians – 12 women and 6 men – they settled on the island, with largely unhappy consequences. Today 47 of their descendants still live there, cultivating gardens of taro and sweet potato. The nearest island is Mangareva in the French Gambier Islands, four days away by boat.

Tonga, a united kingdom

Traditional Polynesian society has a strongly hierarchical structure. This social organisation has remained intact in Tonga, whose king, Taufa'ahau Tupou IV, is the current head of a dynasty that has reigned here since 1845.

When King Taufa'ahau Tupou IV was crowned in 1967, he inherited from his mother – the famous Queen Salote Tupou III – an institution with remarkably solid foundations. An absolute monarch, he is assisted by 33 hereditary nobles who hold the key posts in the country. The system became more accountable in the 1990s, under pressure from a pro-democracy movement, but even now elected representatives form only a minority in the Legislative Assembly. The liberalisation of the regime has been a recurrent theme of the nation's politics, but generally the Tongans are happy with their ancestral system and accept the strict rules and code of conduct that surround the hereditary aristocracy.

Royal domain
King Taufa'ahau Tupou IV sits on a traditional tapa *mat in front of his palace.*

Market day *Tonga is not a wealthy country, but there is no shortage of food.*

Sunday singing

Just about everywhere else in Polynesia, missionaries and priests have succeeded in eroding traditional power. In Tonga, by contrast, they were its greatest ally, from the moment that Chief Taufa'ahau, later King George Tupou I, was converted by Wesleyan missionaries in 1831. With their support and advice, Tupou I created a constitutional government of nobles and commoners, and signed treaties of friendship, first with Germany, then Britain (which later took on the role of protector) and the USA, so keeping colonisers at bay. Thus Tupou I created a stable and unified Christian Tonga, before dying at the age of 97 in 1893.

Every Sunday the current king attends a Wesleyan church. Sunday is sacrosanct in Tonga – no one may work, trade or play, and the only sign of vigorous activity is the singing in the churches. Faithful to the Christian virtues of moderation and simplicity, Tongans live modestly in small homes surrounded by vegetable gardens and pigs – which are treated as pets until they are served up at feasts – against a luxuriant backdrop of greenery and flowers.

The queen in the rain

Millions of Britons remember Queen Salote Tupou III with great affection. At the coronation of Queen Elizabeth II in 1953, televised across the nation, most of the visiting dignitaries sat inside their carriages, protected from the rain. But Queen Salote rode in an open carriage, smiling and waving at the crowds. She was following traditional Tongan etiquette, which dictates that you should not imitate anyone to whom you owe respect. Elizabeth was riding in an enclosed carriage, so Queen Salote would not. At that time Queen Salote had been on the throne for 35 years, and until her death in 1965 she ruled with exemplary clear-sightedness and benevolence. Adored by her subjects and admired abroad, she was an outstanding figure of the Pacific in the 20th century.

Prim and proper *Neiafu, on Vava'u, is the main town of the northern islands of Tonga. The Roman Catholic church is one of its largest buildings. Sunday is reserved for saying mass, and visiting family and friends – and no man will ever be seen shirtless in public, even in the hottest weather.*

Samoa, at the heart of Polynesia

Some 15 islands, at the centre of the Pacific and of Polynesia, make up the two Samoas. In the west lies the independent nation of Samoa – the first Polynesian state to gain independence; in the east lies American Samoa.

Traditional livelihood *Fishing remains a major pursuit and the nets have to be meticulously maintained.*

Robert Louis Stevenson: Tusitala

Robert Louis Stevenson (1850-94), author of *Treasure Island*, sailed the ocean with his family in search of a climate to benefit his poor health. He settled on Apia, where he spent the last four years of his life. Local people called him Tusitala, 'teller of tales'. His house, Vailima ('five waters'), served as the governor's residence under the Germans and under the New Zealand administration. It has now been restored and made into the Robert Louis Stevenson Museum.

Life and death *Symbol of life throughout the Pacific, a breadfruit tree provides shade in a cemetery in Falefa, on Upolu island, Samoa.*

The Samoan islands encapsulate the split personality of the Pacific. The independent nation of Samoa has retained its traditional way of life. American Samoa has accepted many of the ways of the dollar world, and its inhabitants enjoy a good standard of living. The islands were dominated by three rival powers – Germany, Britain and the USA – in the late 19th century, and were formally divided between Germany and the USA in 1899. New Zealand took over the administration of Western Samoa from Germany during the First World War.

The strength of tradition

Western Samoa (known as Samoa since 1997) became the first Pacific nation to win its independence, granted by New Zealand in 1962; it has remained a member of the Commonwealth. The country consists of nine islands covering 1133 sq miles (2935 km²), which support a population of 180 000. The two main islands, Upolu and Savai'i, are swathed in forest that grows out of the fertile black lava. Most of the villages have churches, but the Samoans follow a way of life handed down from ancestral times, governed by a set of customs known as the *fa'a Samoa*. The typical village house is the open-sided, oval-shaped *fale* – a roofed shelter on a stone platform. Life is built around the extended family (*aiga*), under the leadership of the clan chief, the all-powerful *matai*.

Samoa, American-style

American Samoa consists of five islands and two eastern atolls, covering 76 sq miles (197 km²). Some 59 000 people live on these islands – and 50 000 of their compatriots live in mainland USA or in Hawaii. They are distributed in villages, primarily on Tutuila, and the capital Pago Pago has a population of only 14 000. The main internal income comes from tuna fishing and processing, but the islands receive considerable subsidies. Dollars, the ubiquitous reminders of the mighty protector, and the *fa'a Samoa* do not always make for happy bedfellows.

Shouldering the burden *Motorised vehicles are still rare in many parts of Samoa, so traditional methods have to suffice.*

Micronesia

Micronesia is one of the least-known corners of the world. The Americans and Japanese fought savage battles over the islands, but the reminders are now limited to a few US military bases. The islands barely appear on the tourist map, so many Micronesians have been able to continue their traditional lives undisturbed.

The Micronesians are not a people, like the Polynesians, but rather a collection of seven large and distinct cultural and linguistic groups. Most of these peoples, nonetheless, share a common ancestry in the great migrations from Southeast Asia that occurred some 2000 to 3000 years ago – perhaps even 6000 years ago. The first Micronesians used their skills as sailors to reach the islands, then settled in villages as farmers and fishermen, leaving traces of their

world in places such as the fortresses of Pohnpei and Kosrae. Most of these communities have subsequently become ethnically diluted by new waves of incomers, from Melanesia, Polynesia and the Philippines; then Europe, North America, Mexico and Japan.

A complicated history

Because they were poor in resources, the Micronesian islands escaped the early phase of European colonisation in the Pacific. Later, Spain, Britain, Germany, Japan and the USA all took an interest in them for strategic reasons. In 1899, after the Spanish-American War, Spain was forced to cede Guam to the USA and to sell the remaining Marianas and the Caroline Islands to Germany.

Cowboy This young Chamorro boy from Guam is riding a water buffalo, or carabao, an animal probably introduced by Jesuit missionaries in the 17th century.

Bird's-eye view Although seemingly impregnable, it is possible to walk up this escarpment in northern Pohnpei. The summit offers a spectacular view of the little town of Kolonia and its coral reef.

In 1914 the Japanese took over all the German protectorates north of the equator, and in 1919 the Treaty of Versailles awarded them the protectorate of the region. During the Second World War they invaded and occupied Guam, the Gilbert Islands and Nauru, and it took all the power of the American military to dislodge them. After the war the Gilbert Islands (now Kiribati) and Ellice Islands (now Tuvalu) were ruled together under British administration; they separated in 1975, and won their independence. The Caroline Islands, Marshall Islands and Marianas became American protectorates, a status shared, if informally, by many others.

Scattered over the sea

Micronesia's 2100 islands lie over 4.6 million sq miles (12 million km²). They form four main archipelagoes: Marianas, Marshall Islands, Caroline Islands and Kiribati. Some are volcanic (Northern Marianas, Pohnpei, Guam), others are continental in origin (Yap, Palau). The majority, however, are atolls. Only 125 are inhabited, with a total population of 500 000. Micronesia has two independent states that are members of the Commonwealth. In addition, there are two US territories and three further independent states.

Worldwide web The IT revolution has reached Micronesian shores too, as here on Falalop Island in the Federated States.

The American atolls

The USA exerts control over five Micronesian states, under a variety of treaties. Some of these island groups are highly developed, playing host both to US military bases and to Japanese tourists. Others have retained essential elements of their traditional culture.

It is mainly the shopping that brings the Japanese to Guam. Tokyo is less than three hours away, and Tumon Bay, the tourist centre, boasts a string of luxury hotels to accommodate them. Huge building sites consume the last available plots of land, as tower blocks reach relentlessly upwards.

The military and tourists

In the early 1960s, Guam was a high-security bastion of US military power, too strategically sensitive to accept foreign visitors. The lifting of controls and the expansion of air links have turned the island, with its resident population of 154 000, into the Japanese equivalent of Monte Carlo. The Japanese account for 80 per cent of the tourists who come here each year to enjoy an American-style land – a quieter, less ostentatious version of Hawaii. The American military personnel, mainly based at Guam's naval station, have a discreet presence, despite numbering 10 000. Each set of outsiders tends to remain sequestered in its own ghetto: the Japanese in their hotels, American soldiers behind the wire surrounding their bases.

In the sidelines of history

Guam forms part of the Marianas island chain, but has been a separate entity since becoming a US possession in 1899. The rest of the chain stretches out to its north, and forms the Northern Marianas, a Commonwealth in Association with the USA. The atomic bombs destined for Hiroshima and Nagasaki were assembled in Guam, but it was the island of Tinian, in the Northern Marianas, that the Flying Fortresses took off from, on the last leg of their journey to Japan. The American military still regularly uses the island for manoeuvres, but Tinian has extended its activities to include a hotel casino, aimed at the Japanese tourists

Teeming with life   The Rock Islands of Palau rise like green mushrooms from the turquoise sea. The shallow waters of the island are rich in marine life, making this a paradise for divers.

who fill the beaches of neighbouring Saipan. Many of them make pilgrimages to two sites on Saipan, Banzai Cliff and Suicide Cliff, from which hundreds of civilians – men, women and children – hurled themselves to their deaths after the Japanese told them they faced rape and torture if captured by the Americans.

The gardens of Palau

To the south of the Marianas lies Palau, which has a rich selection of Micronesia's flora and fauna. The vivid greens of its lush vegetation sparkle with orchids and parrots, and there are crocodiles in the mangrove swamps. Iridescent giant clams lie in the lagoon. At the Rock Islands, to the south of the current capital, Koror, a cluster of more than 200 islets rises from the sea. The tops of these outcrops, undercut by erosion, bristle with a thick crown of rain forest.

However, the idyll is haunted by the ghost of war. Palau saw some of the most intense fighting of the Second World War, as the US advanced on Japan. Some 15 600 men lost their lives, 13 600 of them Japanese. In 1947, the island became part of the UN Trust Territory of the Pacific islands, under US administration; it became independent in 1981. A new capital, to replace that of Koror, is due to be completed on the island of Babelthuap in 2004.

Captured   A boy admires his captive frigate bird.

*Topless shopper   Well-stocked supermarkets
have opened on many islands.*

Stone money and betel

Although lying just half an hour by air
from Guam, the islands in the Yap group
present an utterly different world. In this
western corner of the Federated States of
Micronesia, the old world of Pacific myth
still prevails, particularly in the outlying
islands. Yap has made stringent efforts to preserve its traditions,
with its outriggers and the traditional-style homes that line the
lagoons. The islanders are encouraged to wear the traditional loin-
cloth, and women leave their breasts uncovered.

Many older Yapese have red teeth from chewing betel nut, a mild
narcotic found all over Asia. Stone money called *rai* is used in the
villages, especially for marriages and to buy land. The 'coins' are
huge stone discs measuring 6-13 ft (2-4 m) in diameter, pierced by
a circular hole.

A diver's heaven

The Chuuk group (formerly spelled Truk) lies in the centre of the
vast collection of islands that make up the Federated States of
Micronesia. It boasts magnificent offshore waters, with fine coral

reefs teeming with marine life – sea anemones, spotted eels, manta
rays. But a lure for many divers is the debris of the Pacific war that
lies scattered in and around the lagoon, where a Japanese fleet
went down in 1944. Japanese and American planes and a mass of
other military hardware lie on the sandy bottom, encrusted with
coral, overgrown with seaweed and inhabited by lobsters and octopuses. Some of the boats were bombed and torn apart before they
sank, but others remain virtually intact, standing upright on their
keels like ghost ships.

The forgotten soldier

Few tourists ever make it to the
remote Talofofo waterfall on
Guam, and fewer still to the cave
nearby where a determined
Japanese soldier lived undetected
for 27 years after the war was
over. Shoichi Yokoi, a sergeant in
the Japanese Imperial Army, was
discovered by a couple of hunters
in the forest in 1972. Yokoi later
explained that he had taken
refuge with some companions
when they heard their country
had surrendered, suspecting that
this was a propaganda ploy by
the Americans. His brothers-in-
arms died, but Yokoi persisted in
his resistance. He taught himself
to weave hibiscus and palm fibres
to make clothes, and nets to trap
fish in the river. He survived
typhoons by sheltering in his cave,
and counted the cycles of the
moon to keep track of time. On
his return to Japan, Yokoi was
fêted as a national hero.

*Under sail   A well-crewed outrigger
in the Satawal islands (Federated
States of Micronesia) changes tack.*

Isolated no longer The islands of Micronesia are served regularly by ships, such as this small cargo boat, the Micro Spirit, which has come close enough to the shore to moor up to a palm.

Treaties and accords

The Republic of the Marshall Islands, the Federated States of Micronesia and the Republic of Palau are independent states, but have all signed Compacts of Free Association with the USA. For the Marshall Islands and the Federated States of Micronesia the economic provisions of these contracts were due to end in 2001 and were subsequently renewed in 2003. The three states exercise considerable autonomy over their internal affairs, but the Americans subsidise them in return for the use of military bases on the islands. Guam is an unincorporated territory of the USA; its people are US citizens but cannot participate in national elections. In 1976 the Northern Marianas became a Commonwealth in Association with the US. It has its own administration and the people have US citizenship.

The atom bomb and bikinis

The Marshall Islands lie scattered along a snaking path just west of the International Date Line. There was little to interest Europeans in the days when they were in search of possessions: mainly flat and desert-dry, the Marshall Islands appeared to lack resources. The Germans, who annexed the islands in 1885, established coconut plantations on them.

The Americans later took possession of the islands for strategic purposes, bringing in fresh water and food, military bases, and also the atomic bomb. The Bikini atoll was chosen as the site for the first postwar atomic tests in 1946. The name became better known for the two-piece bathing suit, which was said to have a similarly explosive effect on male onlookers. This light-hearted reference aside, the tests on Bikini and nearby Enewetak created huge environmental and health problems. The tests stopped in 1958, but over 50 years later, the inhabitants of the atolls of Rongelap and Utirik, to the east of Bikini and Enewetak, continue to receive treatment for the after-effects of being exposed to radioactivity. A concrete dome on the islet of Runit covers a pile of radioactive earth and debris recovered from nearby Enewetak. It has been calculated that its contents will remain radioactive for 50 000 years.

Glittering falls The Kipirohi Falls, on Pohnpei, in the Federated States of Micronesia.

US firing range

Like a pearl necklace upon the waves, Kwajalein consists of a hundred or so islands ringing an immense lagoon. The atoll was turned into a firing range. Intercontinental ballistic missiles launched from California were targeted on the surrounding sea, usually landing at night and bathing the island with unearthly shafts of light. Some 3000 Americans live on the islands, enjoying all the suburban comforts that they might expect in Los Angeles – a baseball pitch, supermarket, cinemas, tennis courts and cocktails in the clubhouse. The 1500 locals who work on the base live at some distance, on the island of Ebeye. They take a ferry to work each morning, but cannot remain in the American enclave once their shift is over. Such are the paradoxes and dilemmas of American Micronesia.

Counting the catch Fishermen squat among the day's haul.

109

Micro-states: sand and guano

Nauru, Kiribati and Tuvalu are among the smallest independent states on the planet. They are also among the lowest-lying, and rising sea levels threaten to engulf them. Phosphate brought Nauru and Kiribati wealth, but the supplies are now nearly exhausted.

The horn sounds even before the car draws to a halt outside the shop. Out shoots the Chinese shopkeeper to make the sale. Originally from Hong Kong, he imports corned beef, rice, tinned fish, soft drinks, video cassettes, plastic mats and bottled water – all of which have made the journey to Nauru by container ship.

Emirs of the Pacific

Nauru hangs like a tiny Chinese lantern from the line of the equator. Unlike many Pacific islands, it has no lagoon to soften its coasts, and no other islands to share its solitude. But for a long time Nauru had an advantage and it made the island very rich indeed.

The riches derived from migrating birds that, over the millennia, deposited thick layers of excrement (guano) on the island – the world's highest-quality phosphate. From the beginning of the 20th century Germans, then New Zealanders, British and Australians exploited this resource. After independence in 1968, successive governments of Nauru did the same, in the knowledge that the phosphate supply was predicted to run out by the end of 2005. During the 1970s and 1980s, island inhabitants, known as the 'emirs' of the Pacific, enjoyed one of the world's highest standards of living and payed no tax. They also became very unhealthy.

The island now faces an uncertain future – the phosphate supply is dwindling and a series of financial crises has left it close to bankruptcy. In 2001, Naura agreed to accommodate asylum seekers for Australia in return for millions of dollars of aid. Whether this

Close to the sea   The Abemama atoll, like most of the atolls of Kiribati, is little more than a sand bank. Its inhabitants are famed for their skill in building pirogues, sailing canoes.

kind of deal will be the island's future source of wealth is unknown. Nowadays, only Nauruan – a language spoken nowhere else – alludes to the ancestral traditions that once existed on the island.

Lunar landscapes

Nauru has been scraped back to its foundations. It is a doughnut of an island, a ring of rocks and sand, hollowed out by excavation, stripped of vegetation, its diminutive horizon fractured by

Unsustainable yields   Some islanders fish using traditional methods – a contrast to the phosphate industry, which has stripped the surface of Nauru to rugged lumps of limestone, once covered under layers of guano.

Nauru, the world's smallest republic

Covering 8 sq miles (21 km²), this tiny state has over 12 000 inhabitants, of whom two-thirds are native-born. The remainder are 'expats' – foreign nationals who come as contract workers. Discovered by Europeans in the late 18th century, Nauru was a whaling base for many years. Annexed by Germany in 1888, it became a British mandate administered by Australia in 1920, was occupied by the Japanese in 1942, and became a UN Trust Territory in 1945 before winning its independence as a republic in 1968.

The outriggers of Kiribati

The Republic of Kiribati is an archipelago of 33 islands and atolls with a total surface area of 313 sq miles (811 km²). A third of the 96 000 population live on the island of Tarawa, where the capital, called Bairiki, is located. In 1943 Tarawa was the scene of a violent battle in the Pacific War, when the US forces recaptured the island from the Japanese. The islanders are Micronesian and speak their own language, called Kiribati. Skilled fishermen, they are also known for their boat-building. They have preserved many of their traditions, and their old way of life based on fishing, farming and strong family bonds. Many live in traditional village houses with palm roofs. The main source of revenue until independence in 1979 came from the phosphate mines on the island of Banaba. These have since closed, but the islanders have continued to benefit from the interest on the capital accumulated from the phosphate sales. Other resources include copra and fishing licences granted to foreign fleets, but the republic is also heavily dependent on international aid.

levels that are already claiming their shores. Many have toyed with abandoning the island to the frigate birds, but for the time being the government has decided to remain, pinning its hopes on being able to rehabilitate the landscape over the next two decades.

Hotels and islands

With the exception of Guam and Saipan, Micronesia has not been a popular tourist destination, but in recent years several new air routes have opened up, bringing even the remoter islands within reach of big cities on both sides of the Pacific. Tuvalu has only a handful of small hostels and guesthouses, and Kiribati does not offer a lot more: visitors can choose between hotels in the capital, Tarawa, or staying with families in village homes equipped with little more than mosquito netting. But gradually tourist traffic is beginning to inspire development, and more hotels are sprouting up around the lagoons.

Local colour *Tourists who come to Tuvalu may be treated to a dance spectacle which reinforces the islanders' Polynesian ancestry.*

Even Kiritimati, a far-flung outpost of Kiribati, is starting to build more hotels. This same atoll was used for British and American nuclear weapons tests between 1956 and 1962, but it has now been judged free of contamination. The reputation of the area's game fishing, scuba diving and conservation areas is causing an increase in tourist numbers.

Tuvalu and its stamps

Tuvalu (formerly the Ellice Islands) consists of nine atolls, spread out over 350 miles (560 km). The total land area is just 9.6 sq miles (25 km²), but its Exclusive Economic Zone covers 290 000 sq miles (750 000 km²). Its highest point is no more than 15 ft (4.5 m) above sea level. The people are Polynesians, who probably came from Samoa in the 14th century. This explains why the Ellice Islands split from the Gilbert Islands in 1975. Today, the population stands at 9600, with a high birthrate of 5.1 per cent. Tuvalu became independent of Britain in 1978; the Queen remains head of state and is represented by a governor-general. The people live from agriculture and fishing. Recently, money has been made from selling the country's internet code 'tv', which is in demand from television companies. They also export a little copra – and a large quantity of postage stamps which show the beauty of the area. International aid accounts for 50 per cent of Tuvalu's revenues.

mine workings and the stumps of limestone (old coral pinnacles) that remain. The land is virtually sterile, except for gardens cultivated mainly by the Chinese community. A meteorological station has just been installed on the island, part of a network of five stations set up to monitor the long-term effects of climate change in the western Pacific, a matter of great interest to Nauru.

Although the island rises to only 213 ft (65 m), most people live on the coast. Like all Pacific islanders, Nauruans are familiar with the cyclones that strip the coconut palms and houses, and the tsunamis that drive inland from the sea. They have learnt to live with such threats, but are at a loss to know how to cope with rising sea

Connections *The island of Tarawa is home to half the population of Kiribati. It is also the hub of the national airline, Air Tungaru.*

CHAPTER 6

ISLAND DREAMS, ISLAND REALITY

The 20th century was a rollercoaster ride for the islands of the Pacific: exchanged like cards by the colonial powers at conferences on the other side of the world; ravaged by the Second World War; abused by nuclear testing; launched on the path of independence, contending with the invasion of Western culture through tourism, television, video cassettes and imported goods. Today, the region encompasses perhaps a greater range of humanity than ever. While surfers slide down the rollers off Waikiki Beach, miners in New Caledonia labour for copper, airline staff in Samoa consult their computers, and villagers in the interior of Papua New Guinea collect bird-of-paradise feathers for their sing-sing regalia. Many of the islands are torn between traditional cultures and clan identity, and the material rewards and broader vision of the wider world. The decisions made in the face of this dilemma have not always been happy ones.

Surf's up, and four brave the swell at Waimea Bay, Oahu.

Hawaii: surfing, golf and shopping

This group of 122 islands has everything that characterises the Pacific: fire-spitting volcanoes, beaches of black and white sand, rich and unique wildlife. It also has its very own mix of surf clubs, skyscrapers, shopping malls, golf courses and ukuleles.

Major islands

The Hawaiian islands stretch out in a line 2000 miles (3200 km) long. The eight biggest islands lie in the south-west of the chain. From east to west, these are: Hawaii (137 000 inhabitants), Maui (115 000), Kahoolawe, Lanai, Molokai, Oahu (the capital island, with 900 000 people), Kauai (56 000) and Niihau.

High life   Some 7 million visitors come to Waikiki, on Oahu, every year to enjoy the heady mix of America in the Pacific.

Surfing Hawaii

Surfing is said to have been invented in Hawaii: Captain Cook saw Polynesian surfers here in 1778. The sport was revived in around 1900, and now the islands have 1600 surfing spots. The most celebrated are along the north shore of Oahu, where Waimea Beach and Sunset Beach, scene of the world championships, are located. Surfers from around the world come to face the challenge.

Hot plunge   Tourists watch the lava of Kilauea flow into the ocean, on Hawaii island.

Once upon a time, every passenger who arrived at Honolulu airport received a *lei*, the garland of fresh frangipani flowers made familiar to the world by the 1960s films of Elvis Presley. It may have lost this little touch, but Hawaii remains otherwise fairly true to its myth: beyond the airport lie the palm trees, the skyscrapers, the well-engineered motorways, the surfing and golf, the sumptuous tropical landscapes, the vast US naval bases and a unique mix of peoples.

Beaches, volcanoes and whales

Most tourists stay in Oahu, in Honolulu itself, or in its suburb Waikiki Beach, with its famous surf beach lined by high-rise hotels. Honolulu is a modern city, American-style, but it still has its local touches: the streets lined with palms, 19th-century buildings, and a picturesque Chinatown. Street bands entertain the sunbathers with their jangling songs played on steel guitar and ukulele.

Just a few miles from Honolulu lies Pearl Harbor. The psychological damage inflicted by Japan's surprise attack on December 7, 1941, is still palpable, particularly in the presence of the sunken USS *Arizona*, in which over a thousand crew lost their lives. It has been left to lie in the harbour as a poignant memorial.

The other islands offer wild and rich landscapes, deserted beaches, and vestiges of the Polynesian past. Hawaii (the 'Big Island') is dominated by its massive volcanoes: the extinct Mauna Kea and active Mauna Loa. Maui offers tranquil beaches and magnificent cliffs that plunge dramatically into the sea, and boat trips that take visitors to see the passing schools of humpback whales. Kauai is the greenest of the Hawaiian islands, its rain forest was used as the setting for the film *Jurassic Park*.

The small, arid island of Niihau, in the far west of the main Hawaiian group, is still privately owned and is the protected home of 300 mainly pure-blooded Hawaiians, who continue to uphold their traditional – but Christianised – culture.

Privileges of the Polynesian melting pot

European settlement in the Pacific has produced a large mixed-race population in many islands. In Tahiti, people of mixed race are known as 'demis' – from the French for halves – and enjoy a privileged status.

Charismatic   *The controversial Gaston Flosse.*

United colours   *Youngsters gathered on the beach for holiday fun symbolise the mixture of races found throughout French Polynesia.*

Gaston Flosse's father was a French trader in mother-of-pearl; his mother was a Polynesian from Mangareva, the main atoll in the Gambier archipelago. He was born in June 1931 at Rikitea, the only village of any size on that atoll, and was brought up speaking French and Tahitian. He married at 20 and had six children. He became a teacher, then went to a Catholic college in Lyon, in France, to further his training. In 1962 he entered politics. His rise to power was impressive: president of the Polynesian Assembly in 1973, deputy at the national parliament in Paris in 1978, secretary of state for the South Pacific in 1986, mayor of Pirae in Tahiti in the 1990s. Pro-nuclear and anti-independent, he ran into controversy during the final round of nuclear tests ordered by President Jacques Chirac in 1995-6, but his support for the tests also gave him bargaining power in his long-term quest to secure greater autonomy for French Polynesia. His irrepressible energies later led to the post of senator in Paris (attending once a month) and president of the Polynesian government – as well as to court cases over abuse of power and kickbacks. Tall, elegant and jovial, Flosse has always felt that he had a special gift for representing his country.

Bilingual   *The Chinese school in Papeete helps to preserve the culture of the Chinese community.*

Controversial beauty

In December 1998, 22-year-old Mareva Galenter, Miss Tahiti, won the Miss France competition. Her success soon ran into controversy. Other contestants suspected the result had been fixed: the public telephone vote (representing a third of the final vote) had gone to another candidate, and it was said the judges' vote was fixed. The dispute tainted the competition, but there were some benefits to be derived from '*La Guerre des Miss*', as the French press called it. The photogenic Mareva became a well-known face, and established a role for herself as a top model. Tahiti was also proud of her, as ambassador for the women of Polynesia.

Mixed society

Interracial marriage has occurred since the first encounters between Polynesians and Europeans in the 17th century. In French Polynesia, mixed families have never been frowned upon. Rather, with a foot in both communities and command of two languages, they have enjoyed a privileged position as intermediaries, and they assist the mutual understanding that both cultures need in order to prosper. The most successful demi businessmen today plough profits back into the islands. Many, like Flosse, also take up public service.

The Chinese, who are the main shopkeepers on the islands, have also mixed with the Polynesians, as well as with the demis and the Europeans. As a result, the population of French Polynesia represents a blending of three continents.

The challenge of the ocean

Explorers, adventurers, solo yachtsmen, circumnavigators, holidaymakers, fishermen, refugees from the pressures of modern life – all sorts of people come to the ports of the Pacific islands, on anything from rafts to luxury cruisers.

When Magellan emerged from the straits that bear his name at the southern tip of South America, after enduring a long battering by icy storms, the ocean that lay before him appeared so calm that he named it Pacific. By a strange stroke of destiny, he managed to cross the entire ocean without encountering a single inhabited island before pitching up in Guam in 1521. Some 250 years later, James Cook fixed the positions of the main islands of the ocean. But the highest accolade for navigation should go to the ancient Polynesians, who made journeys of thousands of miles in their voyages of exploration – all the more remarkable for being primarily eastwards, into the prevailing winds.

The routes and journeys of the early Pacific mariners have long been the subject of speculation. In the middle of the 20th century, the Norwegian Thor Heyerdahl, convinced (mistakenly) that the Pacific people came originally from South America, not from Asia, decided to retrace the route that they might have taken by raft. His *Kon Tiki*, built along the lines of rafts used by the Incas to travel down the coast of South America, sailed from Peru in 1947. Three and a half months and 5000 miles (8000 km) later it reached the island of Raroia, in the Tuamotu chain of French Polynesia, somewhat to the north of the expected destination. The raft missed the only channel into the lagoon and was wrecked on the coral reef.

Back in the 1930s, the French adventurer Éric de Bisschop had sailed from Cannes to Honolulu in a hand-built Polynesian canoe, called *Kaimiloa*, and he likewise developed a theory that the Polynesians may have sailed east to west. The story of the *Kon Tiki* inspired him to attempt Heyerdahl's journey in reverse. In 1956 he set sail from Polynesia on board a sailing raft called *Tahiti Nui*. He

Safe haven *Yacht crews can enjoy a little rest and relaxation in a sheltered bay.*

reached the coast of Chile some months later, but lost his craft as he approached the shore. Two years later he tried to return by the same route and set sail on another raft, *Tahiti Nui II*. He was forced to dismantle it in mid-ocean to create a smaller raft, baptised *Tahiti Nui III*. This foundered on the reef of Rakahanga, in the Cook Islands, where de Bisschop died.

The journeys of the ancient Pacific navigators were better replicated in 1976. An American and Polynesian team built a 60 ft (18 m) traditional, twin-hulled sailing canoe (or *wa'a kaulua*), called *Hokule'a*, and an international – but mainly Polynesian – crew sailed it from Hawaii to Tahiti, a remarkable voyage of 3000 miles (4800 km), which demonstrated the feasibility of regular long-distance travel in this kind of craft.

Windsurf wonder *Tahitian Robert Teritehau beat off rivals to become world champion.*

Muscle power *Crews dig their paddles into the sea at the start of Hawaiki Nui, the big annual canoe race in French Polynesia.*

Solitary outrigger *A fisherman of Malakula (Vanuatu) makes for shallow waters in his search for a catch.*

Canoe marathon

In French Polynesia one of the big annual events is the canoe race called Hawaiki Nui, which takes place in the Society Islands in November. Some 60 boats take part in this challenging race, which links four islands in three stages, over three days (Huahine to Raiatea, then on to Taha'a, then to Bora Bora). To cover the 72 mile (116 km) course, the six-man teams have to paddle for a total of about ten hours. At each start and finish excited crowds cheer on the teams. Most participants come from nearby islands, but the Hawaiians are also regular competitors, and ferocious contestants. Even rowers from Europe now participate. In 1994, the German Olympic kayak team took part, and its eighth place demonstrated that the standard of rowing at the Hawaiki Nui is very high indeed – and that the Tahitians were not about to allow themselves to be dethroned.

Solo navigators, pleasure yachts and sea gypsies

In 1895 the Canadian Joshua Slocum began his great solo journey on a wooden sloop. With just a sextant, a compass and an alarm clock as his instruments of navigation, he travelled some 50 000 miles (80 000 km) across the world's seas. During his long Pacific crossing, Slocum stopped at the Marquesas, the Tuamotus and in the Samoan islands. He later published his adventures in his great classic of the sea, *Sailing Alone Around the World* (1900).

The French yachtsman and travel writer Bernard Moitessier was inspired by this book to name his yacht, a 40 ft (12 m) ketch, the *Joshua*. In 1968, poised to win a round-the-world yacht race, he abandoned it to retrace his hero's journey, landing at Tahiti after ten months of sailing. He spent the next 18 years sailing around the Pacific and wrote two books recounting his experiences.

Travelling around any bay in the Pacific, it is not unusual to find a boat at anchor. Often these are the boats of a new generation of sea gypsies, for whom sailing has become a way of life. The boat is a floating home, which can change its backdrop – beach, port, open sea – at the whim of its captain. Others are inspired by similar dreams, but pursue them from the luxury of a cruise ship.

Living the dream

The promise of a simple, more authentic way of life has inspired many to turn to the Pacific as a refuge from the Western world. A painter, a singer and a millionaire are among those who have built havens for themselves in the islands.

Warmer climes *French polar explorer Paul-Emile Victor at home on Bora Bora.*

Memories *Paul Gauguin recorded his life in Tahiti in a book called* Noa Noa.

On June 9, 1891, after two months at sea, Paul Gauguin (1848-1903) arrived in Tahiti. He was 43 years old. Papeete did not live up to his dream of the primitive life, but he buried his disappointment in the embrace of the beautiful Teha'amana and focused on his art. During this euphoric period of his life, he painted 66 pictures. But he became dogged by ill-health and poverty, and in 1893 begged to be repatriated. Back in France, he lived off a surprise legacy from an uncle, again grew restless and

returned to Tahiti in 1895, only to find his companion gone. Gauguin continued to paint, but in ever greater distress: in 1897 he tried to commit suicide by swallowing arsenic, but the attempt failed. In June 1901 he resettled on the island of Hiva Oa, in the Marquesas. There he painted and sculpted and regularly talked through the night with visitors, drinking absinthe. He also angered the authorities for taking sides with the locals. He died, lonely and tormented, in 1903. But his paintings only hint at his torment: indeed, Gauguin's images of Polynesia, and his portrayal of its sensual mysteries, made a lasting impression on the world and inspired others to follow him.

Jacques, Paulo and Malcolm

The cemetery on Hiva Oa is also the last resting place of another celebrity. Belgian singer-songwriter Jacques Brel (1929-78) chose to be buried near Gauguin, whom he referred to affectionately as Paulo. Brel became increasingly irritated by the pressures that went with fame. In November 1975 he visited Hiva Oa on his yacht, and, attracted by the calm and serenity of the island, decided to settle there. His song *Les Marquises* (*The Marquesas*), which he recorded shortly before his early death from lung cancer, paints a moving picture of the tranquillity of his adoptive home.

American publishing magnate Malcolm S. Forbes chose Laucala, a little island in Fiji, as his hideaway, paying a million dollars for it in 1972. His 3000 acre (1200 ha) empire has 250 inhabitants, a church, a shop and a herd of feral goats. He built a school, several luxurious, traditional-style houses for tourists, and a landing strip. A frequent visitor, he became so attached to the island that when he died his ashes were placed in a clearing close to his little house.

A new life

The much-travelled journalist Jerry Hulse was a travel editor with the *Los Angeles Times*. On March 1, 1998, he wrote an article from Kauai, one of the most beautiful Hawaiian islands. He told his readers that he was contemplating retiring there. He had planned to write a novel, but found he preferred to run on the beach and meditate on the landscape, or do volunteer work for the community. A month before taking his decision, he was still hesitating between the smog of Los Angeles and listening to the island breezes. On March 31 he took the plunge. After 39 years of work, he handed in his resignation to realise a childhood dream.

New horizons *Many people have opted to take time out to sail the Pacific, sometimes with all the family as willing companions.*

Kava, Polynesia's pepper grog

Kava is an intoxicating and narcotic drink made from a pepper plant. It used to be reserved for traditional ceremonies, but now it has become a popular and perfectly legal tipple. The pharmaceutical industry is also taking an interest.

Aura of respectability

In October 1988, kava producers set up the Regional Kava Council to promote collaboration in all areas of the trade: techniques of cultivation, harvesting and production, the control of pests, storage, quality control and pricing. There was also talk of protecting 'intellectual property rights' in kava – especially the hybrid forms of the plants.

Kava is made from the roots of a kind of pepper, or peppermint, plant, *Piper methysticum*, that grows wild in Vanuatu. Thanks to hybridisation, 85 varieties have now been developed, each with a different strength or effect.

Raw material Pepper-plant roots are the basis of kava production.

Varying traditions

Kava is particularly popular in Vanuatu, Fiji, Samoa and Tonga, and is also found in Micronesia. In Vanuatu the drink is prepared from fresh green roots. Traditionally, they are chewed and spat out, or simply grated, then mixed with water. The mash is not fermented – kava is a narcotic, not an alcohol. Its intoxicating effect is said to give access to the spirit world of the ancestors. Special kava ceremonies are part of traditional life, governed by rituals, and kava accompanies all key rites of passage. The roots are also cherished as gifts in ritual exchanges, and kava plays an important role in traditional medicine. The Fijian version, called *yaqona*, is made from dried roots and the mix is filtered through a strainer. It is considered rather innocuous compared to the brews of Vanuatu – powdered kava mixes can even be bought in Fiji's markets.

Prohibition by missionaries and colonial administrations failed to stamp out kava-drinking. Indeed, rather the opposite: kava became a symbol of the struggle for independence in Vanuatu during the 1970s. These days its consumption is tolerated, even encouraged, by local authorities, who prefer its pacifying effects to those of alcohol or cannabis. Kava relaxes, it makes people jolly, clear-minded, peaceable and never aggressive. Nonetheless, it is not entirely inoffensive: if abused, it can have serious side effects. One 'shell' too many leaves a drinker incapacitated – although it does not cause a hangover

A medicine and an industry

The medicinal and dietary properties of *Piper methysticum* – working as a non-addictive soporific, a tranquilliser, an anti-depressant, an analgesic, a suppresser of anxiety and hunger – have been studied by various pharmaceutical groups. Since the 1970s it has been used in over-the-counter remedies. Kava thus has become a growing source of income for the producing countries: Vanuatu, Fiji, Samoa, Tonga and the Federated States of Micronesia. In Fiji, the value of exports in recent years has been in excess of US$20 million, and is rising. In Vanuatu, it provides work for 6000 farmers and export revenues from kava now exceed those of copra.

Taking a 'shell' at the *nakamal*

At sunset, Melanesians head for the kava bar – called a *nakamal* in Vanuatu – to have a 'shell'. Traditionally, kava, a greenish or greyish liquid with a bitter, earthy taste, is served in half a coconut shell. Seated around a fire, drinkers knock back the entire contents of the shell in one go, then spit on the ground to give thanks to the spirits. They contemplate the flames and the stars, eat snacks, converse in low voices and, with numbed mouth and limbs, let themselves drift with the flow of the gentle tropical night.

Island challenge Rugby players from Tonga (above), and from Samoa and Fiji (left), present a serious challenge to bigger nations when they come to the World Cup.

Rugby warriors take on the world

Fiji, Tonga and Samoa play rugby at international level, and with great passion and talent. The sport complements the tough athleticism of these descendants of the Polynesian and Melanesian warriors of old.

The rugby world has long been familiar with the formidable commitment, strength and courage of the Maori players among New Zealand's All Blacks – the team famed above all for their intimidating pre-match *haka*, a Maori war dance. But the Rugby World Cup has revealed that there is plenty more, and equally explosive, talent in other islands of the Pacific – in Fiji, Tonga and Samoa. They may be tiny nations, with a total population of little over a million, but their teams have charged onto the international rugby scene with the force of a cyclone.

All three teams play a quick, open, inventive and aggressive game, and they also have well-honed technical skills – a combination that has sometimes delivered a nasty shock to the old rugby-playing nations. Their powerfully built players polish their skills in passing, tackling and general strategy by playing seven-aside rugby, a sport at which the islanders show a special talent.

Foreign mercenaries

A fair number of players from the Pacific islands play in clubs abroad – and even in foreign national teams. Some of the greatest rugby players of New Zealand have been of Samoan or Tongan origins, their parents having emigrated from the islands. Estimates suggest that 60 per cent of players regularly come from the islands. This includes two of the most famous All Black players ever. Michael Niko Jones, called the 'Iceman', a star of the 1980s and 1990s, has a New Zealander father and a Samoan mother, and the superstar Jonah Lomu who was born in Auckland in 1975 to parents who came from Tonga. At 6 ft 5 in (1.9 m) and weighing 260 lb (118 kg), this great winger is exceptionally powerful and remarkably fleet of foot. A rare kidney condition has led to a current withdrawal from the world of rugby.

The Wallabies of Australia have also drawn players from the islands, including players of Tongan descent such as Willie Ofahengaue, George Smith, Tontai Kefu and his brother Steve (their father was in the Tongan team that beat Australia in 1973).

Some islanders have even gone to play in European teams. The most famous of these is Ratu (chief) Emori Bolobolo, who as a winger for Stade Français became the first Fijian to play in a French championship-winning team, in 1998.

Intimidating their rivals Samoa is a nursery for rugby talent. At least a quarter of New Zealand's All Blacks have Samoan origins. Here the national team prepares to unleash its talent.

The sporting spirit

What do a football star and a stone-lifter have in common? The same satisfaction in sporting achievement. And sport offers a rare opportunity to meet people from other island nations.

Local heroes *The rise of a few players to international status has boosted soccer in New Caledonia.*

Athletes from 22 Pacific island nations and territories took part in the 13th South Pacific Games, held in Suva in 2003. At first, the atmosphere was tentative: groups of athletes and their coaches mingled in their tracksuits; competitors eyed each other timidly, exchanging polite greetings. The Samoans spoke English, the Tahitians French, but they discovered similarities in their respective traditional languages. Rivalry became more intense in the stadium, but a feeling of fraternity prevailed. All the participants found they shared common values and even common ancestors. Nonetheless, national pride and identity remained strong.

This microcosm of the Pacific world has been played out regularly since the first Games in 1963, in changing locations: Fiji, New Caledonia, Tahiti, Samoa, Papua New Guinea. Each time (now every four years), the Games become more professional: the facilities and organisation improve, the standard of performance rises, more records are broken. But intensive training techniques have not yet reached the Pacific islands and financial interest in sport is rare. The competitions may be hotly contested, but they retain an air of sportsmanship. The most commonly heard message at the end of the 2003 Games was: 'See you in Samoa in 2007!'

Stars of the world, stars of the village

Football was not a feature of the 2003 Suva games, but is a popular sport in the South Pacific, with its own share of heroes. Two exceptional players from New Caledonia have played in the French national team. Jacques Zimako played for the French club Saint-Étienne, and for France on several occasions. But the greatest Kanak star is Christian Karembeu, who has participated in football at the highest level – and for France when it won the World Cup in 1998.

The Pacific islanders' passion for sport manifests itself in games that are entirely local in origin. On Rurutu, in the Austral Islands of French Polynesia, men lift stones as a trial of strength. Each January a competition is held in every village, then the best contestants congregate at a large clearing in the south of the island, where the official stones are lined up. The heaviest weighs 286 lb (130 kg), and some are coated in oil to make the task more difficult. Women also compete, lifting up to 132 lb (60 kg).

Rock of ages *Stone-lifting is practised as a sport on Rurutu (Austral Islands). The same blocks of stone have served many generations of competitors.*

The original bungee jump

Nangol, or land diving, is an ancient forerunner of bungee jumping. It has been practised since time immemorial in the Pentecost Islands of Vanuatu. In April and May, after the yam harvest, young men throw themselves headfirst from an 80 ft (25 m) scaffold made of branches. At the foot is a large circle of deeply dug earth, to serve as a landing bed – but this should not be needed. The diver has a pair of liana vines attached to his ankles that will break his fall just above the ground – a bone-shuddering halt that is softened only by the stretching of the vines and the bending of the scaffold. Just before a diver takes the plunge, he is in a state of ritual limbo, and free to speak his mind, to criticise elders or refute allegations. The gods then have the perfect opportunity to punish him if he is wrong.

Where Celluloid fails

The islands of the Pacific present a picture of tranquil beauty. Paradoxically, many of the movies filmed against this backdrop are tales of violent conflict.

The mutiny on the *Bounty*, that fascinating episode of history, has been made into a film three times. On each occasion the story of the tempestuous relationship between Captain Bligh and his second-in-command Fletcher Christian has placed two great actors in opposition to each other. The 1935 version brought Charles Laughton's Bligh up against Clark Gable – the last film he made without his legendary moustache. The next, filmed in 1962 on Tahiti and Bora Bora, painted a sumptuous, travel-brochure picture of Polynesia. Trevor Howard played an intransigent and cruel Bligh to Marlon Brando's charismatic Christian. Despite a large budget of $27 million dollars, and a very long production schedule lasting 18 months, the film was the least successful of the three *Bounty* movies. But Brando, enraptured by the tranquil

Contravening tradition Tabu *(1931), Friedrich Murnau's last film, paints a sensitive picture of pre-colonial Polynesia. Although never patronising, it is ultimately a Western view of the Pacific.*

beauty of the South Seas, decided to buy Tetiaroa, a small atoll to the north of Tahiti, as a result of this experience. The third film was made in 1983, on the island of Moorea in French Polynesia. Here Anthony Hopkins played a more sympathetic, if misguided, Bligh to Mel Gibson's Christian – permitting a more considered exploration of the clash of individuals and cultures.

War movies' mixed record

War torn The attack on Pearl Harbor, in Tora! Tora! Tora! *(1970).*

The Pacific War has fascinated film-makers since 1945, and there have been a number of new contributions to the canon in recent years. *The Thin Red Line* (1998), directed by Terence Malick and based on James Jones' novel, tells of one of the most harrowing episodes of the war: the battle for Guadalcanal. Opening sequences show the magnificent landscapes of the island before plunging a young soldier into it to face the brutality of the battle: the dual themes of natural splendour and human violence run through the film. Disney's film *Pearl Harbor* (2001) tried less successfully to place the historical facts within the context of the love lives of participants, but the action sequences were widely admired.

History repeats itself Marlon Brando *played Fletcher Christian in* Mutiny on the Bounty *(1962). The experience changed Brando's life: he married his leading lady Tarita Teriipaia, and moved to Polynesia.*

Tamed idol *The rebel of rock 'n' roll, Elvis Presley pursued a less turbulent career after his period of military service (1958-60). The exotic Pacific environment was deemed to suit his new image as a sentimental romantic, as seen here in* Paradise Hawaiian Style *(1965).*

Death of a director

The *Bounty* story has a disproportionate place in movie history. The great heroes of Pacific exploration have been ignored, as has the odyssey of the first Polynesians in the conquest of their new world. Despite its promise as a location, the Pacific has not been well served by the film industry. *South Pacific* (1958), the film of the stage hit based on James Michener's novel, is remembered more for its songs than for cinematic quality. In 1979 *Hurricane*, a major Hollywood production, was made in Tahiti, but despite a big budget and several stars, including Mia Farrow and Trevor Howard, the film was a flop. Kevin Reynolds' *Rapa Nui* (1994) told a love story-cum-epic set in Easter Island, where it was filmed, with similar results.

But there is a major exception to this rather dismal roll call. Friedrich Murnau's *Tabu*, filmed on Bora Bora in 1931, is considered a classic. Codirected with the pioneer documentary film-maker Robert Flaherty, and using a cast of Polynesians, Murnau applied his famous emotionally charged camera technique to create a deeply sensual tale, beautifully filmed, of an impossible love between a young man and woman. Their relationship challenges convention and ends tragically. When Murnau suddenly died shortly after making the film, rumour suggested that he had transgressed.

Truth versus fiction

A number of documentary films about the Pacific bear witness to the physical beauty of the islands and the unique nature of their cultures. Two Australian film-makers, Bob Connelly and Robin Anderson, put together a remarkable film called *First Contact* (1983) using footage taken by Mick and Dan Leahy when they went to the Highlands of Papua New Guinea in 1933. Then, in 1983-91, they made a documentary trilogy that followed on from this, starting with *Joe Leahy's Neighbours*. It is the story of Mick Leahy's son by a Highland woman, and the efforts of the people to come to terms with the modern world.

Star backing *The success of the 1980s television series* Magnum *owed much to its star, Tom Selleck, playing a private detective, but also to its exotic setting in Hawaii.*

Reality behind the filmset

Most of the small island nations of the Pacific have modest natural and human resources. Economic production is minimal, limited to subsistence agriculture and fishing, a little tourism and perhaps one export crop, such as sugar or copra. The income from these rarely matches domestic needs. As much as 50 per cent of the revenue of some countries is derived from foreign aid, and development prospects depend entirely on such subsidies.

The economic life of the Pacific runs at two speeds – if not three or four. On the one hand there are the wealthy foreign settlers, the descendants of the colonial class or more recent 'expat' arrivals, and those local people who have succeeded in hooking into the new economy. On the other are the villagers, living off traditional gardening or fishing, in the undeveloped hinterland, where conditions have barely changed since colonial days. New underclasses are also emerging: young islanders who remain permanently unemployed or underpaid; the disaffected urban poor; and immigrant labourers, mainly

Getting by *Many in Tahiti barely scrape a living.*

from Asia, working for minimal wages.

The population growth in the Pacific is relatively high, averaging 1.9 per cent. Every year there are 150 000 new babies, a figure that equates with the number of young people who cannot find work. Meanwhile, those who are trained – technicians, civil servants, medical staff – tend to leave the islands to seek their fortunes elsewhere. Thus the hospitals of Fiji, for example, have to recruit doctors and nurses from the Philippines, China and India.

Nuclear testing and the fallout

From 1946 to 1996, the Americans, the British and the French tested nearly 300 nuclear weapons in the Pacific. The physical and political fallout from these tests is still being felt.

New dawn   The first hydrogen bomb was detonated on Enewetak in 1952.

The Americans exploded 67 nuclear bombs in the atolls of Bikini and Enewetak in the Marshall Islands between 1946 and 1958; the British (and their American allies) exploded 24 in the Christmas Islands (Kiritimati) and Malden Islands in the Kiribati group between 1956 and 1962. All these tests were atmospheric. The French, forced to find a new test site after Algeria became independent in 1962, carried out 200 explosions in the Polynesian atolls of Fangataufa and Mururoa between 1966 and 1996, of which 44 were atmospheric (1966-74) and the remainder underground. There was very little consultation with local people over the decision to carry out these tests: the pressures of the Cold War and Western defence were considered adequate justification.

Medical research has revealed exceptionally high levels of cancer among the people exposed to the radiation, notably the inhabitants of Rongelap and Utrik atolls in the Marshall Islands, who were downwind of a hydrogen bomb explosion on Bikini in 1954. Also military personnel involved in the tests were affected, particularly in Kiribati. The Americans generally accepted full responsibility for the problems that resulted, and have given the islanders financial compensation. But still the islanders feel that not enough has been done. The French and British, for their part, continue to insist that their tests had no long-term negative effects.

The Bikini story

In February 1946 Commodore Ben H. Wyatt, US military governor of the Marshall Islands, arrived on Bikini atoll and asked the 167 inhabitants if they would agree to leave their home temporarily for the 'benefit of all mankind', because President Truman had chosen it for atomic tests. Some 55 years later, they have still not returned. First they were moved from Bikini to Rongerik atoll, where they became sick from the food, then to Kwajalein, then to Kili Island. In the 1970s the Americans declared that the radioactivity on Bikini had reduced to zero and encouraged the islanders to go home. In 1972 a group of families did return to their ancestral land, and were shocked to see the extent of the damage. But in 1978 they were once again evacuated when high levels of caesium were found in crops. The USA launched a new initiative to clean up the atoll, and in 1998 a report by the UN's International Atomic Energy Agency said that Bikini was clear of radioactivity. Not surprisingly, the islanders remain unconvinced.

Site clearance   The French nuclear testing site on Mururoa was finally dismantled after the last test in 1996, following an international outcry.

The Pacific: nuclear-free zone

From the 1970s, the peoples of the region, with the support of international organisations such as Greenpeace, began to mobilise against all nuclear presence in the Pacific, and particularly against the French, who ignored pressure to stop testing weapons. In 1985, the Pacific nations adopted a treaty that proclaimed the South Pacific a 'nuclear-free zone'. But France continued testing on Mururoa until 1996, eventually signing the treaty and dismantling its nuclear stations in Polynesia in 1997-8.

Taking to the streets   Nuclear protesters in Papeete, Tahiti, in September 1995.

The lure of distant opportunity drains talent

The islands often prove too small to match the ambitions of the young people of the Pacific. They have inherited the adventurous spirit of their ancestors and, like them, they leave their native islands to seek new opportunities. Many never return.

Steven is Samoan. He went through school in the capital, Apia, and passed his exams. Many young people of his generation have similarly been to school, and are similarly qualified, but there are simply not enough jobs to go round. Like one in three of his compatriots, Steven considers emigrating. The USA holds little hope: people from Samoa used to be able to get jobs in American Samoa, and used this as a kind of back door to the USA. But now American Samoa has imposed much tighter restrictions on immigration from neighbouring islands. Instead, Steven decides to go to Australia, where one of his uncles has been living since 1970. But first he has to continue his studies to earn the qualifications he needs to obtain a visa. His uncle suggests he trains as a nurse, like himself, but Steven opts for massage. After three years of study, his knowledge and physical strength make him well qualified to work as a masseur. He goes to Australia, integrates successfully and takes Australian citizenship, joining the 80 000 other Pacific islanders who have become Australians.

The lure of the cities

A large proportion of the population from the Polynesian and Micronesian islands now live

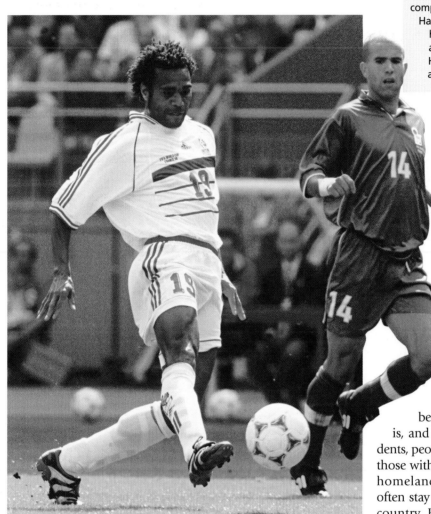

Winning ways Christian Karembeu is perhaps the world's most famous Kanak. He played in the French soccer team that won the 1998 World Cup.

abroad – in the USA, Australia and New Zealand. They are often drawn to the big cities because that is where the work is, and assimilation is easier. Students, people with qualifications, and those with sporting talent leave their homelands happily enough, and often stay for good in their adoptive country. Having set up home, they may encourage other members of their family to follow. In Melanesia, emigration is less pronounced, with the exception of Fiji. In 1968, at independence, a large number of Fijian Indians left for the USA, and a trickle have followed since. In all these small Pacific countries the loss of trained and experienced personnel has severe repercussions: it takes years to train replacements, and it is expensive to recruit from abroad.

But the emigrants do at least send money back home. These contributions may be modest, but they add up, and play a significant role in the national revenue of the islands. And sometimes these countries benefit directly from experience gained by their nationals abroad. A number of emigrants do return home – out of nostalgia for the country of their birth, their traditional food, or their families. Steven is thinking about it. He has even bought a plot of land on Samoa – perhaps for when he retires.

Not enough The limitations of their island may prove too constraining for these children of Kiritimati.

CHAPTER 7

ART AND CULTURE

The people of the Pacific islands believe that the natural world of the land, the sea, the stars, plants, animals and human beings, and the supernatural world of spirits and gods, are inextricably linked and in constant communion. This concept is central to their social, cultural, religious and artistic practices. Land ownership, fishing rights, tribal hierarchies, alliances and rituals are all based on the mythology of the clan, as communicated by the ancestor gods and interpreted by the chiefs. This rich spiritual life manifests itself in dance, music and singing, as well as in daily invocations. Sacred objects such as masks, drums, flutes and costumes are fashioned and decorated as stipulated by the rituals. Even ordinary daily objects are made in accordance with strict conventions, because they too are part of the spiritual world.

The horn-like call of the conch shell is a familiar sound in the Pacific islands.

The stone giants of Easter Island

The hundreds of stone heads, many of them colossal, that dot the landscape of Easter Island are a unique archaeological marvel. Sculpted by the Polynesian inhabitants of the island, their original significance remains a mystery.

Since their discovery in 1722 by the Dutch navigator Jacob Roggeveen, the unique stone statues of Easter Island (also called Rapa Nui by the indigenous people) have intrigued generations of visitors. Cook landed here in 1774, and wondered how the islanders, who appeared to have no mechanical equipment, had managed not only to erect the heads, but also to place large cylindrical stones on top of them. He speculated that they had used stone ramps and scaffolding. The French explorer La Pérouse came to a similar conclusion in 1786. But then came the Peruvian slave-traders, known as 'blackbirders', the missionaries, and the diseases that decimated the population. They combined to destroy what vestigial knowledge of Easter Island culture remained – and with it the secret of the statues.

Unearthly statistics

There are almost 1000 statues, or *moai*, in all. They were carved from the yellowish volcanic rock in a quarry on the extinct volcano of Rano Raraku and taken to their chosen site. They were mounted in lines of four to six statues on stone plinths, called *ahu*, facing inland with their backs to the sea. All these statues were later knocked over during a period of island turmoil, perhaps by earthquakes – though many have been re-erected in modern times. Others were abandoned along the path from the quarry, and 300 lie unfinished in the quarry, as if work on them had been interrupted.

Almost all the statues appear to be male figures. The smallest measures 6 ft 5 in (1.9 m); the largest is 33 ft (10 m) tall and weighs 90 tons. There is an unfinished *moai* which weighs 300 tons and is

The mysterious *rongorongo*

Another of Easter Island's mysteries are the *rongorongo*: wooden tablets covered in symbols or hieroglyphs. They have not been fully deciphered, but are thought to record sacred fertility chants. Only 25 of them have survived.

Silent witnesses *Only through recent work by historians and archaeologists has it been possible to demonstrate conclusively how the statues were made and erected.*

69 ft (21 m) long. Some 60 of these heads are topped by cylinders, or *pukao*, a ceremonial topknot of contrasting red stone from Punapau volcano. Most of the heads have lost their eyes, but originally the *moai* were not blind: the sculptors added eyeballs of white coral, shell or stone so that they could look at the sky.

A total of 245 *ahu* were erected along the coasts of the island. Some of these platforms are bounded by vertical walls made of large blocks of stone set in place without mortar. The similarity between these constructions and the walls built by the Incas at Cuzco, Peru, suggested to the Norwegian Thor Heyerdahl that the Easter Islanders came originally from South America. But most archaeologists believe that the *ahu* are a form of *marae*, the open-air altars of the Polynesians found in many of the archipelagoes to the west.

The death of a civilisation

Archaeological work undertaken from 1886, and since supported by modern carbon dating, has identified three periods of Easter Island history. In the earliest, between the 5th and 8th centuries AD, the first sailors and settlers arrived. They had endured a long voyage: Easter Island lies more than 2000 miles (3200 km) from the nearest main group of islands to the west (now French Polynesia), and about the same distance from the coast of Chile to the east. They were rewarded with a fertile island covered with forest, and established the *ahu* as their altars. The second period

Surviving eyes *Most of the heads have lost their white eyes. Coral eyes deteriorated more quickly than stone ones.*

Witness to a changing landscape *The statues are a ubiquitous presence on Easter Island, standing incongruously alongside modern structures.*

Where do Easter Islanders come from?

The first settlers came to the island on their sailing canoes between 450 and 750 AD. A few historians still hold that they came from Peru, as Thor Heyerdahl suggested. But most researchers are convinced that they came from Polynesia in a continuation of the eastward migrations that spanned the eastern Pacific. Linguistic and plant analysis, together with more recent genetic research, appears to confirm this theory.

Visiting Easter Island

Some 17 000 tourists visit the island every year. It can be reached by direct flights from Tahiti and Chile. Mataveri Airport, opened in 1967, has a big runway, extended by the Americans as an emergency landing place for the space shuttle. The capital, Hanga Roa, has tourist facilities and attractions which include hotels, guesthouses, a pizzeria, souvenir shops, a disco and an anthropological museum. Visitors can travel around by tour bus, hire car, motorbike, bicycle or horseback. The Parque Nacional Rapa Nui, established in 1935 to preserve the archaeological inheritance, covers two-thirds of the island's 24 sq miles (62 km²).

(12th-17th centuries) saw the erection of the statues on the *ahu*. Some 6000-10 000 people, perhaps more, now lived on the island, ruled by a powerful and sacrosanct aristocracy. The third period covered the disintegration of this society into clan warfare, famine and cannibalism, perhaps triggered by overpopulation. The tribes rebelled against the ruling élite, overturned many of the statues and decapitated others. The *moai* cult may have been supplanted by the birdman cult, which was centred on the ceremonial centre of Orongo, in the far south-west of the island. Here, numerous relief carvings of bird-headed men have been sculpted on the rocks.

This era coincided with the arrival of Europeans. When Roggeveen reached the island it had a population of about 4000, but many of the *moai* were still standing; by the time the Europeans arrived as settlers in the 1860s no *moai* remained on its plinth, and the island had been stripped of its dense forest.

The debate continues

The history of Easter Island is still debated by archaeologists. A number of theories have been advanced to explain how the statues were made, transported and raised onto their sites. Recent experiments have demonstrated that it would have been fairly easy to carry out this task using the natural resources of the island and mass labour. The sculptures were all carved out of soft volcanic rock, using tools made of the very hard stone from the Orito volcano. As for transporting them, archaeologists believe they may have been rolled on logs or hauled over wooden planks lubricated with palm oil. At their chosen site, they could have been eased into position using wooden levers and stone or earth ramps – rather as Cook and La Pérouse had surmised.

Reinstated *The* moai *are now being restored to their original positions.*

The Venice of the Pacific

The Federated States of Micronesia possess two archaeological wonders: the deserted lagoon cities of Nan Madol (on the island of Pohnpei) and Lelu (on Kosrae).

A network of canals Nan Madol is built on 92 artificial islets. Canoes can still navigate the canals that surround them.

Pohnpei is a volcanic island, well-watered, mossy and green. Rising out of the lagoon of Temwen, on the south-east side of the island, are the ruins of a city built in coral and basalt, and abandoned by a vanished civilisation.

The city and its canals

Nan Madol is a 500-year-old lake city, built on nearly a hundred artificial islets raised on the tidal flats and reef heads. The city is made up of rectangular walled compounds, which are separated by a grid of artificial canals. Each compound served a different function, and the whole site covers a broad rectangle nearly 1 mile (1.6 km) long.

At high tide, tourist boats can slide along these canals past the remains of a complex and ordered urban society. They pass the Nan Douwas, the massive temple fortress with walls 25 ft (7.5 m) high, containing huge royal burial chambers; the priest's quarter and cemetery; the servants' quarters; the coconut-oil factory; the workshop where outrigger canoes were built; government offices; a medical centre; a residence for visiting dignitaries; a magical pool, said to have revealed the secrets of the islands to the chief when he bathed there; and another pool where the sacred eel, fed on turtle flesh, served as a messenger between gods and humans.

The stones of Nan Madol

The walls of the city have a distinctive construction: they are largely composed of polygonal blocks of basalt – formed naturally by volcanic cooling. Some of the blocks are 25 ft (7.6 m) long and weigh 50 tons.

According to legend, Nan Madol was built by two magicians, the brothers Olo-chipa and Olo-chopa. They made the stones fly through the air, and when they came down they arranged themselves in the shape of the city's walls. Archaeologists have a more pragmatic explanation: the stone blocks were brought here by raft from quarries on Pohnpei. Although recent carbon dating shows that the site of Nan Madol has been inhabited from about 200 AD, the town was built between the 12th and 15th centuries, when the archipelago was ruled by a notoriously cruel dynasty of Micronesian kings, the Saudeleurs. It is thought that in about 1520 the Saudeleurs were overthrown by the chief of Kosrae, Isokelelel, who established a new regime on Pohnpei, and that Nan Madol was later abandoned.

Built to last The walls of Nan Madol's fortress show a particularly robust example of the building methods used in the city. Lengths of basalt have been laid like the logs of a log cabin, and the gaps filled with smaller blocks and rubble.

The royal city of Lelu

Some 300 miles (480 km) to the east of Nan Madol is another stone city on the partly artificial island of Lelu, just off Kosrae. From the 14th to the 19th centuries, huge enclosures were built with hexagonal blocks of basalt – similar to those of Nan Madol – to form the power base of the island chief and his nobles. Much of the ruined city now lies obscured by tropical vegetation. It includes a fortress with the remains of a palace, dwelling compounds, the site of the chief's feasting house, meeting houses and flat-topped pyramids that served as temporary tombs.

Water world Nan Madol's foundations are now cleared of invasive mangroves to reveal how the island compounds once looked.

Kanak homes

The traditional dwelling of New Caledonia, referred to by the French word *case*, is round, with a conical roof supported by wooden columns and a huge central pillar. The walls and roof are made from woven palm fronds, or from the bark of the niaouli tree. Access to the house is through an opening between carved wooden door jambs, called *talés*, spanned by a very low lintel. People entering have to lower their head, which is considered a mark of respect. The roof is topped by a finial sculpted in the shape of the clan emblem.

Many hands House-building is undertaken by the community.

A family home A fare, on the Fijian island of Yasawa.

Houses in harmony with Nature

In Samoa it is called a fale, *in Tahiti a* fare, *in New Caledonia a* case: *the wooden, thatch-roofed dwellings of the Pacific are a living tradition. Each island, and even each clan, has its own distinctive version.*

The three key symbols of island life are the palm tree, the outrigger canoe and the thatched village dwelling. They are all linked: wood from the palm trees is used to construct the boats and the frames of houses, fronds are used for sails and thatch. Palm fibres are used to bind both the beams of houses and the masts of boats. Village houses, whether dwellings or public meeting houses, are built – if not always entirely of palms – of light, plant-based materials. Set around a communal space shaded with trees, they are effectively extensions of their natural surroundings.

Thatch and wood

In a traditional Pacific island house, vertical wooden poles provide the basic frame and support a wooden framework for the sloping roof, over which is laid a layer of palm fronds, or other plaited leaves.

In Samoa, the *fales* have an oval or round ground plan, and are built on stone platforms made of blocks of coral or lava. They are open-sided, with woven mats that can be lowered like blinds, to keep out storms. Mats are also used to sleep

on, and the edge of the platform serves as seating. Personal possessions are few, and may all be stored in a single trunk. Every village also has a large community building. In Micronesia, the traditional dwellings are often A-frame in design, with the sloping roof reaching almost to the ground. In the Highlands of New Guinea, they may be elaborately decorated with carvings and paintings. In some villages, longhouses accommodate several families.

The biggest and most important building in any traditional village in Papua New Guinea is the *haus tambaran*, the spirit house. Men alone have access to the interior, reached through a very small entrance in the front of the building. Inside, the walls, pillars and beams are painted with scenes and figures depicting the spirits. Sacred objects such as masks, sculptures and musical instruments hang from the walls. This is where warriors traditionally sleep before doing battle, and boys likewise come here in the period leading up to their initiation rites.

Public space In Melanesia, the communal house is by far the largest in the village.

Modern and traditional

The Tjibaou Cultural Centre in New Caledonia, which overlooks the lagoon of Nouméa, is one of the most exciting examples of modern architecture in the Pacific. It occupies ten buildings inspired by the traditional village houses of the island, as well as by sailing canoes and shells.

Traditional dress *Ready for inauguration day.*

The Tjibaou Cultural Centre is a memorial to the pro-independence leader of the Kanaks, Jean-Marie Tjibaou. Signatory to the crucial Matignon Accords of 1988, he was assassinated in 1989 by a disaffected Kanak, whose son had been tortured and killed by French thugs the preceding year. The Centre was commissioned to fulfil the desire of both the French and the Kanaks to create a place in which the Melanesian culture of New Caledonia could be gathered, presented and promoted. President François Mitterrand included the Centre as one of his grand building projects and it received a grant of 320 million francs.

The basic idea for the Centre was devised by a Kanak team led by Marie-Claude Tjibaou, widow of Jean-Marie. It was built on land donated by the municipality of Nouméa, and the running costs – 35 million francs a year – are shared by New Caledonia and France.

A Melanesian village

The Centre is located at the tip of the Tina peninsula, overlooking the lagoon. Designed by the Italian architect Renzo Piano, its basic layout echoes the traditional Melanesian village – or rather a set of three villages. It consists primarily of ten giant *cases* rising to 72-108 ft (22-33 m), each with a surface area of 592-1506 sq ft (55-140 m²), constructed of the tropical hardwood iroko on steel girders. They

line up along an avenue that stretches for 251 yd (230 m), evoking the central thoroughfare between village houses. The buildings are designed to withstand windspeeds of 143 mph (230 km/h).

The first 'village' is devoted to art, the second is a media centre, and the third has been set aside for administration and for young visitors. Low-rise buildings, opening onto a garden, house exhibition halls, which include a rich collection of contemporary regional art, plus a 400-seat theatre. A 'Path of Legends' leads through the garden, which reflects the immense range of Melanesia's plant life, with candelabra pines, kaoris, coconut palms, and taro and yam gardens. Three traditional *cases* nearby represent the chiefdoms of the three Caledonian provinces.

The Centre was inaugurated on May 4, 1998, the ninth anniversary of the death of Tjibaou, with a ceremony that brought together delegations from all of Caledonia and the French Pacific territories. Lionel Jospin, the French prime minister, and leading Caledonian and Kanak leaders also attended. That same day they signed the Nouméa Accords, which reinforced the Matignon Accords and set out the peaceful democratic process that the archipelago will follow for the next two decades.

Great leader *Jean-Marie Tjibaou, whose memory is honoured by the Tjibaou Cultural Centre.*

Respect for location *Despite their considerable size, the buildings fit comfortably with their surroundings. The use of natural materials was central to the design concept.*

Renzo Piano, an Italian kanak

The Italian architect Renzo Piano was awarded the task of building the Centre. Famous, together with Richard Rogers, for the Pompidou Centre (1971) in Paris, he has worked on many buildings around the world, including the Kansai International Airport Terminal (1994) at Osaka, Japan. After visiting the site at Nouméa he based his design on the traditional architecture and village layout of New Caledonia, but interpreted it in a modern, stylised way. His structure echoes the Kanak model in texture and form, open to the landscape, the sky and the wind – symbolising an openness to the cultures of the Pacific.

The art of tattooing

Adventurous tourists are often tempted to return from the Pacific with an indelible souvenir inscribed onto their shoulder or ankle. But in the home of tattooing, this is not simply a decorative art: it is the expression of a very old cultural tradition.

Tapa

The paper mulberry tree (*Broussonetia papyrifera*), or sometimes the breadfruit tree or banyan, is used to make the precious cloth called *tapa*. The bark is stripped away, scraped, softened in water, and then beaten with a mallet and meshed together to make large, thin sheets of a felt-like material. Traditional motifs – similar to tattoos – are painted onto the sheets, each island having distinctive and instantly recognisable designs. Before Europeans brought cloth, *tapa* was used to make the skirt-like wrap called a pareo (or pareu), used in traditional ceremonies.

Decorative art Tattooing has become popular again, as a symbolic, and indelible, expression of the Pacific heritage.

When Jonas was born on the island of Upolu, in Samoa, his grandmother put aside some soot from a burnt candlenut – an essential ingredient of the dye for his future tattoo – and placed it on a dry coconut shell. Now that Jonas has reached the age of 15, his grandmother presents him with the shell so that he can have his first tattoo. He hands this precious treasure to the *tufuga*, the man in the village who makes tattoos. The application of the design follows a solemn ritual. Surrounded by friends and family, who have come to give him support with chatter and chants, Jonas is made to lie down on a mat on the ground. The tattoo is engraved into his skin with the sharp points of a tattoo comb made from sharks' teeth or pieces of shell. The *tufuga* learned his art from his father and he enjoys great prestige in the village. For Jonas, the experience is very painful, but it proves his courage.

Status symbol

Before missionaries came to the Pacific, tattooing was a common practice. The word tattoo comes from the Polynesian *tatau*, which translates roughly as 'opening a wound'. The practice served various functions in Pacific island society: it played a part in coming-of-age rites; it indicated status in the community; and it was a sign of prowess as a warrior or hunter. As they always attested to the standing of their wearer, tattoos were also a valuable asset in attracting women. Efforts by missionary priests to stamp out the practice

were largely successful and the art of tattooing went into decline. But now it is being revived, adopted by the young as a way of asserting their pride in their cultural identity.

The art of tattooing is found throughout the region. The traditional motifs are geometric patterns and stylised images inspired by nature and spiritual beliefs – stars, plants, animals, human or mythical figures. In the Marquesas, a man might have his body completely covered with tattoos, a process that takes many years to complete; while women tend only to have tattoos on parts of the body that are normally concealed. In the Solomons, on the island of Malaita, the skin is broken to make 'scar tattoos' without pigment. In the northern Solomons, some men are tattooed with black or blue patterns beneath their eyes, and the women have their breasts tattooed. Tourists who appreciate the artistry of these patterns, but are not inclined to endure the pain, can buy original patterns in the shops of cities like Papeete – but in the form of transfers.

Making the mark A traditional tattoo is applied with the sharp points of a rake-like tattoo comb.

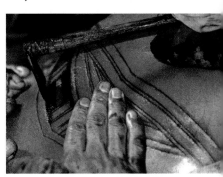

The art of Vanuatu and Papua New Guinea

The traditional art of the Pacific is hugely varied, the product of exceptional inventiveness and creative vitality. The Melanesians are particularly gifted artists, and Vanuatu and Papua New Guinea also boast rich artistic traditions.

Ritual mask *Papuan masks like this are used in ancestor cult rituals, and the skill in carving them has now been adapted for the tourist market.*

The masks of Ambrym

Masks and headdresses are a central feature of the dances and ceremonies of Ambrym, in Vanuatu, especially those involving yam cultivation rites. The masks are made out of wood pulp and mashed fruit. The artist first makes a basic framework with strips of wood, usually from the breadfruit tree, or tree fern; then he covers the framework with the dough. This is made from lianas and wood that have been soaked, grated and pounded into pulp, then mixed with coconut milk, breadfruit juice, fruit pastes and sap. The dough is then modelled into shape and, once dry, painted with bright colours and decorated with pigs' tusks, feathers, and banana fibre (for the hair). Most of the masks are faces, and they represent ancestral spirits. Some of them are designed for comic effect, with wide-open, grinning mouths, laughing eyes and crinkled noses.

In traditional societies of the Pacific islands, paintings, sculptures, masks and costumes are never simply aesthetic. Like everything else, they are linked to the spiritual world and to clan mythology. Because art is an expression of religious beliefs, it is treated with considerable respect. In Melanesia, as in many other parts of the region, there are strong social rules that govern how art is made, how it looks, and how it should be treated. This applies even to the decorative embellishments added to ordinary everyday objects, such as tools and utensils, or the prows of outrigger canoes.

To a casual observer, the vibrant appearance of the region's art belies its complex cultural context. A Westerner cannot hope to understand this context fully. The central focus of Melanesian art, for example, is not so much the objects themselves as the performance for which they are produced. The main form of artistic expression is in fact the public rituals and ceremonies. Objects that are made for these events may even be destroyed after use. Given that they are produced to accompany dance and singing, these props – which include masks, headdresses and drums – have to make a strong visual impact, and this explains much of the exuberant boldness of the art.

Red-eye *The museum of Port Vila, the capital of Vanuatu, has a rich collection of traditional art.*

Serious art *Only men produce the masks and sculptures. Such works are not intended for exhibition, but for use in ceremonies.*

134

Few countries can match Papua New Guinea for the range and vitality of its art. Masks are made of wood inlaid with shells and bone, or of clay-covered basketwork, modelled, painted with bright colours, and embellished with beads, feathers and plant fibres. The Asaro mudmen of the Eastern Highlands make strange, helmet-like masks out of grey clay. The Trobriand islanders are famed for their carved and polished wooden bowls. Sculptors in New Ireland produce elaborate figures for funerary rites. In Bougainville they weave *buka* baskets, said to be the finest in the Pacific. Perhaps the greatest exhibition of Papuan artistic creativity can be witnessed at a festival on mainland Papua, when all the clans congregate in full regalia.

Watching over you *The Polynesian tiki is an emblem and an amulet. It represents the ancestors, and brings a positive force.*

An evolving tradition

Both the Polynesians and Micronesians have used soft volcanic rock and fossil coral for sculpture, and have even tackled the much harder jade to make small carvings. In Melanesia, artists tend to use short-lived materials – bamboo, tree-fern wood, dough made out of vegetable matter, unfired clay, all painted with water-based pigment. The work is not made for posterity: it splits, rots, peels and falls apart in the damp and humid climate.

Missionaries had a profound effect on Melanesian art – on both its legacy and its evolution. Disapproving of anything that they interpreted as idolatry, they destroyed countless sculptures and other work connected to the ancestor cults. Anthropologists sent some pieces of art home to the great ethnographic collections, but although this preserved them from destruction, it denied the societies that created the work a large slice of their cultural legacy.

Some parts of Melanesia escaped the influence of the missionaries, and artistic traditions have carried on regardless. Some enthusiasts of Melanesian art complain that the quality has deteriorated – an effect linked to the disappearance of many rituals and the growth of the tourist art market. Others argue that Melanesian art is undergoing something of a renaissance, and not simply in terms of the sheer volume of work being produced. Art has become an important means by which Pacific islanders can express and assert their own unique cultural identity, and not all the works that are produced for the tourist trade are assembly-line products lacking significance or merit.

Living art is always in a state of perpetual evolution. The artists of Vanuatu and Papua New Guinea have learnt to integrate with modern commerce by adopting Western techniques, materials and something of the Western approach to art. But their work is still ultimately linked to the spirit world and ancient mythology – and still retains the original vision that goes with that tradition.

Music and dance from the heart

In the Pacific, all big events are accompanied by music and dance. Today, musicians playing traditional music are celebrating their cultural identity.

The *pilou* is a ceremonial form of traditional music and dance in New Caledonia in which the participants invoke their ancestors to perpetuate clan ties. The choir and percussionists take their places in the middle of the performing area, a large flat expanse of grass or sand. There are about 20 male dancers: their bodies are painted and adorned with flowers, foliage, feathers and shells, and they wear shimmering outfits that undulate and flutter with their energetic movements, producing a rustling sound to accompany the stamping of their feet. The *pilou* taps such forces of energy that it can induce a state of mind close to a trance. In the colonial era the priests found it unsettling and it was banned by the authorities. Today, it is no longer prohibited, and it permits young Kanaks to perpetuate an important element of their cultural heritage.

Rhythm sticks *Bamboos held in the hand beat out the tempo on the ground to accompamy dancers.*

Voices and shells

Since the dawn of Pacific history, music and dance have been central to initiation rites, marriages, name-giving ceremonies and funerals. Several musical instruments distinguish Pacific traditions. Percussion plays an important role: the Polynesians used skin drums, but more recently the slit drum (made of hollowed wood) has been adopted. Large bamboos are used to beat the ground, following the rhythm of the drums. Flutes, or panpipes in the Solomons, produce a rhythmic, soft and melodic sound. The conch, a common shell that is found in the lagoons, is also fashioned into an instrument: its soft, ringing call is said to represent the voice of a chief or an ancestor.

But perhaps the supreme instrument of the Pacific is the human voice. Traditional songs recount the legends of the ancients, linking them to familiar aspects of daily life. The islanders' obvious pleasure in singing was a great boon to the missionaries, who could lure parishioners into church on the promise of hymn-singing, to which they brought their own enthusiastic and polyphonic style.

Singing, chanting and clapping accompanies many traditional dances. These often enact stories and serious matters such as the destructive force of a cyclone, or preparing for war.

Kanéka

In 1975 Jean-Marie Tjibaou proposed establishing for New Caledonia a 'vast cultural inventory that would facilitate an endeavour to rediscover and redefine identity'. It was in this spirit that kanéka was born, a blend of Kanak tradition and international contemporary music. The most obvious non-Kanak element is the guitar, which American forces introduced to New Caledonia during the Pacific War. The guitar is now the most common instrument played by the Kanaks, but kanéka uses traditional percussion, replacing or complementing the drumkit. Dozens of groups now play kanéka. They practise their compositions in the villages, then perform them

Giant drum

In Vanuatu there is a kind of huge drum that exists nowhere else in the Pacific. Carved from the trunk of a breadfruit tree, the lower part is hollowed out and a slit inserted, while the upper part is sculpted with stylised faces, often with disc-like eyes. The drum may be 10-20 ft (3-6 m) in height. It is held vertically and struck with a wooden stick: the wider the slit, the higher the note. A concert of several drums is very impressive. The rhythms overlap and weave in and out of each other, following patterns handed down through the generations. The international reputation of these drums has preserved the tradition, but making drums for foreign markets has decimated the old breadfruit trees of Ambrym and Malekula, from which sacred drums are made.

Early learning *Young Papuans on the island of Fergusson are learning the ancestral rhythms from an early age.*

The rhythm of time *In some parts of Melanesia dance has retained its traditional character and produces spectacles of exceptional intensity.*

at festivals, or record them in studios. Different sensitivities emerge, according to whether the group likes traditional or modern music; whether they like hard-hitting or escapist lyrics. But in this search, kanéka helps them to define their own identity. With the help of radio and cassettes, and concerts, it has become the leading form of contemporary musical expression for the Kanaks.

Reggae and tamure

Reggae has also had a major influence in the Pacific, and especially in Melanesia. Since Bob Marley spread this style of Jamaican music around the world in the 1970s, most Black peoples have identified with it and borrowed its distinctive rhythms. 'Pacific reggae' has had a major impact on the creation of a popular contemporary Melanesian sound, from Fiji to Papua New Guinea.

In Polynesia, singing has always played an important part in daily life. Tahitian music creates a life-enhancing, carefree mood. At informal gatherings known as *bringues*, friends and family produce their ukuleles and guitars and make their own versions of traditional songs and current hits. But Tahiti is perhaps more famous for the tamure, a traditional dance accompanied by drums, which thrills tourists with its dynamic sensuality.

Male voice choir *Pacific music accommodated the religious songs of the missionaries. This men's choir in the Solomon Islands is off to sing at a wedding.*

Moïse Wadra: a pioneer

Moïse Wadra is one of the pioneers of kanéka. Born in Guama, on the island of Maré, in the 1970s, he attempted to live in Nouméa but quickly returned home and spent time composing work that was recorded in 1991. His dynamism and originality shine through his music. Initially influenced by folk and Tahitian music, Moïse has kept this lightness of touch in his own compositions. He uses a synthesiser like panpipes; the guitar and base provide acoustic sound. Often in the Pacific it is the voice that gives identity to music. Moïse's voice is soft and gravelly, and his melodies are drawn from various sources, but all are traditional songs.

Adapting to new ways

Pacific culture places a high value on community and hospitality, symbolised by the exchange of gifts. How have the islanders managed to live with the Western model, which places much greater value on individualism?

In the Pacific, visits exchanged between villages or islands follow a strict pattern of protocol, albeit carried out with casual ease. As part of the exchange of hospitality, men will sit around a speaker, often the clan chief, who will make a welcoming speech and explain the reason for the meeting. Throughout the speech, the listeners encourage the speaker with nasal 'mm' sounds, as if they are making conversation on the telephone. The larger the group, the greater the volume of the 'mms', giving the impression of collective assent. Successive speakers will be similarly encouraged by the listeners. The women take no part in the proceedings, but may watch from the side.

Meetings such as these are accompanied by an exchange of gifts, which are prominently displayed in front of those for whom they are intended. By tradition, the gifts should be similar. In the past,

Bearing gifts *In the Trobriand Islands of Papua New Guinea, presents form a key part of social exchange between the islands.*

they consisted of precious shells or feathers, or items made of woven vegetable fibre, such as bags. Nowadays, they might include banknotes and cloth, but the original sentiment remains intact: exchange symbolises the will to unite in friendship.

Uneasy compromise

The code of social obligations, or custom, is part of tradition. Custom governs the relationships between individuals within the clan and with those outside it. It also dictates how the rites of passage – birth, initiation, marriage, death – are commemorated. Traditional ways are easily maintained in remote communities, but close proximity to the modern world produces a conflict of interests. Villagers in Samoa take or borrow property, for example, because they believe it is owned by the community. This is a cause of complaint from tourists, who accuse them of stealing.

Young people find it hard to reconcile traditional and Western values. They are tempted to keep for themselves the income they earn from working, but tradition tells them to share it with their extended family. The debate continues, but it seems inevitable that traditional values will have to show some flexibility if they are to be maintained in the face of an increasingly changing environment.

Welcome touches *Traditional gestures of welcome, such as the* **lei** *(garland) of flowers, are warmly appreciated by tourists.*

Segregation *Traditionally, mealtimes are shared, but men and women eat separately.*

Gifts or bribes?

For a politician, receiving gifts in the customary manner can be misconstrued and risks attracting attention from the legal authorities. Marie-Noëlle Ferrière-Patterson was appointed ombudsman in Vanuatu, to see that the law was observed in such matters. She applied the rules to the letter, unmoved by the argument that gifts are linked to an established tradition of respect to chiefs, or are a valid way of thanking someone for a favour. Her enquiries caused the fall of the government in 1996, and the exposure of kickbacks received by government ministers remains an ongoing political issue.

Coconut with everything

The culinary arts of the Pacific derive from the copious ingredients of the lagoons and the sea, the gardens and the coconut palms. Dishes have to be adaptable to mass catering, because meals are an opportunity to bring the whole tribe together.

*B*ougna, a mixture of braised vegetables, meat and coconut milk, is a traditional Melanesian dish. Taro, yams or sweet potatoes are peeled, sliced and spread over a bed of banana leaves. Pieces of chicken, pork or fish are added, then coconut milk is sprinkled over. The mixture is then wrapped in banana leaves and sealed.

The method of cooking *bougna* is ingenious. To make the earth oven, or *umu* as it is known locally, a hole is dug in the ground, 8 in (20 cm) deep and with a width that corresponds to the size of the banana-leaf bundle. The hole is then filled with wood, which is set alight. Large pebbles are placed on the embers, and when they are hot, the bundle is placed on them. More banana leaves are then laid on top and the oven is sealed with a layer of sand. The dish takes 3-4 hours to cook, depending on its size. When the envelope is finally opened, the delicious scents of the *bougna* fill the air. Everyone considers it worth the wait.

Food parcels Bougna, *a speciality of Kanak cuisine, is prepared with great care and patience.*

Raw fish and fresh coconut

One of the great dishes of French Polynesia is a salad, called *ia ota*, made with raw fish perfumed with coconut milk. The preferred fish is red tuna. Cut into cubes and rinsed in sea water, the fish is allowed to marinate for a few minutes in lemon juice, and is then sprinkled with coconut milk, a touch of vinegar, salt and pepper. Then it is mixed with little pieces of chopped tomato, cucumber and green onion, and finally garnished with parsley.

While coconut milk is the dominant flavour of Pacific cooking, coconut is used in a variety of other ways. The heart of the palm is excellent in salads; the white pulp of a young nut makes a good dessert. Coconut water provides a refreshing drink, again especially if taken from a young, green coconut – excellent for hikers at the end of a long walk. Some coconuts may contain as much as 2 pints (1 litre) of liquid – which is why coconuts are so cherished on small atolls where fresh water is scarce.

Presentation *Fresh tiare flowers are sold in divisions of 100, wrapped in little parcels of leaves.*

The tiare welcome

*T*he gardenia tiare (*Gardenia tahitensis*) is the emblem of Tahiti. This small white, star-shaped flower has such a pungent scent that it is often the first sensation to strike a traveller on arrival – and one that will forever conjure memories of the islands. It is closely associated with the traditional welcoming ceremony of Tahiti. Particularly honoured guests may receive a whole garland (or *lei*) of tiare flowers. When a plane arrives, a hostess may offer each of the passengers a tiare. People will often wear a single tiare over one ear. According to custom, it is worn behind the left ear if the wearer is unattached, and behind the right one if already spoken for. Steeping the flowers in coconut oil produces the essence called *monoï*, used in the manufacture of local cosmetics (soaps, shampoos, suntan cream). Tahitian women use it to scent their hair.

Fresh delivery *Women on Yap share out the fish that the men have just brought in. The fish is usually cooked simply, by grilling it over an open fire.*

Maps, Facts and Figures

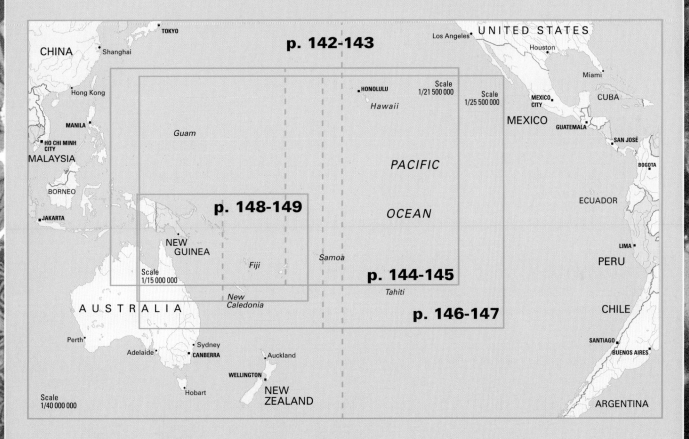

CHINA
TOKYO
Shanghai
Hong Kong

p. 142-143

UNITED STATES
Los Angeles
Houston

Miami

MANILA

HONOLULU

Hawaii

Scale
1/21 500 000

Scale
1/25 500 000

MEXICO
CITY

CUBA

HO CHI MINH
CITY

MALAYSIA

Guam

MEXICO

GUATEMALA

SAN JOSÉ

BORNEO

PACIFIC

BOGOTA

JAKARTA

p. 148-149

OCEAN

ECUADOR

NEW
GUINEA

Fiji

Samoa

LIMA

Scale
1/15 000 000

*New
Caledonia*

p. 144-145

Tahiti

PERU

AUSTRALIA

p. 146-147

CHILE

Perth

Sydney

Auckland

SANTIAGO

Adelaide

CANBERRA

BUENOS AIRES

WELLINGTON

Hobart

NEW
ZEALAND

Scale
1/40 000 000

ARGENTINA

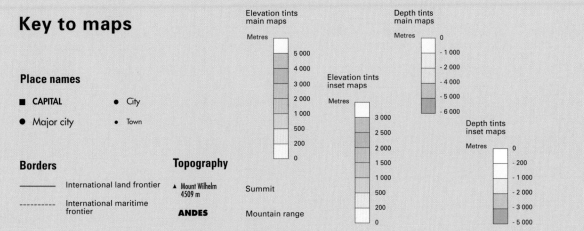

Key to maps

Place names

■ **CAPITAL**   ● City

● **Major city**   • Town

Borders

——————— International land frontier

- - - - - - - International maritime
frontier

Topography

▲ Mount Wilhelm
4509 m   Summit

ANDES   Mountain range

**Elevation tints
main maps**

Metres

5 000
4 000
3 000
2 000
1 000
500
200
0

**Elevation tints
inset maps**

Metres

3 000
2 500
2 000
1 500
1 000
500
200
0

**Depth tints
main maps**

Metres

0
- 1 000
- 2 000
- 4 000
- 5 000
- 6 000

**Depth tints
inset maps**

Metres

0
- 200
- 1 000
- 2 000
- 3 000
- 5 000

Oceania • The Pacific

CHINA
Lanzhou
Xi'an
Huang He
Chengdu
Dongting Hu
Chang Jiang
Wuhan
Nanjing
Shanghai
Chongqing
Changsha
Poyang Hu
Hangzhou
Kunming
Red River
Canton
Macau · Hong Kong
HANOI
Haiphong
LAOS
Gulf of Tonking
VIETNAM
HAINAN
THAILAND
Mekong
CAMBODIA
Tônlé Sap
PHNUM PENH
Ho Chi Minh

SOUTH KOREA
Pusan
Osaka · Nagoya
TOKYO
JAPAN
YELLOW SEA
CHEJU-DO
Korea Strait
Sata-misaki
OSUMI-SHOTÓ
EAST CHINA SEA
RYUKYU IS.
SAKISHIMA-SHOTÓ
OKINAWA
TAIPEI
Taiwan Strait
TAIWAN
Luzon Strait
BATAN ISLANDS
BABUYAN ISLANDS
PARACEL ISLANDS
LUZON
MANILA
MINDORO
CALAMIAN GROUP
PHILIPPINES
SAMAR
Philippine Trench
MINDANAO
SULU SEA
Balabac Strait
SULU ARCHIPELAGO
SANGIR
KEPULAUAN TALAUD
CELEBES SEA

PHILIPPINE SEA

OGASAWARA-SHOTÓ (BONIN ISLANDS) (JAPAN)
KAZAN-RETTO (VOLCANO ISLANDS) (JAPAN)
MINAMI-TORI (MARCUS) (JAPAN)
KURE ATOLL
MIDWAY ISLANDS (USA)
LISIANSKI

WAKE ISLAND (USA)

MARIANAS ISLANDS
TINIAN
ROTA
GUAM (USA)
YAP
NGULU
PALAU
ULITHI
SOROL
WOLEAI
EAURIPIK
NGATIK
CHUUK
HALL IS
OROLUK
MORTLOCK IS
SENYAVIN
POHNPEI
KOSRAE
EBON
KAPINGAMARANGI
PACIFI
TAONGI
BIKINI
BIKAR
ENEWETAK
UJELANG
KWAJALEIN
MALOELAP
MARSHALL ISLANDS
MAKIN
GILBERT ISLANDS
N'AURU
OCEAN I.
HOWLAND I. (USA)
BAKER I. (USA)
KIRIBATI
KANTON (USA)
PHO
ISLAN

BRUNEI
MALAYSIA
SINGAPORE
SUMATERA
Palembang
BORNEO
Makassar Strait
SULAWESI
BURU
SERAM
Manado
HALMAHERA
MOROTAI
MAPIA
MOLUCCA SEA
NEW GUINEA
Puncak Jaya 5 030 m
Peg. Van Rees
Peg. Maoke
ADMIRALITY ISLANDS
BISMARCK ARCHIPELAGO
NEW IRELAND
Melanesian Basin

JAVA SEA
Selat Sunda
JAKARTA
Surabaya
JAVA
BALI
BANDA SEA
FLORES SEA
KEP. KAI
KEP. ARU
KEP. BARAT DAYA
YAMDENA
PALAU DOLAK
KEP. BABAR
INDONESIA
GREATER SUNDA IS
CHRISTMAS I. (AUST.)
SAWU SEA
ROTE
LESSER SUNDA IS
TIMOR SEA
PAPUA NEW GUINEA
Gulf of Papua
Port Moresby
Torres Strait
Cape York
NEW BRITAIN
BOUGAINVILLE
CHOISEUL
ISABEL
NEW GEORGIA
MALAITA
GUADALCANAL
MAKIRA
RENNELL
SOLOMON ISLANDS
TUVALU
ROTUMA
SAMOA
ÎLES DE HOORN
AM SA

Sunda Trench
MELVILLE I.
BATHURST I.
Point Blaze
Darwin
Arnhem Land
ARAFURA SEA
Gulf of Carpentaria
CAPE YORK PENINSULA
TAGULA
D'ENTRECASTEAUX ISLANDS
CORAL SEA
Cairns
SANTA CRUZ ISLANDS
BANKS ISLANDS
ESPIRITU SANTO
MALAKULA
EFATÉ
VANUATU
ERROMANGO
VANUA LEVU
FIJI
VITI LEVU
SUVA
TONGA
ÎLES CHESTERFIELD

ASHMORE & CARTIER IS.
BONAPARTE ARCH.
BUCCANEER ARCH.
Cape Lévêque
Kimberley Plateau
Fitzroy
DAMPIER ARCH.
BARROW I.
DIRK HARTOG ISLAND
Tropic of Capricorn
TANAMI DESERT
GREAT SANDY DESERT
GIBSON DESERT
Alice Springs
Great Dividing Range
ÎLES LOYAUTE
NOUMÉA
MATTHEW I.
HUNTER I.
NEW CALEDONIA (FRANCE)
New Caledonia Trough

Perth Basin
Perth
Darling Range
Bluff Knoll 1 096 m
Cape Leeuwin
GREAT VICTORIA DESERT
SIMPSON DESERT
Lake Eyre
Nullarbor Plain
AUSTRALIA
Great Australian Bight
Darling
Murray
Lachlan
FRASER I.
Brisbane
LORD HOWE I. (AUST.)
Sydney
CANBERRA
Adelaide
KANGAROO ISLAND
Melbourne
Great Dividing Range
TASMAN SEA
NORFOLK ISLAND (AUST.)
KERMADEC ISLANDS (N.Z.)
North Cape
Auckland
East Cape
NEW ZEALAND
NORTH ISLAND

KING I.
Bass Strait
FURNEAUX GROUP
TASMANIA
Hobart
Storm Bay
Cape Farewell
Karamea Bight
Mt Cook 3 764 m
Southern Alps
Christchurch
West Cape
SOUTH ISLAND
CHATHAM IS (N.Z.)
WELLINGTON
STEWART ISLAND
ANTIPODES IS (N.Z.)
BOUNTY IS (N.Z.)

0   350   700 miles
0   400   800   1 200 km

F   G   H   I   J

Los Angeles
San Diego
Phoenix
El Paso
Dallas
USA
Memphis
Mississippi
Atlanta
Cape Hatteras
Cape Lookout
Cape Fear
BERMUDA (UK)

GUADALUPE (MEXICO)
Colorado
Houston
New Orleans
Cape Canaveral
ATLANTIC OCEAN

BAJA CALIFORNIA
Rio Grande
Gulf of Mexico
Tampa
Miami
THE BAHAMAS
TURKS
AND CAICOS
Tropic of Cancer

Sierra Madre Occidental
Sierra Madre Oriental
Monterrey
Cabo San Lucas
Cape Sable
Straits of Florida
LA HABANA
CUBA
HAITI
20°

Tampico
Guadalajara
MEXICO
Mérida
Bahía de Campeche
Yucatan
Cap Cruz
PORT-AU-PRINCE
DOM. REP.

ISLAS REVILLAGIGEDO
Sierra Madre del Sur
MEXICO
BELIZE
Gulf of Honduras
CAYMAN IS
JAMAICA KINGSTON
SANTO DOMINGO

HONOLULU
MAUI
HAWAII
WAIIAN IS

Golfo de Tehuantepec
GUATEMALA
GUATEMALA
EL SALVADOR
SAN SALVADOR
HONDURAS
TEGUCIGALPA
NICARAGUA
Lago de Nicaragua
CARIBBEAN SEA

MANAGUA
SAN JOSÉ
PANAMÁ

O C E A N

CLIPPERTON (FRANCE)
COSTA RICA
PANAMÁ
Golfo de Panamá
Magdalena

ISLA DE COCO
Medellín
BOGOTÁ

GMAN REEF (USA)
MYRA ATOLL (USA)
TERAINA
TABUAERAN
KIRITIMATI
ISLA DE MALPELO
Cali
COLOMBIA

JARVIS (USA)
ISABELA
SANTA CRUZ
ECUADOR
QUITO
Putumayo
Napo
0°

MALDEN
STARBUCK
GALAPAGOS ISLANDS (ECUADOR)
Guayaquil
Golfo de Guayaquil
▲ Chimborazo 6 310 m
Marañón

TONGAREVA
VOSTOK
ÎLES MARQUISES
Trujillo
BRAZIL

FLINT
ÎLES PALLISER
ÎLES TUAMOTU
LIMA
PERU

ROW K NDS
TAHITI
SOCIETY ISLANDS
ÎLES DU DUC DE GLOUCESTER
GROUPE ACTÉON
20°

TEMATANGI
MORANE
ÎLES AUSTRALES
ÎLES GAMBIER
HENDERSON (UK)
Antofagasta
ISLAS DE LOS DESVENTURA DOS (CHILE)
ATACAMA DESERT

FRENCH POLYNESIA
PITCAIRN (UK)
DUCIE (UK)
EASTER ISLAND (CHILE)
ISLA SALA Y GOMEZ (CHILE)
Salado

CHILE
Aconcagua 6 959 m
Córdoba
Uruguay

JUAN FERNÁNDEZ ISLANDS (CHILE)
Valparaíso
SANTIAGO
Rosario
BUENOS AIRES
MONTEVIDEO

Concepción
ARGENTINA
Mar del Plata
Río Negro
40°

A N D E S
Golfo San Matías
Peninsula Valdes
Bahía Blanca

ISLA DE CHILOE
ARCHIPELAGO DE LOS CHONOS
Golfo de San Jorge
Cabo Tres Puntas

▲ Cerro San Valentín 4 058 m
ISLA WELLINGTON

Micronesia

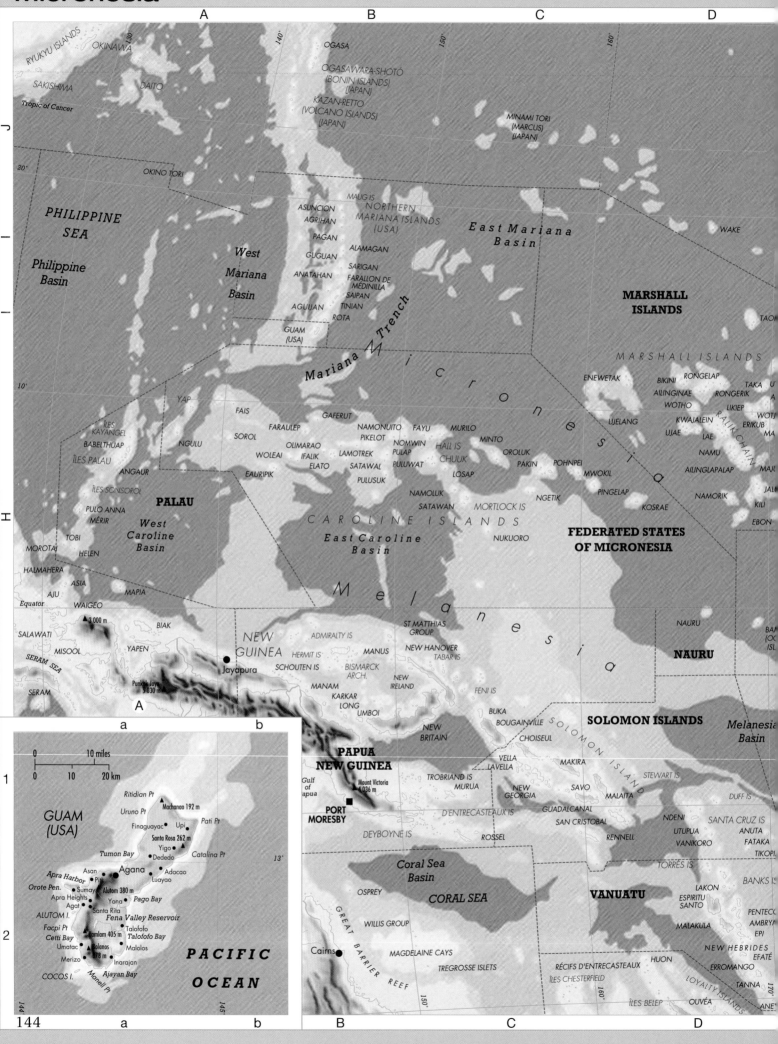

RYUKYU ISLANDS
OKINAWA
SAKISHIMA
DAITO
Tropic of Cancer

OGASA
OGASAWARA-SHOTÓ
(BONIN ISLANDS)
(JAPAN)
KAZAN-RETTO
(VOLCANO ISLANDS)
(JAPAN)

MINAMI TORI
(MARCUS)
(JAPAN)

OKINO TORI

PHILIPPINE
SEA

Philippine
Basin

ASUNCION
AGRIHAN
PAGAN
GUGUAN
ANATAHAN

MAUG IS
NORTHERN
MARIANA ISLANDS
(USA)

East Mariana
Basin

WAKE

West
Mariana
Basin

ALAMAGAN
SARIGAN
FARALLON DE
MÉDINILLA
SAIPAN
AGUIJAN
TINIAN
ROTA

GUAM
(USA)

Mariana Trench

Micronesia

MARSHALL
ISLANDS

TAO

MARSHALL ISLANDS

ENEWETAK
AILINGINAE
WOTHO
UJELANG

BIKINI
RONGELAP
RONGERIK
LIKIEP
KWAJALEIN
UJAE
LAE
NAMU

TAKA
WOTJ
ERIKUB
MA

RALIK CHAIN

YAP
FAIS
GAFERUT
NAMONUITO
FAYU
MURILO
MINTO

ÎLES
KAYANGEL
BABELTHUAP
ÎLES PALAU
NGULU
SOROL
FARAULEP
PIKELOT
NOMWIN
HALL IS
OROLUK
PAKIN
POHNPEI
MWOKIL

ANGAUR
WOLEAI
OLIMARAO
IFALIK
LAMOTREK
PULAP
PULUWAT
CHUUK
LOSAP
PINGELAP

AILINGLAPALAP
NAMU
NAMORIK
KILI
EBON
JAL

ÎLES SONSOROL
EAURIPIK
ELATO
SATAWAL
PULUSUK

PALAU
PULO ANNA
MÉRIR
West
Caroline
Basin
TOBI
HELEN

NAMOLUK
SATAWAN
NGETIK
KOSRAE

CAROLINE ISLANDS

East Caroline
Basin

MORTLOCK IS
NUKUORO

FEDERATED STATES
OF MICRONESIA

MOROTAI
HALMAHERA
ASIA
MAPIA
AJU
Equator
WAIGEO

▲ 3 000 m

Melanesia

SALAWATI
MISOOL
SERAM SEA
SERAM

YAPEN
BIAK

NEW
GUINEA
Jayapura ●
Puncak Jaya
5 030 m ▲

ADMIRALTY IS
HERMIT IS
SCHOUTEN IS
MANAM
KARKAR
LONG
UMBOI

ST MATTHIAS
GROUP
MANUS
BISMARCK
ARCH.
NEW
IRELAND

NEW HANOVER
TABAR IS

FENI IS

NAURU

NAURU

BA
(OC
ISL

Melanesia

BUKA
BOUGAINVILLE
NEW
BRITAIN
CHOISEUL
VELLA
LAVELLA

SOLOMON ISLANDS

SOLOMON ISLAND

Melanesia
Basin

PAPUA
NEW GUINEA

Gulf of
Papua
Mount Victoria
4 036 m ▲

PORT
MORESBY ■

TROBRIAND IS
MURUA
D'ENTRECASTEAUX IS
DEYBOYNE IS
ROSSEL

MAKIRA
NEW
GEORGIA
GUADALCANAL
SAN CRISTOBAL
RENNELL

SAVO
MALAITA

STEWART IS

DUFF IS

NDENI
SANTA CRUZ
UTUPUA
VANIKORO

ANUTA
FATAKA
TIKOPI

TORRES IS

Coral Sea
Basin

CORAL SEA

OSPREY

GREAT BARRIER REEF

WILLIS GROUP

Cairns ●

MAGDELAINE CAYS
TREGROSSE ISLETS

VANUATU

LAKON
ESPIRITU
SANTO

PENTECO
AMBRY
EPI

NEW HEBRIDES
EFATÉ

BANKS IS

RÉCIFS D'ENTRECASTEAUX
ÎLES CHESTERFIELD

MALAKULA
HUON
ÎLES BELEP
OUVÉA

ERROMANGO
TANNA
LOYALTY ISLANDS
ANE

Inset: GUAM

0 · 10 miles
0 · 10 · 20 km

GUAM
(USA)

Ritidian Pt
Uruno Pt
Finaguayac ●
Machanao 192 m ▲
Upi ●
Pati Pt
Santa Rosa 262 m ▲
Yigo ●
Catalina Pt
Dededo ●
Tumon Bay
Agana ●
Apra Harbor
Asan ● Piti
Adacao ●
Luayao
Orote Pen.
Sumay ●
Alutom 380 m ▲
Apra Heights
Yona ●
Pago Bay
Agat ● Santa Rita
ALUTOM I.
Fena Valley Reservoir
Facpi Pt
Tamlam 405 m ▲
Talofofo
Cetti Bay
Solanos ▲
Talofofo Bay
Umatac ●
678 m ▲
Malolos
Merizo ●
Inarajan
COCOS I.
Ajayan Bay
Monell Pt

PACIFIC
OCEAN

180° *170°* *160°* *150°*

KURE
ATOLL

PEARL AND HERMES ATOLL

MIDWAY ISLANDS
(USA)

LISIANSKI LAYSAN

MARO

GARDNER
PINNACLES

NECKER

FRENCH FRIGATE SH. NIHOA

Tropic of Cancer

H A W A I I A N   I S L A N D S

NIIHAU KAUAI OAHU MOLOKAI

KAULA Honolulu ● LANAI MAUI

KAHOOLAWE

▲ 4 205 m

HAWAII

20°

JOHNSTON ATOLL
(USA)

PACIFIC OCEAN

C e n t r a l

P a c i f i c

B a s i n

10°

KINGMAN REEF (USA)

PALMYRA ATOLL (USA

TERAINA

TABUAERAN

TARITARI

ARAKEI
ARAWA
AIANA
ABEMAMA
ARANUKA

HOWLAND I (USA)

BAKER I (USA)

KIRITIMATI
(CHRISTMAS ISLAND)

JARVIS
(USA)

Equator

UTI BERU

NEA NIKUNAU

NOTOA AMANA ARORAE

KIRIBATI

WINSLOW

KANTON (USA)

P H O E N I X   I S L A N D S ENDERBURY
BIRNIE

ORONA RAWAKI

NIKUMARORO MANRA

MALDEN

STARBUCK

L I N E   I S L A N D S

NANUMEA NIUTAO

ANUMANGA

NUI VAITUPU

P o l y n e s i a

VALU NUKUFETAU

FUNAFUTI

ÎLES TUVALU

NUKULAELAE

NIULAKITA

ATAFU

TOKELAU
(N.Z.)

NUKUNONU

FAKAOFO

SWAINS

NASSAU

PENRHYN

RAKAHANGA

PUKAPUKA MANIHIKI

*NORTHERN
COOK ISLANDS*

SUWARROW

VOSTOK

CAROLINE

FLINT

10°

ROTUMA

WALLIS AND FUTUNA
ISLANDS
(FRANCE)

WALLIS
(FR.) UVÉA

FUTUNA ALOFI

ÎLES DE HORN

SAMOA

SAVAI'I UPOLU

*MANUA
ISLANDS*

TUTUILA

*COOK ISLANDS
(N.Z.)*

*ÎLES SOUS-
LE-VENT* *ÎLES DU ROI GEORGES*

ÎLES PALLISER MATAIVA AHE MANIHI

MOTU ONE RANGIROA KAUKURA APATAKI

MAUPITI BORA
BORA MAKATEA NIAU ARATIKA

HUAHINE FAKARAVA TAHANEA

MAUPIHAA RAIATEA TETIAROA

VANUA LEVU

FIJI

YASAWA
GROUP KORO

VITI LEVU

RINGGOLD IS

*LAU
GROUP*

TAFAHI

TONGA

FONUALEI

VAVA'U

TONGA
IS

ANTIOPE

PALMERSTON

AITUTAKI

MANUAE

SOCIETY ISLANDS

MOOREA

MAIAO TAHITI

ÎLES DU VENT

KADAVU

FIJI

VATOA

180°

ÎLES HA'APAI

NUE
(N.Z.)

BEVERIDGE

*SOUTHERN
COOK
ISLANDS*

TAKUTEA

ATIU MAUKE

MITIARO

HÉRÉHÉRÉTUÉ

150°

20°

ÎLES NOMUKA

170°

orth
iji
asin

North
iji
asin

*C e n t r a l
P a c i f i c
B a s i n*

Polynesia

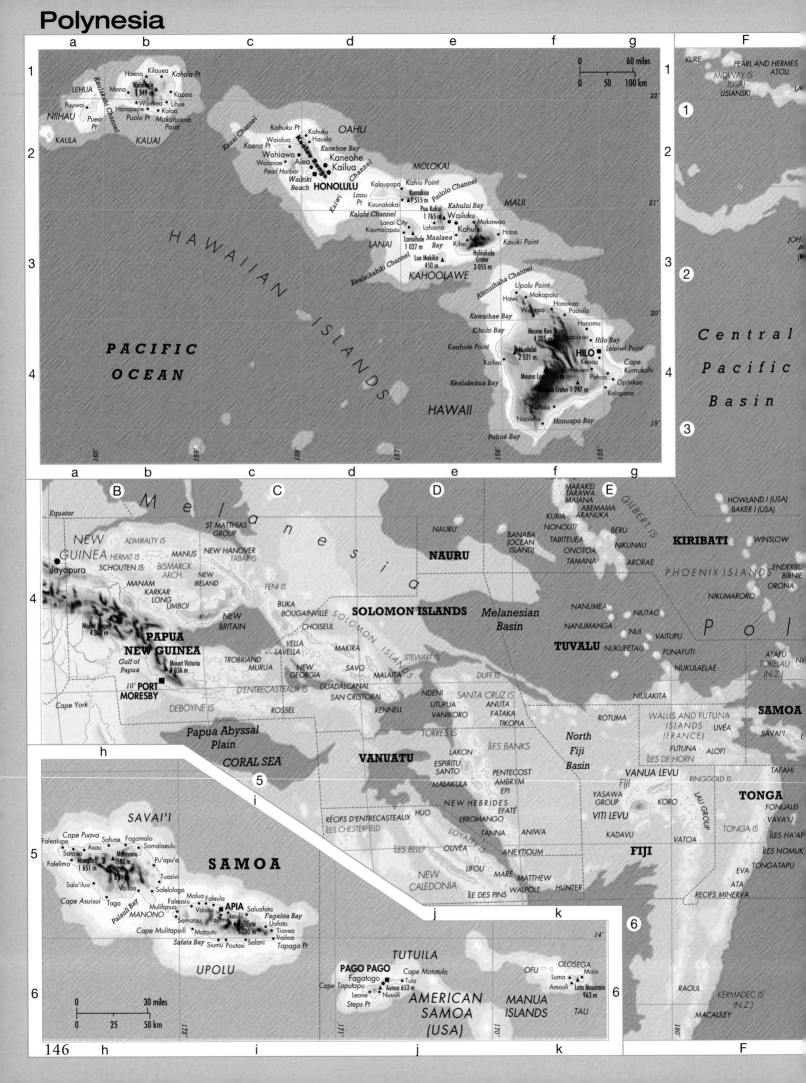

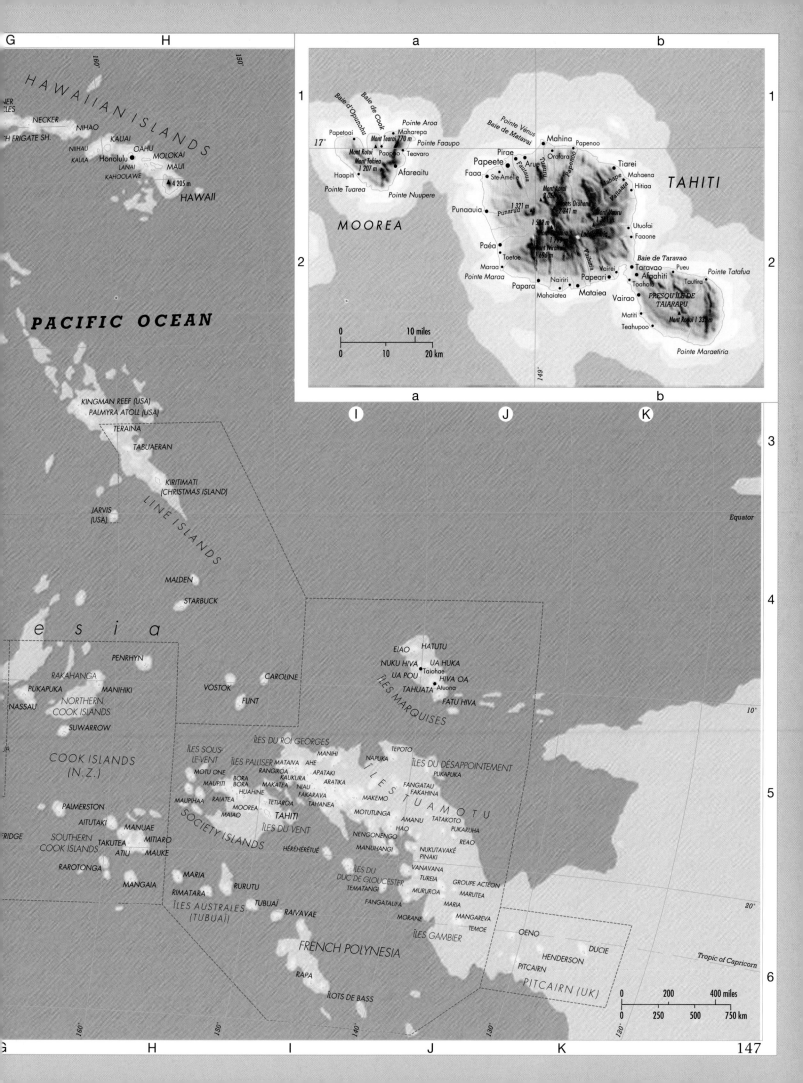

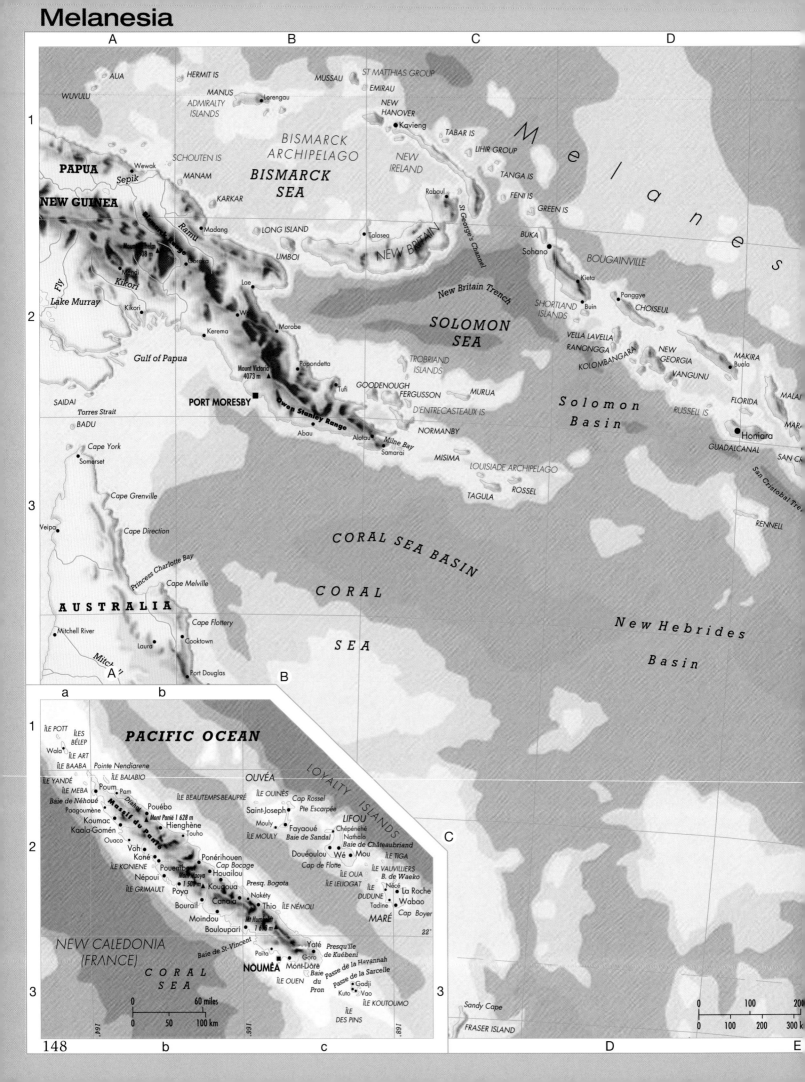

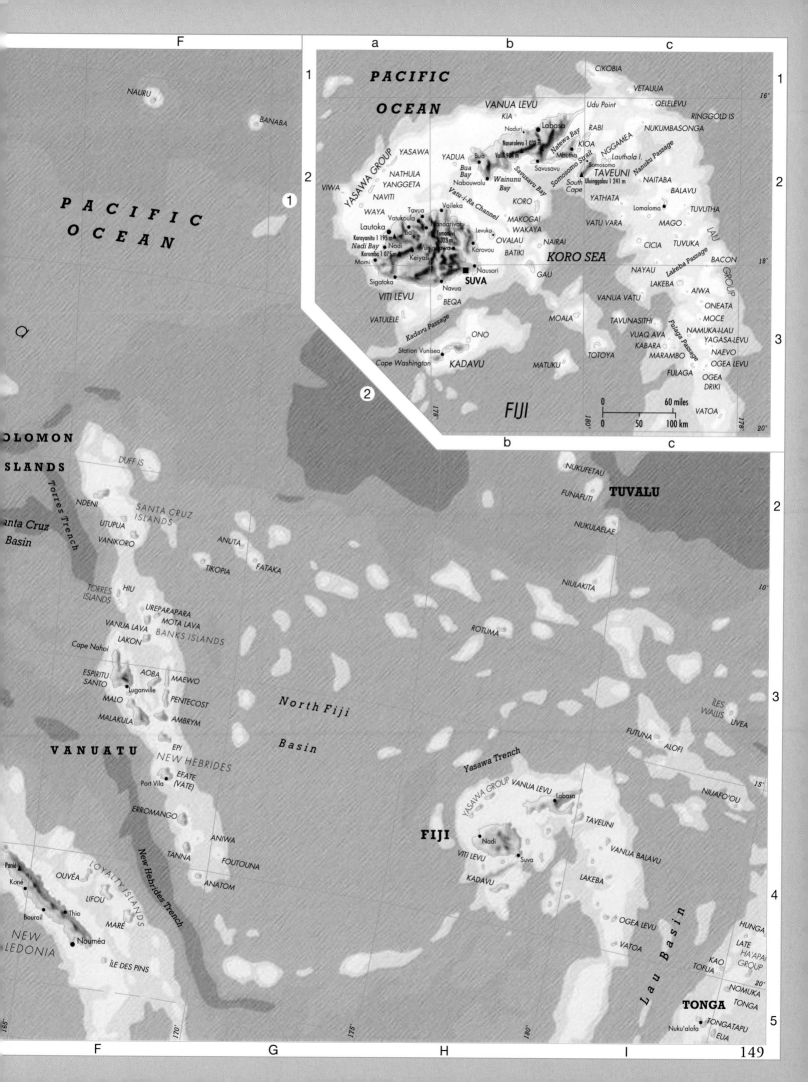

PACIFIC

OCEAN

CIKOBIA

VETAUUA

VANUA LEVU

Udu Point

QELELEVU

KIA

RINGGOLD IS

Naduri

Labasa

RABI

NUKUMBASONGA

YASAWA GROUP

YASAWA

YADUA

Bua

Nasorolevu 1 032 m

Natewa Bay

KIOA

NGGAMEA

Lauthala I.

Somosomo

Vatih 904 m

Mbutha

NATHULA

YANGGETA

Bua
Bay

Nabouwalu

Wainunu
Bay

Savusavu Bay

Savusavu

Somosomo Strait

TAVEUNI

Uluinggalau 1 241 m

NAITABA

NAVITI

South
Cape

BALAVU

WAYA

Tavua

Vatukoula

Vaileka

Vatu-i-Ra Channel

KORO

YATHATA

Lomaloma

TUVUTHA

VIWA

Ba

Lautoka

Yandarivatu

Levuka

MAKOGAI

WAKAYA

MAGO

Koroyanitu 1 195 m

Tomaniivi
1 323 m

Vunindawa

OVALAU

CICIA

TUVUKA

Nadi Bay

Nadi

Korovou

NAIRAI

Koromba 1 075 m

Keiyasi

BATIKI

KORO SEA

NAYAU

LAKEBA

Momi

Sigatoka

SUVA

Nausori

GAU

AIWA

Navua

Lakeba Passage

BACON

VITI LEVU

BEQA

VANUA VATU

ONEATA

VATULELE

Kadavu Passage

ONO

MOALA

TAVUNASITHI

MOCE

Station Vunisea

VUAQ AVA

NAMUKA-I-LAU

YAGASA-LEVU

Cape Washington

KADAVU

MATUKU

TOTOYA

KABARA

Fulaga Passage

NAEVO

MARAMBO

OGEA LEVU

FULAGA

OGEA
DRIKI

FIJI

VATOA

LAU GROUP

0   60 miles

0 50 100 km

PACIFIC

OCEAN

NAURU

BANABA

S O L O M O N

I S L A N D S

DUFF IS

NUKUFETAU

FUNAFUTI

TUVALU

NDENI

SANTA CRUZ

ISLANDS

NUKULAELAE

Santa Cruz
Basin

Torres Trench

UTUPUA

VANIKORO

ANUTA

NIULAKITA

TIKOPIA

FATAKA

TORRES
ISLANDS

HIU

UREPARAPARA

MOTA LAVA

ROTUMA

ÎLES
WALLIS

VANUA LAVA

BANKS ISLANDS

UVEA

LAKON

Cape Nahoi

AOBA

MAEWO

N o r t h   F i j i

FUTUNA

ALOFI

ESPIRITU
SANTO

Luganville

PENTECOST

B a s i n

MALO

MALAKULA

AMBRYM

Yasawa Trench

NIUAFO'OU

VANUATU

EPI

NEW HEBRIDES

YASAWA GROUP

VANUA LEVU

Labasa

Port Vila

EFATE
(VATE)

FIJI

TAVEUNI

ERROMANGO

Nadi

VANUA BALAVU

ANIWA

**NEW
CALEDONIA**

Panié

Koné

OUVÉA

LIFOU

TANNA

FOUTOUNA

Suva

New Hebrides Trench

VITI LEVU

LAKEBA

Bourail

Thio

LOYALTY ISLANDS

MARÉ

ANATOM

KADAVU

OGEA LEVU

L a u   B a s i n

HUNGA

Nouméa

VATOA

LATE

ÎLE DES PINS

HA'APAI
GROUP

KAO

TOFUA

NOMUKA

TONGA

TONGA

TONGATAPU

Nuku'alofa

EUA

Countries and territories of the Pacific

The islands of the Pacific represent a region of great diversity – political, social, economic and cultural. Inhabited by just 0.2 per cent of the world's population, they include some of the smallest nations, scattered over a vast region, but also see themselves as a community.

MICRONESIA

FEDERATED STATES OF MICRONESIA
Area: 271 sq miles (702 km²)
Capital: Palikir
Currency: U.S. dollar
Population: 107 500
Status: republic in free association with U.S.

GUAM
Area: 209 sq miles (541 km²)
Capital: Agana
Currency: U.S. dollar
Population: 157 557
Status: unincorporated U.S. territory

KIRIBATI
Area: 266 sq miles (690 km²)
Capital: Tarawa
Currency: Australian dollar
Population: 96 335
Status: republic

MARSHALL ISLANDS
Area: 70 sq miles (181 km²)
Capital: Majuro
Currency: U.S. dollar
Population: 56 429
Status: republic in free association with U.S.

NAURU
Area: 8 sq miles (21 km²)
Capital: No offical capital
Currency: Australian dollar
Population: 13 329
Status: republic

GUAM

NORTHERN MARIANAS

MARSHALL ISLANDS

PALAU

FEDERATED STATES OF MICRONESIA

MICRONESIA

Howland Island (
Baker Island (U.S

KIRIBATI

PAPUA NEW GUINEA

NAURU

BANABA

SOLOMON ISLANDS

TUVALU

TOKELAU

VANUATU

WALLIS AND FUTUNA

SAMOA

AMERIC
SAMOA

MELANESIA

NEW CALEDONIA

FIJI

TONGA

NIU

MELANESIA

SOLOMON Islands .
Area: 11 583 sq miles (30 000 km²) **Population:** 432 200
Capital: Honiara
Status: monarchy
Currency: Solomon Islands dollar

FIJI
Area: 7066 sq miles (18 300 km²) **Population:** 830 000
Capital: Suva
Status: republic
Currency: Fiji dollar

VANUATU
Area: 5699 sq miles (14 760km²) **Population:** 202 200
Capital: Port Vila
Status: republic
Currency: vatu

NEW CALEDONIA
Area: 7376 sq miles (19 103 km²)
Capital: Nouméa
Currency: French Pacific franc (CFP)
Population: 210 798
Status: French Territorial Collectivity

PAPUA NEW GUINEA
Area: 178 703 sq miles (462 840 km²)
Capital: Port Moresby
Currency: kina
Population: 5 190 000
Status: monarchy

NORTHERN MARIANAS

Area: 184 sq miles (477 km²) **Population:** 69 000
Capital: Garapan **Status:** United States
Currency: U.S. dollar Commonwealth

PALAU
Area: 188 sq miles (487 km²) **Population:** 19 976
Capital: Due to move to **Status:** republic in free
Babeldaob island in 2004 association with U.S.
Currency: U.S. dollar

AMERICAN SAMOA
Area: 76 sq miles (197 km²) **Population:** 57 000
Capital: Pago Pago **Status:** unincorporated U.S.
Currency: U.S. dollar territory

COOK ISLANDS
Area: 93 sq miles (240 km²) **Population:** 21 008
Capital: Avarua **Status:** state in free asso-
Currency: New Zealand dollar ciation with New Zealand

EASTER ISLAND
Area: 63 sq miles (162 km²) **Population:** 3000
Capital: Hanga Roa **Status:** province of Chile
Currency: Chilean peso

FRENCH POLYNESIA
Area: 1609 sq miles (4167 km²) **Population:** 262 125
Capital: Papeete **Status:** French overseas
Currency: French Pacific franc (CFP) territory

HAWAII
Area: 6409 sq miles (16 600 km²) **Population:** 1 211 537
Capital: Honolulu **Status:** U.S. state
Currency: U.S. dollar

NIUE
Area: 100 sq miles (260 km²) **Population:** 2145
Capital: Alofi **Status:** state in free asso-
Currency: New Zealand dollar ciation with New Zealand

PITCAIRN
Area: 1.8 sq miles (2.8 km²) **Population:** 47
Capital: Adamstown **Status:** British colony
Currency: New Zealand dollar

SAMOA
Area: 1097 sq miles (2842 km²) **Population :** 180 000
Capital: Apia **Status:** monarchy
Currency: tala

TOKELAU
Area: 4 sq miles (10 km²) **Population:** 1418
Currency: New Zealand dollar **Status:** New Zealand
territory

TONGA
Area: 289 sq miles (748 km²) **Population:** 108 141
Capital: Nukualofa **Status:** monarchy
Currency: pa'anga

TUVALU
Area: 11 sq miles (26 km²) **Population:** 11 146
Capital: Funafuti **Status:** monarchy
Currency: Tuvalu dollar/Australian dollar

WALLIS AND FUTUNA
Area: 106 sq miles (274 km²) **Population:** 15 734
Capital: Mata-Utu **Status:** French overseas
Currency: French Pacific franc (CFP) territory

POLYNESIA

HAWAII

Kingman Reef
Palmyra Atoll
(U.S.)

Jarvis Island
(U.S.)

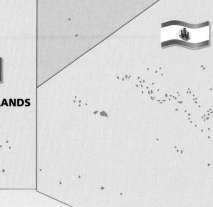

FRENCH
POLYNESIA

OOK ISLANDS

PITCAIRN

EASTER ISLAND

French territory

Commonwealth

Land and ocean

Spread across an ocean that is bigger that the planet's entire land area, there are tens of thousands of islands in the Pacific, some of them substantial, most microscopic. The total combined land area of 221 506 sq miles (573 700 km²) is only a little bigger than that of France.

THE DISTRIBUTION OF LANDMASSES ▼

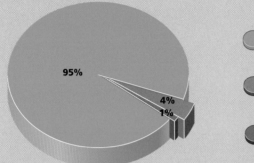

95%

4%

1%

Melanesia
210 425 sq mile
(545 000 km²)

Polynesia
9884 sq miles
(25 600 km²)

Micronesia
1197 sq miles
(3100 km²)

LAND AREAS AND THEIR EXCLUSIVE ECONOMIC ZONES

Many of the nations and territories of the Pacific may be small in terms of land area, but they have huge areas of ocean attached to them, called Exclusive Economic Zones (EEZ), established under a UN convention called the Law of the Sea (1982).

	Area (sq miles/km²)	EEZ (sq miles/km²)	Proportion
Papua New Guinea	178 703/462 840	1 196 900/3 100 000	14.9 % (x6)
French Polynesia	1609/4167	1 930 500/5 000 000	0.08 % (x1200)
Cook Islands	93/240	772 200/2 000 000	0.01 % (x9804)
Tuvalu	11/26	501 900/1 300 000	0.0015 % (x50 000)

Some of the territories, such as Niue, consist of just one island. Others, such as French Polynesia or the Federated States of Micronesia, are composed of hundreds of islands, grouped into several archipelagoes and spread out over colossal areas of sea. It takes 12 hours to fly across the region, from Los Angeles to Sydney, during which the sea appears like a great blue desert peppered by rare specks of land.

The climate

The Pacific islands lie, for the most part, between the tropics, and have a hot and humid climate. On average 78 in (2000 mm) of rain falls every year. Temperatures vary only moderately over the year: 23-31°C (73-88°F) in hotter months and 18-28°C (64-83°F) in cooler months. These differences mark the two seasons. The Northern Hemisphere has its cooler months between November and April; the Southern Hemisphere in May to October. Easter Island has a temperate climate, and an average temperature of 21°C (69°F).

High mountains, low atolls

The highest mountains are on the large islands of Melanesia, but there are also substantial peaks in Hawaii. By contrast, many islands are so low that they are under threat from rising sea levels.

The International Date Line

Time is calculated from the prime meridian that runs through Greenwich in London, a line that also represents 0° of longitude. Time to the east of the prime meridian is ahead of Greenwich; to the west it is behind. Around the other side of the world, on the line of 180° of longitude, the two times run into each other, so that time on the east of 180° of longitude is 24 hours behind time to the west of it – so crossing 180° of longitude from east to west and jumping ahead a whole day. The line of 180° of longitude passes right through the middle of the Pacific Ocean and through some island countries, such as Kiribati and Fiji. Because it would be inconvenient to have two different days in one country, to avoid this the International Date Line has been drawn along a crooked path.

ISLANDS ON WHICH THE HIGHEST POINT IS OVER 6562 FT (2000 M) ▼

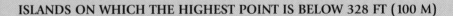

4508 m
Mount Wilhelm

4208 m
Mauna Kea

2447 m
Mount Makara-komburu

2241 m
Mont Orohena

Papua New Guinea

Hawaii

Solomon Islands

French Polynesia

ISLANDS ON WHICH THE HIGHEST POINT IS BELOW 328 FT (100 M) ▼

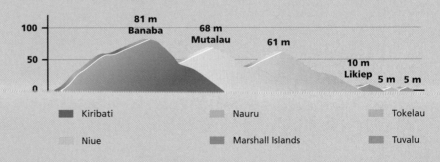

81 m
Banaba

68 m
Mutalau

61 m

10 m
Likiep

5 m   5 m

Kiribati

Niue

Nauru

Marshall Islands

Tokelau

Tuvalu

Population profiles

The Pacific islands have a total population of 9.2 million people, expected to rise to 10 million by 2012. Although descended from common ancestors, the island peoples have developed distinct national differences, which are manifested in their ethnic make-up, languages, culture and demography.

More than 4 million people live in Papua New Guinea and only about 50 on Pitcairn. Melanesia, with its larger islands, and 95 per cent of the total landmass of the region, is more heavily populated than any other region of the Pacific. Athough they have smaller net populations, many islands in Micronesia and Polynesia have much higher population densities. Proportionately, the smaller islands have higher levels of emigration, which has a major impact on the islands that the migrants leave behind. The population of the Cook Islands, for example, is under 20 000, but there are 30 000 Cook Islanders living in New Zealand and a further 20 000 in Australia.

Age profiles
The age pyramids below, comparing the populations of Papua New Guinea and Fiji, show substantial differences in their age structure. In Papua New Guinea 71 per cent of the population is below the age of 44. By contrast, Fiji has a much higher proportion of older people. The difference reflects the fact that Fiji is one of the more developed nations in the Pacific, and Papua is among the least developed. In Fiji, 40 per cent of women use birth control, and the relatively well-developed health services, available to all, keep older people healthier for longer.

Life expectancy
The average life expectancy across the Pacific is marginally higher than the world average, but there are large disparities between the islands. Generally, the territories administered by outside powers enjoy a higher life expectancy because of better health facilities (which were often an off-shoot of military bases). Also, they tend to have better standards of living, in terms of material comforts, which are derived to some extent from greater opportunities to work in public services.

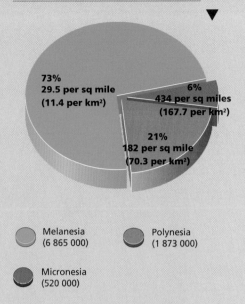

73%
29.5 per sq mile
(11.4 per km²)

6%
434 per sq miles
(167.7 per km²)

21%
182 per sq mile
(70.3 per km²)

Melanesia (6 865 000)

Polynesia (1 873 000)

Micronesia (520 000)

Hence on Guam, life expectancy for men is 18 years longer than in Papua New Guinea; for women, there is a disparity of 20 years.

LIFE EXPECTANCY		
	Men	Women
Papua New Guinea	54 years	56 years
Vanuatu	66 years	69 years
Nauru	56 years	63 years
Tonga	66 years	70 years
French Polynesia	68 years	73 years
Guam	72 years	76 years

Literacy
The literacy levels in the Pacific are surprising: statistics for the islands often exceed even those of the world's richest countries, although some noticeably lag behind. As in health, Papua New Guinea brings up the rear. Improvements in educational facilities mean that younger generations have a higher overall literacy level than their elders, which will raise averages over time. This is particularly true of Papua New Guinea.

AGE PYRAMIDS ▼

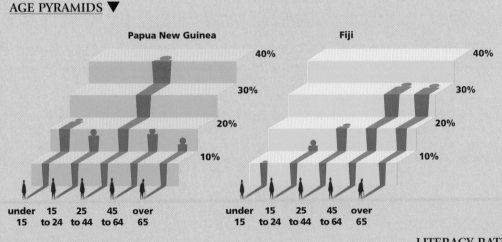

Papua New Guinea

40%
30%
20%
10%

under 15 | 15 to 24 | 25 to 44 | 45 to 64 | over 65

Fiji

40%
30%
20%
10%

under 15 | 15 to 24 | 25 to 44 | 45 to 64 | over 65

LITERACY RATES IN THE PACIFIC ▼

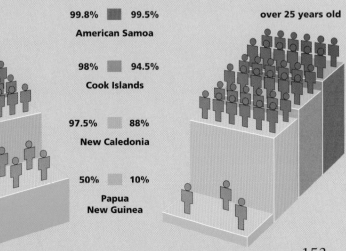

15–24 years old

over 25 years old

99.8% ■ 99.5%
American Samoa

98% ■ 94.5%
Cook Islands

97.5% ■ 88%
New Caledonia

50% ■ 10%
Papua New Guinea

URBAN AND RURAL POPULATIONS		

On the Pacific islands there are very few towns with a population in excess of 100 000. Many of the larger urban centres have barely 10 000 inhabitants and remain very closely connected to their rural hinterland.

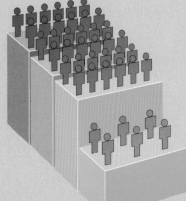

Population:	urban (%)	rural (%)
Palau	72	29
Marshall Islands	69	31
American Samoa	50	50
Tonga	41	59
Federated States of Micronesia	27	72
Solomon Islands	18	83

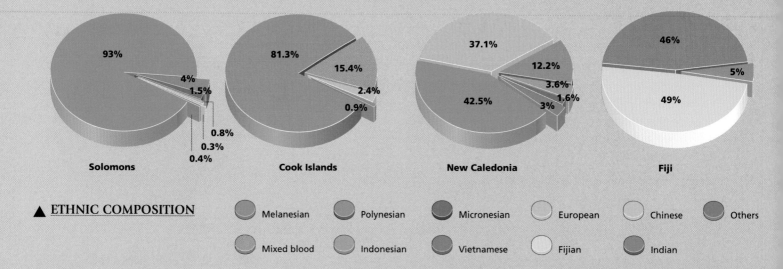

Solomons 93% 4% 1.5% 0.8% 0.3% 0.4%

Cook Islands 81.3% 15.4% 2.4% 0.9%

New Caledonia 37.1% 42.5% 12.2% 3.6% 1.6% 3%

Fiji 46% 49% 5%

▲ ETHNIC COMPOSITION

- Melanesian
- Polynesian
- Micronesian
- European
- Chinese
- Others
- Mixed blood
- Indonesian
- Vietnamese
- Fijian
- Indian

Ethnic composition

Because of their geographical isolation, indigenous populations have remained in the majority in most islands – with the exception of Fiji, New Caledonia and Hawaii, where large numbers of immigrants arrived to develop the resources. In Fiji, most came from the Indian subcontinent; in New Caledonia, they came mainly from Europe. In Hawaii, 20 per cent of the people are of mixed Polynesian descent; there are large minorities of Caucasians and Japanese; and pure blood Hawaiians constitute less that 1 per cent of the total.

NUMBER OF
LANGUAGES FOUND
IN MELANESIA ▼

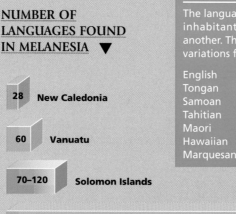

28 **New Caledonia**

60 **Vanuatu**

70–120 **Solomon Islands**

715 **Papua New Guinea**

THE POLYNESIAN LANGUAGES

The languages of Polynesia are sufficiently similar to permit inhabitants from one island to understand those from another. This selection gives some idea of the uniformity and variations found in certain common words:

English	house	island	woman	land
Tongan	fale	motu	fefine	fonua
Samoan	fale	motu	fafine	fanua
Tahitian	fare	motu	vahine	fenua
Maori	whare	motu	wahine	whenua
Hawaiian	hale	moku	wahine	honua
Marquesan	hae	motu	vehine	henua

Health

Changes in diet and lifestyle over the past half century have led to an increase in those suffering from high blood pressure, diabetes and cardiovascular problems. Access to medical services is sometimes extremely limited, with damaging implications for the fight against infectious diseases such as diarrhoea, dengue fever (a tropical disease transmitted by mosquitoes), malaria, tuberculosis and pneumonia. The situation is often made worse by the lack of clean fresh water and poor sanitation. There are major disparities across the region, and generally health is better in the dependent territories where Western standards of medicine and hygiene are more prevalent.

A multitude of languages

Melanesia has just 0.1 per cent of the world's population, but one-third of its spoken languages. Pacific culture was historically entirely oral: the absence of writing meant that language was never fixed or standardised, and developed according to local use. The use of pidgin (in Papua, the Solomons, Vanuatu) evolved from the need to create a lingua franca to span the multitude of local languages, initially for the purpose of trade. Polynesian, by contrast, forms a family of languages with a remarkable volume of shared features, given the huge distances between islands. Paradoxically, the only writing that has been found is on the remotest island of them all, Easter Island, in the form of carved hieroglyphs.

THE MAIN RELIGIOUS
DENOMINATIONS ▶

Religions

Missionaries targeted the region with such success that it is now the most Christian part of the world outside Europe, and traditional religions have been almost completely supplanted. There is a complex patchwork of Christian beliefs: Roman Catholic, Anglican, Presbyterian, Seventh Day Adventist, Jehovah's Witnesses, Mormons, Assemblies of God (Pentecostal), and Church of Christ.

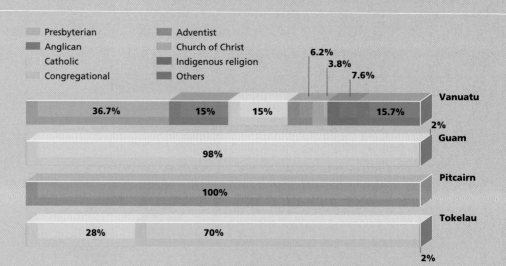

- Presbyterian
- Anglican
- Catholic
- Congregational
- Adventist
- Church of Christ
- Indigenous religion
- Others

Vanuatu 36.7% 15% 15% 15.7% 6.2% 3.8% 7.6%

Guam 98% 2%

Pitcairn 100%

Tokelau 28% 70% 2%

Economies dependent on the rest of the world

The economies of the Pacific islands have been shaped by their geographic isolation as well as by the threat of cyclones and seismic activity – all of which discourage foreign investment. Except for the large islands of Melanesia, they are poor in natural resources: the most promising development sector is tourism.

The gross domestic product of the Pacific islands shows marked disparities. Although most people still live from subsistence farming and fishing, as their ancestors did, income from external sources has a major impact on the GDP figures. In the case of Guam, this income comes largely from tourism and revenue from the US military presence.

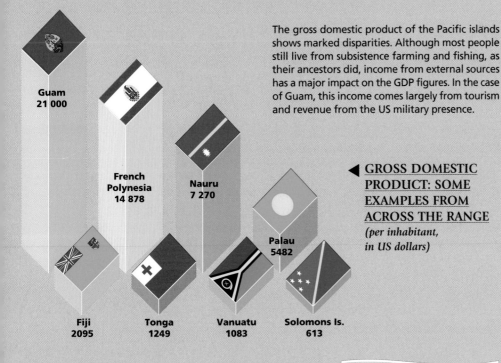

◀ **GROSS DOMESTIC PRODUCT: SOME EXAMPLES FROM ACROSS THE RANGE**
(per inhabitant, in US dollars)

- Guam 21 000
- French Polynesia 14 878
- Nauru 7 270
- Palau 5482
- Fiji 2095
- Tonga 1249
- Vanuatu 1083
- Solomons Is. 613

EXPORTS OF TIMBER PRODUCTS FROM MELANESIA ▼
(in millions of US dollars, and as a percentage of total exports)

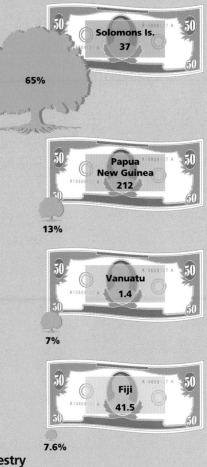

- Solomons Is. 37 — 65%
- Papua New Guinea 212 — 13%
- Vanuatu 1.4 — 7%
- Fiji 41.5 — 7.6%

EXPORTS OF FISH ▶
(in millions of US dollars, and as a percentage of total exports. Figures for 2000-2002)

Fishing

Fish exports, primarily tuna, provide a growing source of income for many states. Fishing fleets are owned mainly by foreign industrial nations with licences to the Exclusive Economic Zones.

Copra

A shrinking market and a drop in the international price for copra have depressed production. Some nations have more or less given up production and turned to other products to take the place of copra, such as timber, vanilla, kava and – in the case of Tonga – pumpkins.

- Federated States of Micronesia 14.4 — 84.8%
- Marshall Islands 0.5 — 7%
- Tonga 0.8 — 12%
- Solomons Is. 10.4 — 18%

Forestry

Timber is one of the principal exports of Melanesia, although the profits are mostly made by foreign nations (notably Malaysia), which do the logging under licence and process the timber elsewhere. Initiatives to readjust this imbalance include the creation of timber processing works on the islands, and local forest exploitation using portable saw mills, which also reduces the environmental impact of logging.

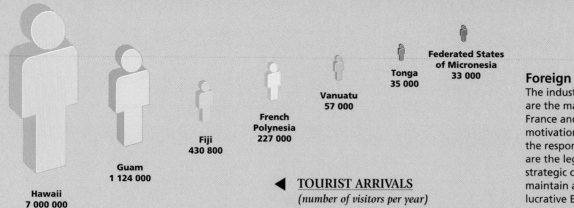

Hawaii
7 000 000

Guam
1 124 000

Fiji
430 800

French
Polynesia
227 000

Vanuatu
57 000

Tonga
35 000

Federated States
of Micronesia
33 000

◀ **TOURIST ARRIVALS**
(number of visitors per year)

Foreign aid

The industrialised countries on the Pacific Rim are the main contributors of foreign aid, but France and Britain are also major donors. The motivations are various: some islands remain the responsibility of foreign nations; others are the legacy of historical links. There are also strategic considerations, and the desire to maintain access to the vast and potentially lucrative Exclusive Economic Zones.

Tourism

The Pacific islands rank among the most desired holiday destinations in the world. Names like Tahiti, Bora Bora and the Cook Islands conjure up images of the perfect tropical holiday setting. But tourist figures tell a rather different story. By far the most visited archipelago is Hawaii, with 7 million visitors a year, followed by Guam. Islands of the south Pacific have relatively modest visitor figures, and tend to cater for a fairly wealthy clientele. Fiji is the most popular, in part because it is a stopover point for long-haul flights, and it has become a popular destination for young travellers on round-the-world trips. Tourism now accounts for about a third of Fiji's annual foreign revenues. To reach remoter islands, travellers either have to be wealthy to afford the air fare, or prepared to accept the more basic standards of local transport and accommodation.

SOURCES OF FOREIGN AID RECEIVED BY TONGA (IN MILLIONS OF US DOLLARS, FIGURES FOR 2001)			
Nations		International organisations	
Japan	11.1	EU	0.7
Australia	5.4	Various development funds	0.4
New Zealand	3.6	Asian Development Bank	0.3

SOURCES OF FOREIGN AID RECEIVED BY VANUATU (IN THOUSANDS OF US DOLLARS, FIGURES FOR 1996)			
Nations		International organisations	
Australia	10 200	EU	4400
France	6000	Asian Development Bank	2600
New Zealand	3700	UN	500
Japan	3400		

IMPORTS AND EXPORTS

(The tail end of the arrows represents imports, and the point of the arrows represents exports, with totals expressed in millions of US dollars.) ▼ ▶

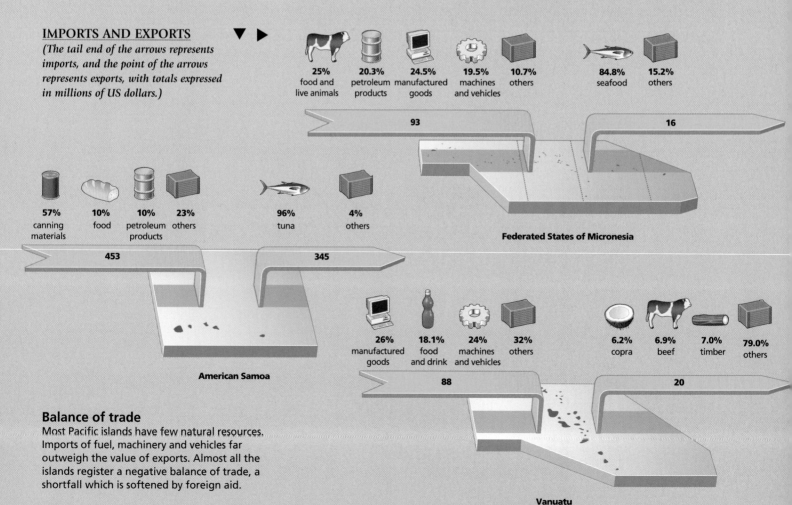

25% food and live animals — 20.3% petroleum products — 24.5% manufactured goods — 19.5% machines and vehicles — 10.7% others — 93

84.8% seafood — 15.2% others — 16

Federated States of Micronesia

57% canning materials — 10% food — 10% petroleum products — 23% others — 453

96% tuna — 4% others — 345

American Samoa

26% manufactured goods — 18.1% food and drink — 24% machines and vehicles — 32% others — 88

6.2% copra — 6.9% beef — 7.0% timber — 79.0% others — 20

Vanuatu

Balance of trade

Most Pacific islands have few natural resources. Imports of fuel, machinery and vehicles far outweigh the value of exports. Almost all the islands register a negative balance of trade, a shortfall which is softened by foreign aid.

Index

Page numbers in *italics* denote illustrations. Alphanumeric references in brackets are the co-ordinates for places in the map section, pp. 140-149

Acknowledgments

Abbreviations: t: top, m: middle, b: bottom, l: left, r: right.

FRONT COVER: Moorea, French Polynesia: HOA-QUI/Altitude/Y. Arthus Bertrand.
BACK COVER: Hawaiki Nui, an annual canoe race in French Polynesia: HOA-QUI/S. Grandadam

Pages 4/5: HOA-QUI/Altitude/Y. Arthus-Bertrand; **6/7:** COSMOS/SPL-T. Van Sant; **8t:** COSMOS/Aspen-J. Aaronson; **8b:** PHONE/Auscape-J. M. La Roque; **8/9:** HOA-QUI/E. Valentin; **10/11:** BIOS/M&C Denis-Huot; **11:** HOA-QUI/Altitude/Y. Arthus-Bertrand; **12t:** PHONE/Auscape-B. Saunders; **12b:** BIOS/P. Kobeh; **12/13:** BIOS/Y. Lefèvre; **14t:** DIAF/B. Simmons; **14b:** BIOS/A. & E. Lapied; **15:** ASK IMAGES/T. Nectoux; **16t:** IRD/M. Lardy; **16/17b:** HOA-QUI/Ph. Bourseiller; **17:** HOA-QUI/I.&V. Krafft; **18t:** COSMOS/P. Menzel; **18/19b:** HOA-QUI/V. Audet; **19t:** PHONE/J.-P. Ferrero; **20:** PHONE/Auscape-J. M. La Roque; **21:** PHONE/J.-P. Ferrero; **22tl:** BRIDGEMAN ART LIBRARY/British Museum, London; **22/23b:** PHONE/Auscape-A. Belcher; **23t:** Coll. VIOLLET; **23ml, 23b:** COSMOS/A. Ryman; **23mr:** MUSEE DE L'HOMME/M. Oster; **24tl:** COSMOS/Aurora-R. Caputo; **24/25tr:** COSMOS/Aurora-P. Essick; **24m:** RMN/J. G. Berizzi; **24b:** Coll. VIOLLET; **25tr:** BRIDGEMAN ART LIBRARY/'Kava ceremony in Tonga' by A. de Sainson/National Gallery of Australia, Canberra; **25ml:** PHONE/Auscape-A. Belcher; **25mr:** COSMOS/A. Ryman; **25b:** LAUROS GIRAUDON; **26tl:** Jean Loup CHARMET/watercolour by Duché de Vancy/Bibliothèque Mazarine, Paris.; **26tr:** Jean Loup CHARMET; **26bl:** EXPLORER/J. L. CHARMET/engraving by Boilly; **26/27b:** BRIDGEMAN ART LIBRARY/Tahitian war canoes by W. Hodges/National Maritime Museum, London; **27t:** BRIDGEMAN ART LIBRARY/'People and monuments of Easter Island' from the atlas of La Pérouse's expedition by Duché de Vancy; **27b:** ND-VIOLLET; **28tl:** Coll. VIOLLET; **28tr:** Jean Loup CHARMET/Bibliothèque des Arts Décoratifs, Paris; **28m:** ASK IMAGES/S. Fautré; **28b:** HOA-QUI/Altitude/Ph. Bourseiller; **29t:** GAMMA/N. Reynard; **29b:** COSMOS/B. Gysembergh; **30tl:** RMN/M. Bellot/Letter from Ch. Giraud/Musée du Louvre, Paris; **30tr:** Jean Loup CHARMET/drawing by Pierre Loti/Collection Loti-Viaud; **30m:** BRIDGEMAN ART LIBRARY/Private collection; **30b:** BRIDGEMAN ART LIBRARY/painting by C. Krieghoff/Bonhams, London; **31t:** RMN/G. Blot/Musée du Louvre, Paris; **31m:** Jean Loup CHARMET/Vve Magnin & Fils éditeurs, Paris; **31b:** Jean Loup CHARMET/Island women, Max Radiguet/Naval history service, Vincennes; **32t:** SYGMA/J.-P. Laffont/Film Tora! Tora! Tora! by Richard Fleisher, 20th Century Fox,1970; **32m:** GAMMA; **32b, 33t:** TALLANDIER; **33m:** Jean Loup CHARMET/Musée des Deux Guerres, Paris; **33bl:** EXPLORER/Coll. Bauer; **33br:** DIAF/Jacobs; **34tl:** DIAF/B. Barbier; **34tr:** GAMMA/Sydney Freelance-Murphy; **34bl:** SYGMA/T. Graham; **34/35b:** PHONE/J.-P Ferrero; **35t:** SYGMA; **35mr:** COSMOS/Contact Press Image/R. Smolan; **35br:** GAMMA/Liaison/Rotolo; **36/37:** BIOS/Lefèvre; **38/39:** PHONE/Auscape-T. Till; **40l:** BIOS/M. & C. Denis-Huot; **40/41t:** HOA-QUI/Altitude/Y. Arthus-Bertrand; **41tr:** DIAF/Pratt-Pries; **41b:** COSMOS/SPL-Nasa; **42l:** HOA-QUI/Altitude/Y. Arthus-Bertrand; **42/43t:** HOA-QUI/Altitude/Ph. Bourseiller; **43m:** HOA-QUI/M. Denis-Huot; **43b:** HOA-QUI/E. Valentin; **44t:** COSMOS/Anzenberger-Schill; **44b:** BIOS/Seitre; **45l:** COSMOS/SPL-J. Mead; **45r:** HOA-QUI/W. Buss; **46t:** HOA-QUI/Altitude/E. Valentin; **46/47b:** HOA-QUI/M. Denis-Huot; **47t:** BIOS/Seitre; **48tl:** BIOS/M. Gunther; **48tr:** PHONE/J.-P. Ferrero; **48b:** GAMMA/C. Voulgaropoulos; **49t:** ASK IMAGES/C. Esther; **49bl:** BIOS/Dani-Jeske; **49br, 50/51:** HOA-QUI/Ph. Bourseiller; **52/53tl:** COSMOS/G. Navaron; **52m, b:** SYGMA/Ch. Durocher; **53b:** COSMOS/SPL-Nasa; **54l:** COSMOS/SPL-K. MacDonald; **54/55:** HOA-QUI/I&V Krafft; **55tr:** COSMOS/Aspect/S. Middleton; **55br:** HOA-QUI/Ph. Bourseiller; **56t:** HOA-QUI/I&V Krafft; **56b:** IRD/M. Monzier; **57t, m:** SYGMA/Austral International; **58l, 58/59t:** IRD/B. Marty; **59m:** COSMOS/SPL-Nasa; **59b:** COSMOS/Aurora-P. Essick; **60/61:** BIOS/F. Bavendam;

62l: BIOS/A. Maywald & Fotonatu; **62m:** BIOS/FNH Gunther; **62/63:** BIOS/Y. Hubert; **63r:** BIOS/K. Schafer-WWF International; **64tr, m, b:** BIOS/Seitre; **65t:** BIOS/D. Heuclin; **65b:** BIOS/Seitre; **66bl:** BIOS/D. Heuclin; **66/67t:** PHONE/J.-P. Ferrero; **66br:** PHONE/A. Visage; **67r:** RAPHO/M. Yamashita; **67b:** DIAF/Wheeler; **68t:** BIOS/E. le Norcy; **68bl:** BIOS/N. Therond; **68m:** PHONE/F. Gohier; **69tl, b:** SYGMA/Ph. Giraud; **69tr:** ASK IMAGES/C. Esther; **70t:** BIOS/F. Bavendam; **70bl:** BIOS/Y. Lefèvre; **70/71b:** BIOS/F&J. L. Ziegler; **71tl:** BIOS/WWF-Donald Miller; **72t:** BIOS/WWF-K. Schaffer; **72b, 73t:** PHONE/F. Gohier; **73b:** PHONE/Auscape-B. Cropp; **74tl:** BIOS/Seitre; **74tr:** BIOS/C. Ruoso; **74tml:** HOA-QUI/Altitude/V. Audet; **74bml:** BIOS/E. Le Noecy; **74b:** BIOS/G. Martin; **74/79:** HOA-QUI/Altitude/Y. Arthus Bertrand; **75tl:** BIOS/Bavendam; **75ml:** BIOS/J. Rotman; **75bl:** IRD/P. Laboute; **75b:** IRD/J. Orempuller; **75mr:** BIOS/Y. Lefèvre; **76tl:** HOA-QUI/Altitude/Y. Arthus Bertrand; **76bl:** JACANA/Maza; **76bl:** BIOS/Mafart-Renodier; **77b:** BIOS/Y. Lefèvre; **77/78b:** PHONE/Auscape/M. Spencer; **78tl:** HOA-QUI/L. Pozzoli; **78tm, tr, mmr, m, br:** BIOS/Y. Lefèvre; **78mr:** BIOS/F. Bavendam; **78br:** BIOS/P. Kobeh; **78bl:** BIOS/Y. Hubert; **79tl:** HOA-QUI/A. Wolf; **79tr:** BIOS/Y. Lefèvre; **79mr:** SYGMA/Girajo; **79b:** JACANA/P. Laboute; **80/81:** SYGMA/Ph. Giraud; **82t:** SYGMA/Frances; **82/83m:** BIOS/G. Martin; **82b:** COSMOS/E. Ferorelli; **83t:** SYGMA/Ph. Giraud; **83br:** SYGMA/F. Pagani; **84tl:** COSMOS/Aurora-R. Caputo; **84tr:** HOA-QUI/W. Buss; **84b:** HOA-QUI/G. Boutin; **85t:** GAMMA/D. Austen; **85bl:** COSMOS/Anzenberger-E. Loccisano; **85br:** BIOS/P. Arnold; **86l:** COSMOS/Wildlight-B. Bohane; **86/87:** HOA-QUI/Altitude/Y. Arthus Bertrand; **87t, m:** COSMOS/Anzenberger-Sattleberger; **88t:** HOA-QUI/W. Buss; **88b:** ASK IMAGES/S. Fautré; **89t:** COSMOS/Westlight-G. Aurness; **89b:** COSMOS/Westlight-R. Watts; **90/91, 92t, b:** COSMOS/Aurora-P. Essick; **93t:** PHONE/J.-P. Ferrero; **93m:** COSMOS/A. Ryman; **93b:** SYGMA/Ph. Giraud; **94t, b:** HOA-QUI/E. Valentin; **94m:** GAMMA/Rivière; **95t, b:** PHONE/Auscape-M. Burgin; **95m:** PHONE/Auscape-A. Belcher; **96t, b:** HOA-QUI/P. de Wilde; **96m:** HOA-QUI/V. Audet; **97t:** COSMOS/Aurora-P. Essick; **97b:** BIOS/F. Gilson; **98t:** COSMOS/Anzenberger-Sattleberger; **98m, b:** ASK IMAGES/S. Fautré; **99t:** HOA-QUI/Altitude/Y. Arthus-Bertrand; **99m:** HOA-QUI/M. Renaudeau; **99b:** PHONE/Auscape-J. M. La Roque; **100t:** SYGMA/Ph. Giraud; **100bl:** HOA-QUI/W. Buss; **100/101b:** HOA-QUI/M. Renaudeau; **101t:** SYGMA/Ph. Giraud; **102t:** SYGMA/Les Stone; **102m:** HOA-QUI/S. Grandadam; **102b:** HOA-QUI/Liaison Int./B. Lewis; **103t:** HOA-QUI/E. Valentin; **103m:** COSMOS/Woodfin Camp-W. Conrad; **103b:** HOA-QUI/W. Buss; **104t:** COSMOS/Impact-C. Cormack; **104m, b:** PHONE/Auscape-J. M. La Roque; **105t:** GAMMA/L. Maresco; **105m:** RAPHO/J. Ducange; **105b:** BIOS/Seitre; **106hl:** RAPHO/M. Yamashita; **106/107t:** COSMOS/Aspen-J. Aaronson; **106b:** DIAF/B. Simmons; **107tr:** SYGMA/JMCP; **107b, 108tl, 108/109t, 108b:** COSMOS/A. Ryman; **109m:** COSMOS/Aspen-J. Aaronson; **109b:** COSMOS/A. Ryman; **110/111t:** EXPLORER/G. Zawadzki; **110bl, br:** EXPLORER/Ph. Leroux; **111m:** SYGMA/T. Graham; **111b:** EXPLORER/G. Zawadzki; **112/113:** VANDYSTADT/S. Cazenave; **114t:** ASK IMAGES/Viest Coll.-Walter Bibikow; **114b:** COSMOS/P. Menzel; **115t:** SYGMA/Ph. Giraud; **115m:** GAMMA/E. Sampers; **115b:** DIAF/B. Barbier; **116t:** VANDYSTADT/S. Cazenave; **116/117m:** HOA-QUI/S. Grandadam; **116b:** SYGMA/Ph. Giraud; **117tr:** HOA-QUI/E. Valentin; **118t:** SYGMA; **118m:** Bridgeman Art Library/Noa Noa by Paul Gauguin/Victoria & Albert Museum, London; **118b:** HOA-QUI/G. Martin-Raguet; **119l:** RAPHO/M. Friede; **119r:** HOA-QUI/G. Boutin; **120tl:** VANDYSTADT/Allsport-A. Pretty; **120tr:** GAMMA/Liaison-M. Giboux; **120b:** VANDYSTADT/Allsport-A.Pretty; **121t:** HOA-QUI/A. Wolf; **121m:** HOA-QUI/V. Audet; **121b:** ASK IMAGES/L. Weyl; **122t:** TCD/Coll Prod-DB/film Tabu by Friedrich Murnau and Robert Flaherty, 1931, photo F.

Crosby & R. Flaherty; **122ml:** TCD/Coll Prod-DB/Film Tora! Tora! Tora! by Richard Fleischer, 20th Century Fox 1970; **122mr:** SYGMA/Sunset Boulevard/Film Mutiny on the Bounty by Lewis Mileston, 1962; **123t:** TCD/Coll Prod-DB/Paradise – Hawaiian Style by Michael Moore, Paramount 1966; **123m:** SYGMA/J. Langevin; **123b:** SYGMA/Sunset Boulevard; **124t:** COSMOS/SPL-Los Alamos Laboratory; **124m, b:** SYGMA/J. Langevin; **125t:** SYGMA/Tempsport/D. Iundt; **125bl:** GAMMA/Asiaweek/A. Munshi; **126/127:** COSMOS/A. Ryman; **128/129t:** HOA-QUI/Icone-Gellié; **128m:** RAPHO/C. Zuber; **128b:** HOA-QUI/Stockshooter; **129tr, b:** HOA-QUI/Icone-Gellié; **130t, b:** PHONE/Auscape-J. M. La Roque; **130m:** DIAF/Simmons; **131t:** COSMOS/A. Ryman; **131m:** BIOS/P. Arnold; **131b:** COSMOS/S. Sibert; **132t, m, b:** SYGMA/J. Langevin; **133t:** PHONE/Auscape-J. M. La Roque; **133m:** HOA-QUI/S. Grandadam; **133b:** COSMOS/A. Ryman; **134tl:** COSMOS/C. Fishman; **134b:** HOA-QUI/E. Valentin/Port-Vila Museum, Vanuatu; **134/135:** COSMOS/C. Fishman; **135:** ASK IMAGES/C. Esther; **136/137t:** COSMOS/Anzenberger-Schill; **136l:** COSMOS/A. Ryman; **136m:** HOA-QUI/Denis-Huot; **137tr:** BIOS/D. Heuclin; **137b:** PHONE/Auscape-M. Burgin; **138t:** Charles LENARS; **138m:** GAMMA/Liaison/Giboux; **138b:** HOA-QUI/S. Grandadam; **139t:** BIOS/Gunther; **139m:** ASK IMAGES/L. Weyl; **139b:** COSMOS/A. Ryman; **140/141:** SYGMA/Ph. Giraud.

Printed and bound in Europe by Arvato Iberia
Colour separations: Station Graphique, Ivry-sur-Seine